Mehmed S. Kaya is Professor at Lillehammer University College. He founded the *Norwegian Journal of Migration Research*, where he has also been editor-in-chief. Kaya has published Muslim Immigrants' Adaptations to the Norwegian Society (Dr. polit. dissertation) and a series of articles in scientific journals. He received his Dr. polit. degree in sociology and social anthropology from the Norwegian University of Scientific and Technology (NTNU) in Trondheim.

'[This] is an original and significant contribution to a field of study that is in dire need of [attention]... The book is a timely description which, from an ethnographic perspective, addresses aspects of traditional Kurd society in a modern transition period. It... describes themes that are rarely addressed when modern regional developments are discussed [such as] kinship, trade relations and the interface between traditional and modern forms of social and political organization. Other important areas that are addressed include religion, gender and modern social relationships... The book makes a significant contribution to these research themes by providing a view of the interrelations and challenges that Zaza Kurds face today.'

Leif Selstad, Associate Professor, University of Stavanger, Norway

The Zaza Kurds of Turkey

A Middle Eastern Minority in a Globalised Society

Mehmed S. Kaya

I.B. TAURIS

LONDON · NEW YORK

New paperback edition published in 2018 by
I.B.Tauris & Co. Ltd
London • New York
www.ibtauris.com

First published in hardback in 2011 by I.B.Tauris & Co. Ltd

ISBN: 978 1 78831 282 0
eISBN: 978 1 78672 956 9
ePDF: 978 0 85772 014 6

A full CIP record for this book is available from the British Library
A full CIP record is available from the Library of Congress

Library of Congress Catalog Card Number: available

Printed and bound by CPI Group (UK) Ltd, Croydon, CR0 4YY

Contents

Illustrations

Important episodes in the history of the Zaza

*c.*600–700 BC Zaza Kurds converted to Zoroastrianism.

641 Kurdistan was occupied by the Arabs. Kurds were forcibly converted to Islam. The Kurds resisted until the turn of the millennium. Until the 1200s, Kurds were called 'infidels' by Arabic authors. Towards the end of the 1600s, the majority of the Kurds converted to Islam.

1920 The victorious powers of the First World War commit themselves to the establishment of a Kurdish state in parts of South-East Turkey and North Iraq with the Sevres Treaty.

1923 The Sevres Treaty was rejected by Kemal Atatürk's Turkey and was replaced by the Lausanne Treaty, which denied national rights to the Kurds. The victors betray the Kurds and Atatürk annexes Kurdistan to Turkey.

1925 Kurds staged a large rebellion against the newly proclaimed Turkish republic. The rebellion was led by the legendary Sheikh Said who was a Zaza and was from Xinus to the north-east of Solhan. The rebellion started in February and spread to several cities in the Kurdish area. The rebels seized several large cities including Bingöl, Xarput (Elazig), large portions of Diyarbekir and a series of smaller cities. Their liberation was short lived. The rebellion was brutally suppressed by the Turkish army after some months by direct orders from Atatürk. Sheikh Said and 48 of his close collaborators were hanged on 28 June of the same year in Diyarbekir.

1930	The Kurds started yet another rebellion around Mount Ararat. The rebellion was led by General Ihsan Nuri who had deserted from the Turkish army. This rebellion lasted for two years before it was suppressed and the leaders fled to Iran and were granted political asylum there.
1937	Another rebellion took place in the Zaza-dominated province of Dersim to the north-west of Dersim. Also at this time there was full popular participation but the rebellion was suppressed brutally after nearly two years. The leadership, along with the colourful personality Seyid Riza, was executed and more than half of the population of Dersim was deported to West Turkey.
1984	The Kurdistan Workers Party (PKK) started an armed struggle against the central government in Ankara. The PKK demanded independence from Turkey. Turkey arrested PKK leader Abdullah Öcalan with American help in Nairobi in February 1999. The PKK declared a unilateral ceasefire in September of the same year, but Turkey answered with military operations and in 2004 the PKK cancelled the unilateral ceasefire. Turkey is not capable of suppressing a Kurdish rebellion for the first time in recent history.

Preface

This book is an ethnographic study of Zaza-speaking Kurds in Turkey, a people almost completely unknown to the international community. In the 1980s, while I was working on my master's degree, which dealt with the Kurds' adaptation to Norway, I discovered that the Zaza minority was virtually invisible in the world literature. Since then I have followed this unknown people closely. However, because of the unstable political situation in Turkey, it would be some years after I learned of this minority before I could start the present work.

When I finally started this project in 2001, I searched through the common catalogue system of the Norwegian libraries (BIBSYS) for literature on the Zaza people. To my great disappointment, I did not find any titles on Zaza Kurds, with the exception of a few linguistic works and even now in 2006, neither Norwegian nor international literature on this subject exists. In the Kurdish literature, the Zaza are treated as a subtopic. This study is therefore concerned with a people who have been almost entirely neglected in the academic literature.

The task of documenting and revealing little-known societies and preserving their memories usually falls to anthropologists. After all, mapping the cultural variation in the world has been a clear goal for social anthropology. But it seems as if the anthropologists themselves have been hiding from this little-known people. There are still blank areas on the map of Western Asia. There are large areas hardly visited by researchers and these areas have been investigated systematically to an even lesser degree. I felt that something should be done about this situation. This said, it must also be added for fairness that since the 1920s the Turkish authorities have effectively prevented research projects concerning the Kurds. The Kurdish question in Turkey is an extremely sensitive one that is still met with discrimination in Turkish society. During my third field work in 2003, I witnessed four researchers, two from Hungary, one from France and one from Belgium, being expelled from the Solhan region, a Zaza area in Eastern Turkey. They wanted to make zoological investigations around Solhan, but were refused by the local Turkish authorities, who expressed the opinion that they could make the same investigations elsewhere in Western Turkey, an area in which the researchers were not interested.

This book is an original work incorporating important empirical data on a little-studied people. The book is topical in several respects: with relation to the current focus on the Middle East question, ethnicity, minorities, the multicultural society and both European and global political development. The subject is a part of the larger minority research that is taking place the world over. It is important to make clear that societies in the Middle East also include large number of minorities within their boundaries. In this book I compare the Zaza minority's situation in the wider context of similar minority groups in the world.

Since the Zaza society has not been the subject of previous research, I had to make certain decisions with respect to which topics should be emphasized. With a holistic perspective (to understand the totality rather than the individual parts in a society) as a starting point I decided to focus on certain central topics, for instance, the Zaza people's own traditional institutions such as patriarchy, sheikhdom, tribal relations, religion, kinship, reciprocity, culture and identity, the relation between the genders, marriage and the economic system, and their relation to the national state and its policies. In other words, the book consists of a series of insights into the Zaza society. Yet this does not mean that the parts are underestimated. They derive their significance from the totality that they constitute in the same way as, for example, when a Zaza patriarchal practice acquires its meaning through a feudal and sheikhal tradition. The topics often overlap. They are interconnected and the dividing lines between them are analytical. Therefore, the chapters are organized in such a fashion as to illuminate each other, and they are put in a wider social context.

Mehmed S. Kaya
Norway

Chapter 1

Introduction

Although the world is contracting and becoming smaller as we acquire insight into an ever-increasing number of cultures, there are still many peoples with their own cultures, lifestyles and social organizations that are totally unknown to many of us. We do not know how social life in other societies manifests itself under completely different circumstances than the ones we are accustomed to. We still know little about other peoples' living conditions, beliefs and traditions. We know little about what and how they think, what their perception of reality is, how they organize their lives, how they perceive themselves and others, how they view their and others' actions, how they view the world, what their social manners are, how the family is organized, how kinship relations function, how they justify their actions, what in life is important for them and so forth.

The interest in cultural differences has been increasing, and this has its own background; during the last 35 years, Western Europe has become a meeting place for people from practically all over the world. These people come from very different cultures and societies. They bring different perceptions of reality with them, and they have different premises. While we do not have sufficient knowledge about all the cultures and the societies that these different people come from, we are acquainted with different cultures to varying degrees. Some of these cultures and societies have already become familiar in Europe. Some are less familiar and some are totally unknown.

A considerable growth in immigration in the second half of the previous century has created a wholly new situation in the wealthiest parts of Europe. This has not only created problems but also an increased interest in new knowledge about other societies, cultures and ways of life. To communicate with people from different cultures, one must have a certain familiarity with their culture and society. Such familiarity contributes to enriching the communication between people. Because in multicultural societies, as Europe has gradually become and would like to present itself, there is a growing demand for cultural expertise. Familiarity with other cultures is an important premise for communicating with people from a different background. Therefore, it is important for each of us to learn a little about other societies, cultures and ways of life, which can help us to better understand from different backgrounds than ours people.

Because of differences in culture, we experience communication problems, misunderstandings and conflicts. It is necessary to learn about each other's backgrounds to avoid such problems, to better understand each other. First, one has to learn about how others live and what their perceptions of reality are, in order to compare them with one's own culture. To learn these things, we must either participate in or really familiarize ourselves with other people's realities, their thinking patterns and lifestyles, on, quite simply, we must try to live as they do. One must nearly remould oneself in another culture both to understand it and to participate in it to the greatest possible extent, even if one does not identify oneself with it. From experience, I know that it is fully possible for one with a foreign background to communicate with people from a different culture, share thoughts and to experiment without insurmountable problems. Understanding people from a culture does not require becoming similar to them. Yet it presupposes that we have fairly strong reservations against our acquired notions and beliefs about what is right and wrong, and what is worth relating to and what is unworthy. What is right for a Norwegian need not be right for a Kurd. Such an attitude is key to entering other peoples' worlds.

Fredrik Barth (1991) has taught us that human beings who are not particularly informed about other cultures value their own culture and way of life highest, without giving any further thought to the subject, and often think that they are the only right ones. Such an understanding of culture has unfortunate aspects. First, this type of opinion acts as a barrier that prevents human beings from learning about other cultures and lifestyles. Second, it will hinder development of increased understanding between cultures. An example we often experience is the following: when we are communicating with people from cultures that we either have not known previously or are less acquainted with, we discover quite quickly that we have been rather ignorant of their culture or way of life. Gradually we discover that their priorities are different than ours, they perceive themselves and the world differently to we do, and they do things differently. Briefly, one will see that there are other mechanisms that govern their lives. The Zaza people, the Kurdish-speaking group in Eastern Turkey on whom this book focuses, are a very relevant example for illustrating the problems presented above. The Zaza largely have their own ancient arrangements that keep the social order by restricting and solving conflicts between people. Their social organization consists of spiritual- and kinship-based authorities similar to feudal systems. The authorities set the norms for their subjects and are sources of both pleasure and grief for them. In this book, I will present information about Zaza social organization, which regulates their social life. The main question is what social arrangements contribute to the endurance of a society that does not have any connections to the state.

Very little is known about the Zaza Kurds and their society. Acquaintance with this people's ways of life, beliefs and traditions provides us with new knowledge about other human beings, cultures and societies. Much of the life philosophy that the Zaza practise conflicts with quite a few fundamental Western ideas but, all the same, we must understand why it is meaningful for those who practise it. First we must know how they live, why their way of living is so different from ours, why they live thus, etc. In this way, we can expand our understanding of other ways of living. Whether we are natives or immigrants, this expansion of our comprehension also raises questions about who exactly 'we' are. The material in this study is meant to provide knowledge for further reflection on and expansion of multicultural understanding. But, first, a short presentation of the Zaza people is in order.

The Zaza region and its population

The Zaza-speaking Kurds are a people who can bring us closer to ancient Middle Eastern civilizations. The Zaza region is an area on which Persians, Armenians, Arabs, Mongols and Turks have left their marks. But these groups have been perceived as intruders and oppressors. Throughout history, the local population has successfully fought against intruders to preserve its distinctive character. They are also very uninfluenced by modernity and are associated with an agricultural lifestyle.

In this book I mainly analyse the Solhan District and attempt to link this community to the surrounding communities (see Figure 1.1). Solhan itself is a small Zaza town and the seat of district administration. By European standards, Solhan is perceived as a small town, with a Turkish administrative unit consisting of a large garrison, governmental quarters housing the offices for the public prosecutor and the magistrate, and other local authorities and the police. The administration in Solhan is, in its turn, subordinated to the governor's office in the province capital Bingöl. The province governor is appointed by the Ministry of the Interior in Ankara and has the formal power, but the real power is in the hands of the military.

About 20,000 people live in Solhan itself and between 70,000 and 80,000 live in about 70 surrounding villages. Administratively, the villages are connected with Solhan. Virtually everyone in the Solhan region belongs to the Zaza population. They are of Kurdish descent and speak a Kurdish dialect, which is referred to by others as either 'Zaza' and 'Dimili', but their own name for the language is 'Kirdki', which means Kurdish. Zaza or Kirdki is widespread as a spoken language among Zaza-speaking Kurds. This dialect is one of the three largest Kurdish dialects and is spoken by approximately 3 million people. The two other dialects are Kurmanji, which has the greatest number of speakers, and Sorani, with the second largest number of speakers. Yet there is a certain disagreement among linguists about whether Zaza is a dialect of Kurdish or not. Most specialists of Kurdish, among others Lerch (1857, 1858), claim that Zaza is a dialect of Kurdish, while a few (e.g. MacKenzie 1962; Paul 1998) assert that Zaza is perhaps a separate language and that the Zaza originally came from North Iran. But newer genetic research (e.g. Nasidze *et al.* 2005) shows that the Zaza are genetically very close to the other Kurdish groups such as those speaking Kurmanji in Turkey and Sorani in Iraq. These investigations also show that the genetic distance between the Zaza and other North Iranian peoples is large.

I investigated closely the disagreement about whether Zaza is a Kurdish dialect or a separate language, especially among the elder section of the population. All rejected categorically the claim that Zaza is a separate language. They were completely convinced that Zaza is a Kurdish dialect. None had ever felt that they were not Kurds. Neither had they previously heard that they were not Kurds. So, it was an unfamiliar proposition for them. Some of them directly said that such statements are Turkish inventions, and indicated what Turkey might want to achieve by such propaganda:

We are abused by the false Turkish propaganda. For 80 years we have heard that Kurds did not exist, that we were mountain Kurds – well, it was something they invented themselves. We were expected to buy it, but we did not. Because of EU membership, we now hear that the Kurds exist after all.

Zaza-speaking Kurds mainly live in Bingöl and its surrounding areas, Solhan, Darě Yěni, Palu, Piran, Dersim and the adjacent areas. The aforementioned areas are considered to be the core areas for the Zaza. Areas such as Aldus (Gerger in Turkish), Kahta, Koluk (Gölbasi) and Besni in the Adiyaman province are also considered to be Zaza areas. Many Zaza also live in parts of Siverek, parts of Xarput (Elazig in Turkish) and parts of the areas north of Diyarbekir. Otherwise Zaza Kurds are thinly distributed throughout the neighbouring provinces of Mush, Erzincan, Malatya and Ruha (Urfa in Turkish, see Figure 1.1). There are no official statistics on the Zaza people, because Kurds are a taboo. It is estimated that around 3 million Zaza-speaking Kurds live in the area.

The Solhan region lies between Bingöl in the south-west and Mush province in the east. The districts of Solhan consist of pastures, lush river valleys surrounded by high mountains partly covered by vegetation with bare summits in the east, west and south. To the north

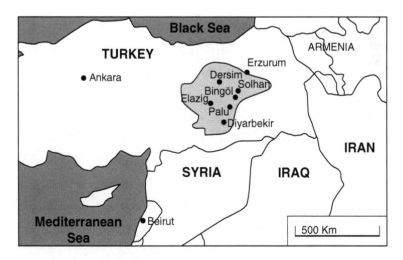

Figure 1.1 Areas where Zaza-speaking Kurds live
Source: Adapted from the original by Martin van Bruinessen (1992).

lies the Mesopotamian highland, with rich water sources that separate valleys and often establish the boundaries between villages. These manifold rivers flow into the Murad River which runs through the districts of Solhan and constitutes one of the largest branches of the Euphrates, on which Turkey has built several gigantic dams and power plants. The area consisting of the town of Solhan and the villages around is called Meneshkut and lies close to the Sherevdin Plateau in the north. The villages that lie to the south and west of the Murad valley are called Wever and Solaxan. In the summer, the vast, beautiful highlands are used both by the villages in Meneshkut and the nomadic Kurdish-speaking Beritan tribes. Beritan tribes have an ecological adaptation and migration pattern that somehow differs from those of the sedentary Zaza pastoralists. The Beritan nomads mainly winter on the plains at the Syrian border and move to the grazing lands on the Sherevdin Plateau in the summer.[1] Grazing lands in Sherevdin (see Figure 1.2) are controlled by the sedentary Zaza, and the Beritan nomads' access to the grazing lands is wholly dependent on the respective relations between them and the sedentary people.

Figure 1.2 The Sherevdin landscape, with a flock of sheep in the middle
Photo: Mehmed S. Kaya.

The low plains have been settled by humans for a long time but nobody knows precisely how long because archaeological excavations have not been allowed. Mountain dwellers live in valleys up to 2,000 metres above sea level. Many of the valleys to the south of Murad River are remote and nearly inaccessible. Here there are quite a few villages that still have little contact with the outside world. The main road from Xarput (Elazig), which serves the trade with Iran, passes through the Solhan region. But people recount that until recently they dared not live near the main road for fear of being seen by the dreaded Turkish gendarmerie. Therefore, they hid their settlements away from it, deep in the valleys and ravines or behind mountains, so that they would not be discovered by the military. Fear compelled them to protect themselves physically from the outside world. However, during the last ten to 15 years, more people have begun living around the main road.

The Zaza are mainly a tribal society. Its people, especially in the mountain villages, are affiliated with tribes and tribal relations are strongly maintained. The right to use the village communal land and outlying fields is collective but usually controlled by prominent village leaders, who are often members of a tribe. It is a society with great social differences: a few rich landowners with power and prestige, and a large majority of small farmers and landless tenants. Most small farmers own from five to eight acres of fertile land. Perhaps up to 40 per cent of the population has become landless in the last 30 years due to the high population increase. The landless live either as tenant farmers or as seasonal workers in the large cities of Southern and Western Turkey. Animal husbandry is their most important livelihood. Each family owns around 50 sheep on average and each nuclear family has six to eight children.

The living standards for most people, including those in the Solhan District, are very low. They can only be compared to the living conditions in Afghanistan and in large areas of Africa. Most people are poor, undernourished or malnourished. The houses they live in are more or less on the same level as the ones Medieval Europeans lived in, that is, they had dirt floors, no indoor plumbing, rustic conditions, and the like, although architecturally they are totally different. The houses lack running water and many do not have toilets. Most people use outhouses or nature itself for this purpose. Women come together to do laundry by the rivers a stone's throw from the villages. People live very close to the animals in their daily lives, nearly side by side. Donkeys, cows and lambs soil around the houses, day and night, year-round.

People here have shorter life spans than does the rest of the population in Turkey. Life expectancy is scarcely more than 50 years. Mortality rates are particularly high among children and women, striking especially the poor. This is due to several reasons but the most important cause is that most people do not have any access to proper health care because the health services are non-existent in the villages. The nearest health service is in Solhan but they seldom receive adequate treatment there, either because they cannot afford it or the health service lacks the necessary expertise. To get better health care, they must travel to the larger cities that are far away, and many cannot afford to do so. In addition, the religious belief that 'one's fate is predestined by Allah' substantially contributes to the high mortality rate. Many are even unaware that their wife or children can be saved by medical science, so they believe that life is determined by fate and its course cannot be changed by man. No developmental work has been done to educate people on how things can be improved.

More than half the population have either never had schooling or are functionally illiterate. About one third of the population has had primary schooling for five years, and less than 1 per cent is educated past this. According to the modern definitions of literacy, the Solhan region can be described as an illiterate society. The low level of education has contributed to the fact that here social arrangements are based on their own experiences, which are totally different from the modern governmental arrangements.

At the same time, I must point out that Zaza society should not be considered to be a simple one. As with all other societies, Zaza Kurds have built up a relatively complicated society. The reader must therefore not derive too simple an interpretation of the description of the society, but try to understand each statement in a larger context of social complexity. Although large sections of the society still live by old values, the totality of the Zaza society consists of many collective units and actors, and diverse relations, including the ones between genders, social processes, ideological currents and creeds. These conditions contribute to producing principles about social formations, hierarchical systems (social hierarchies), forms of government, forms of communication and production, and social arrangements to order these social relations. A religion such as Islam is not a single entity that can be understood in a simple way, but encompasses a series of religious expressions and relations that must be understood according to the Zaza people's difficult situation in Turkey.

Likewise, kinship is not to be understood as a simple phenomenon of the patriarchal or matriarchal type. Instead, these concepts must be interpreted contextually as expressions for the dominant social relations. These relations may vary according to groups, individuals and single incidents.

Nor are the relations between men and women are not unambiguous and simple to understand, although they can appear to be traditional. Gender relations are marked by religious and traditional notions, as they are at the same time connected with practical tasks, and are subject of exchange, cooperation and discussions to different sorts. The view on gender is connected with ethical and philosophical reflections about human behaviour, but at the same time it may be tied to the debate on the meeting between the Kurdish society and modern and global development. Therefore, this book's intention is to show how members of the Zaza Kurdish society try to solve their tasks and meet challenges in the context of grave problems experienced through oppression by the nationalistic Turkish state. That the Kurds have managed to maintain a society providing a certain degree of security and living space is a condition that calls for reflection and afterthought by the reader.

Field work

This work is based on observation through participation in the local communities around the Solhan District. To understand the Zaza society, I have carried out field work both in Solhan and in many villages around it. The villages are situated both in mountain valleys with limited means of communication with the outside world, and in the plains. I have visited also other Zaza areas such as Palu, Xarput, Darĕ Yĕni and Dersim. Further, I have lived among Zaza-speaking Kurds in the large Turkish cities and have visited the neighbouring large Kurdish cities such as Diyarbekir, Antep and Erzurum. These cities are markets to which the Zaza are tied economically and which also have sizeable Zaza populations.

In connection with my field work, I stayed among Zaza-speaking Kurds four times. My shortest stay lasted three weeks, the longest four months. Altogether, I stayed for a total of eight months in the Zaza areas. My sojourns made it possible to collect data, observe social interaction between people and note my impressions. In order to acquire inside information about the actors, I participated both passively and actively, depending on the situation, but with suitable closeness or distance. Further, I continuously followed the Kurdish and Turkish media until recently. In this book, I will try to describe, analyse and explain the social organization that the Zaza society is built upon by means of these methods, including collecting secondary data and information through review of documents, and conducting interviews with representatives from the communities during field trips, linguistic analysis from interviews, statements and speeches in media and public debate. Written material from Turkish and Kurdish media and other institutions are used as supplementary to the field work. These data complement each other.

In this work, I will also utilize my previous experience and knowledge of the Zaza society. It is not just through field work that I came to know it. I was born and partly raised in this area but left it in my youth early in the 1970s. All the same, I have had close connections with this society and know it as an insider. In the 1970s, I visited the Solhan region several times but for other reasons. Prior to my research, my last visit to the area was in June 1979. I had come to the region via Iran on an assignment from a Norwegian newspaper when I was arrested and confined to a military prison in the city of Xarput (Elazig). This happened after I was denounced by two men from the Solaxan tribe. Both were members of the Nationalistic Action Party (MHP). I was charged with sympathizing with the Kurdish cause. After 21 days in prison, I was put on trial by a military tribunal in Xarput and released. The following day, I journeyed home to Norway. The year after (1980), the military *coup d'état* was staged and I did not travel to Turkey during this period. This period of my existence in exile lasted until June 2000 when I visited Solhan again, that is after 21 years.

In connection with the field work I also wish to point out a few important aspects of my stay among Zaza speakers. Through the field work I achieved fellowship with the people I got to know and partly lived with for some time. This made it possible for me to form a comprehensive picture of the social interaction patterns and the social organization that makes up the Zaza society. Their society appeared to me to be a manageable and transparent entity, which made it possible to carry out the field work. This furnishes the basis for an account of the human diversity of the Zaza people.

The topics are organized in such a way that many of their aspects overlap and illuminate each other, and this has been a challenge, especially with respect to context and entirety. That I had to include many topics in this work does not necessarily mean that the demands of a monograph on a delineated subject, for example, specialization and professional differentiation, are not fulfilled. In order to comprehend a people that has not been studied previously and so that further studies can follow, one must start from the beginning, so to speak.

The significance of this study does not lie upon the history of the Zaza minority but their contribution to our understanding of differences and common features of human existence. An increased understanding of the manners of human existence has everlasting importance.

Chapter 2

Kinship

In the last seven to eight years, I have become particularly interested in the Zaza society of the Kurds. But gradually I reached the conclusion that in order to understand how this society functions, I had to study the kinship systems among the Zaza people because like every traditional society the Zaza society is also based on kinship, in some contexts even more so. The Zaza do not have their own modern institutions such as a legal administration, organized work life and political organizations, which in most cases regulate the social life, but what they are preoccupied with is regulated by persons distinguished by virtue of the roles they play as members of kinship groups, sheikhdoms or other types of commonality. In the Zaza society there are some fundamental social units and institutions, as in every other traditional society. Kinship, family and household are especially fundamental, but local community is also perceived as an important fellowship. The relations between them are extremely close. A person's primary affiliation, relations and social ties are connected with these institutions and units.

Kinship systems based on consanguinity or bonds of descent influence many of the interpersonal relations in the Zaza society. Therefore, knowledge of kinship systems is crucial in order to understand this society. The concept of descent is totally central. When I started my field work, one of my very first impressions was that the Zaza society is organized on the basis of descent through and through. Inheritance and property, all types of offices (both political and other types, e.g. offices of trust), social affairs, positions and roles, and even the composition of the local community are to a great extent based on kinship. As if this were not enough, religion (Islam) has also become kinship-based in this area. There are few or no institutions that are not based on kinship relations.

The Zaza institutions are decisively built on descent, which regulates the principles for creation of groups, interactions between the groups and the position of persons within different groups. In short, people are formed by their traditional institutions. For example, if you are related to the sheikhdom on the paternal side then you are also perceived as a sort of sheikh. It is immaterial whether you are a close or distant relation of the sheikh. (Questions connected with sheikhdom are examined in Chapter 5.) Organization of the Zaza society is substantially different from that in Europe. In European societies, one has differentiated institutions for economy, politics, family, socializing, etc. But in the Zaza society, all these melt into one entity. Large sections of the social life are more or less organized through kinship, for example, social organization is based on biologically related social units. This relatedness prevails first and foremost in the distribution of rights, obligations and opportunities in the society. But it is also applicable in all kinds of social contexts.

Kinship systems

Consequently, social life among the Zaza people is organized around kinship bonds and marriage alliances, but different kinship lines have different statuses, for example, kinship through the paternal side is considered to be far more important than the maternal side. They confer different rights and obligations. Belonging to the paternal side confers more rights and obligations, while belonging to the maternal side does less so.

For comprehending the Zaza society, it is also necessary to have knowledge about gender- and age-based relations. All these relations define which roles and tasks one will have. Although some researchers (see for example, Gellner 1987) claim that kinship has only to do with biology, all the same I will concentrate on the social aspects. Biology is matter and reproduction, something significant in itself. However, what is important in this study is what human beings do with their biological bonds, how they use them in their social relations and social behaviour in the sense of status and roles, and how these bonds influence the way their lives are organized. My starting point is, therefore, how kinship relations with in the Zaza society are expressed in social and cultural contexts. When necessary, the Zaza society will be compared to other societies as much as possible. I am aware that it is problematic to compare a society that is mainly based on kinship with patrilineal relations, such as the

Zaza society, to societies in which matrilineal relations dominate. Therefore, it is more productive to compare the Zaza society to other relevant Islamic societies that are also organized through patrilineal relations.

Biological kinship is a driving force, maybe the most important foundation of local identity that regulates the social relations in the Zaza society. Kinship functions as an organizing principle for the society. As superior principles, kinship relations influence how a child is to be raised, how the child will be socialized in the primary group it belongs to, how social relations are based on proximity, loyalty and solidarity within the group, how and to what extent one is integrated into the community one is associated with, and how property is inherited. Furthermore, when one looks more closely into the Zaza society one discovers quickly that social, economic and religious processes are interwoven with kinship relations. Rules of descent play a considerable role here. Many people still follow the rules of descent when they contract marriages. Rules of descent also prevail in cases of distribution of rights and obligations and their transfer between generations, distribution of power and authority, influence on decision-making processes in a family or a tribe, voting in elections, settlement and friendly gatherings, etc. By studying these circumstances, we will discover the 'principles for transference of rights' that will decide whether patrilineal or matrilineal type of kinship relations dominate in the Zaza society.

All cultures and societies have developed categories of persons that are considered to be more closely related to one, and norms of how certain kinsfolk are to behave towards others (see e.g. Keesing 1975). Among Zaza-speaking Kurds, this categorization is more important than in many other cultures. Therefore, I will first discuss how kinship is perceived among Zaza-speaking Kurds. What does kinship mean for them and why do they consider themselves to be related to someone else?

In modern societies, a person's rank and status often depend on what the person contributes or achieves. On the contrary in the Zaza society, innate or ascribed rank and status are very often more significant. People are assigned rank and attributes according to their family and kin in this society, and there is little room for standing out individually. If a person with a Zaza background is to be judged, one must first know to which family the person belongs, to whom the person is related, to which tribe he belongs, to whom he is married, who his mother is or to which family his mother belongs, whether he has brothers and, if so, who they are, who his grandfather is, whether he has uncles, children, sisters and so forth. It is these affiliations that are used as a basis for deciding the status of the person. Such affiliations are often more important than what the person does. In the Zaza society, a person is someone only by virtue of kinship. This entails that individual achievement is less important and the person is judged to a lesser degree as an individual and mainly as a member of his kinship group.

Zaza-speaking Kurds emphasize kinship greatly as we understand it. For them, it is very important to have as many relatives as possible, not only to provide status and prestige, but it is also fundamentally important. People are dedicated to taking care of their relatives, and having relatives is much appreciated.

Interest in kinship relations is expressed in a great many situations. Usually it is expressed when new acquaintances are made. For example, when you get acquainted with a person it is not long before he tells you to whom he is related. This becomes part of the presentation itself. First, he starts with the most prominent person among his relatives, declaring that he is the son, brother, uncle, nephew or some more distant relative of the prominent person in the group. The presentation usually has an air of boasting and pride. By connecting himself with the particular kin as a member, he aims partly at being recognized more easily, but he simultaneously gives an obvious impression of raising himself a few notches above from what the case would have been if he had presented himself as an individual. For there is certainly someone among his kinsfolk who has a better renown and he prefers to be a part of it.

It is extremely seldom that people present themselves as individuals if they do not hold authority or power. These people do not need to connect themselves directly to their kin because they are already well known. If you present yourself as an individual and are not known already, you are immediately asked to whom you are related. Alternatively, if you are known rather positively and have some reputation, you get the two following types of reactions:

Yes, I know who you are or have heard about you. You are known for that and that. Your honour is intact and so forth, because you are the son, nephew, uncle of, are related to that honourable, brave, fearless, honest or famous person or kin.

The other type of reaction will be of this kind:

I do not know you or knew not much about you, but I know or know about that person or those among your kinsfolk. They were and are such and such, they are known for it. They are occupied with this and that.

The point is that one is always identified with one's kin. You are nothing without your kin but exist by virtue of being related to somebody. If you have been successful on your own so that you do not need to be recognized by help of someone among your kin, the kinsfolk receive the honour because, without them, you could not achieve anything whatsoever.

As the examples above indicate, kinship prevails in all types of bonds between people in the Zaza society. Kinship relations are so dominating that they decisively constitute, so to speak, all life. Many ask why kinship is tremendously important among the Zaza and how this large group of people, which is spread over wide areas without any strong ties to the centralized Turkish state, all the same manages to function as an integrated society. I believe the answer lies partly in the kinship system since this group of people is organized through kinship and partly in the fact that the Zaza society lacks its own modern institutions such as a legal administration, a modern economic market with financial institutions, organized work life, cultural and educational institutions, etc. Non-existence of their own institutions is also the explanation for the tragedy of the Kurds. Although the Turkish state has established some institutions, such as a kind of a legal administration, schools, health service and some banks, these appear to be so foreign, corrupt and oppressive that people do not particularly associate with them. Moreover, the established Turkish institutions are of such inferior quality that they are ranked as second class by the people of Western Turkey. Educational institutions such as universities throughout the Kurdish area can in no way compare with the European universities.

Interwoven kinship relations and non-existence of modern institutions are the main reason that a large part of the Zaza society is regulated through traditional institutions such as sheikhdom, the tribal system and the Islamic law Sharia (or Sheriat, as the Zaza people pronounce it). Respectively, these institutions are ruled by hereditary sheikhs, mullahs and leaders of small and large tribes by virtue of their roles as representatives of authorities or members of kinship groups. These are not elected but co-opted by virtue of their being either members of a prominent sheikhal family, being a tribal chief or a 'competent' interpreter of Islamic law.

The principles of the Zaza Kurdish kinship model

The kinship system still functions as a fundamental institution among Zaza-speaking Kurds. What is the basis for kinship and why do people feel such a strong attachment to their relatives?

As mentioned above, the majority of the people do not associate with the Turkish institutions that exist here. My plain impression was that people act consciously to avoid dependence upon the Turkish institutions. There are many reasons for this. First and foremost, it is because these Turkish institutions are, so to speak, entirely alien to the people. These institutions are not integrated into the Kurdish culture and do not aim at developing their culture, either; on the contrary, they are assigned an important task in impeding the Kurdish culture. This has created a great distance between the people and the state institutions. Furthermore, there are many questions connected with the social order that are not addressed by the Turkish laws and regulations. Therefore, people are forced to solve their own problems. They do this by use of kinship systems they have developed over generations. The kinship system is based on principles of descent, morals and group belonging. Therefore, it is important to understand the foundations of the kinship system and how it functions.

The Kurdish-speaking Zaza kinship system is fundamentally based on the idea of consanguinity. Zaza-speaking Kurds have a deeply anchored belief that 'patrilineal blood relations provide genuine belonging, care and protection against evil powers', as people in Meneshkut often express. This is attested by the following sayings as well: *'Eqrebe ti baste tiwa* ('Your relatives are your backbone')' and *'Be eqrebe ti zere coy ti nivesena'* ('Only your relatives think of you in difficult times'). These premises have made people in Meneshkut organize their own large and small organizations and interwoven fellowships based on kinship. At the same time, consanguine fellowships constitute a framework for social and cultural actions, because actions by the members are regulated decisively by the established norms and rules of the fellowship, which aim at keeping them together.

An example of how an individual's behaviour is regulated or controlled through cultural norms or rules is given here: Fatma was a young girl about 16 years old. Suddenly she became ill. She started behaving rather wildly. She cursed openly, yelled, hit people, spat on people's faces and soon began tearing off her clothes. People believed that Fatma was possessed by evil spirits. As in many other cultures, evil spirits are associated with magic or the devil. At this time, Fatma's father worked abroad. At home, her mother did not know how she could tackle the girl's health condition. Therefore, the kinsfolk had to gather to find a solution to Fatma's situation. After some days, the girl was sent to a holy grave with a hope for a cure. They did not believe that a visit to a physician could help the girl. Although the girl had maternal uncles living in the same village, she was accompanied by a paternal cousin.

The girl did not improve particularly after the visit to the holy grave. In the end, after intense recommendation by someone from the village, she was sent to a physician in a large city some distance away. She was also accompanied by the same person. She received some analgesic tablets at the doctor's and gradually calmed down.

The interesting aspect of this example is that the girl was not sent with one of the maternal uncles who, according to the common western conception, is a closer relative, but with a paternal cousin who is biologically somehow more distant. Why? In such cases, everyone immediately questions why the maternal uncles did not turn up. They are after all biologically closer to the girl than the paternal cousin. Was it impractical for them? What is the basis for this?

The answer is probably due to culture. There are acquired norms and rules that legitimize who is to accompany the girl. When biologically conditioned rules do not function as in this case, it means it is the cultural rules that apply. That the paternal cousin had to accompany the girl both to the holy grave and to the physician can be described as a symbolic action. Symbolic actions such as customs, usage, social norms, values and idioms make up a substantial part of the Zaza culture. That Fatma is accompanied on her journeys therefore symbolizes something else. It constitutes a cultural fellowship or a symbolical system (see Geertz 1963; Schneider 1984 n1) that consists of norms and social rules about how responsibility is to be distributed, how obligations are to be fulfilled and how the interaction between the members within the cultural fellowship is to proceed, among other things. In this way, kinship based on patrilineal descent creates the foundation for a cultural fellowship that is perceived as a framework for membership, trust and belonging that regulates the members' actions. The members endeavour to avoid violating the norms and trust, as is exemplified with Fatma's case. Since escorting

Fatma is a result of their cultural interpretations, if the paternal cousin had not escorted her to the holy grave or to the physician, it would be construed as a violation of norms and trust, and this would mean loss of face, dignity and honour for the father's side.

However, patrilineal kinship is more than that. It forms the further basis for a much more functional ideology. The example of Fatma illustrates a well-established power relation based on patrilineal blood ties. This power relation, that is the belief in or the view about the blood ties to the paternal line, which we can as well call the *patrilineal ideology*, has a rather dominating position in the cultural landscape. One of its foremost tasks is to legitimize the social order within the fellowship. When the paternal cousin has a preferential right to escort Fatma to the holy grave and to the physician, this implies a patrilineal power relation, which demonstrates that it is the members of the father's family who have power over and obligations to, as well as responsibilities towards, the girl, and not the members of the mother's family. In this manner, the patrilineal ideology erects its dominant position in the cultural landscape. Therefore, patrilineal ideology manifests itself as an important part of the foundation and organization of fellowships based on descent.

Kinship categories

Today's anthropological studies are more focused on changes and processes in kinship systems (Smedal 2000). This renewed focus started after organizational structure of kinship had been thoroughly charted in the first part of 1900s (see for example, Fortes 1945; Evans-Pritchard 1951; Radcliffe-Brown 1952). Since no previous study has been undertaken among Zaza-speaking Kurds in Solhan, it is important to chart their organizational structure first. Therefore, I take the principles of forming descent groups as my starting point. This will illuminate the roles of kinship and lineage in the ever-changing social life. Principles of forming descent groups are so fundamental in the Zaza-speaking society that they heavily influence how various informal social institutions, such as lineage, rules of marriage and settlement, ownership relations, system of production, exchange processes, etc., are formed. This comprehensive composition of the kinship system does not have to do with property and land only, as some western researchers have claimed (see e.g. Leach 1961). Beyond property and land, it has to do with the need to care for and protect group members, and power and belonging in the group. In many

Middle Eastern and South Asian societies, there are many types of fellowships in which membership is defined on the basis of kinship. Fellowships, both large and small, are further categorized following the patrilineal ideology. This ideology in the Zaza-speaking society is based on a fundamental idea, namely the sexually determined substance (blood, semen, genes, food, spirit, social heritage, division of labour, social relations, etc.) and how it is generated and transmitted. Although both the mother and the father contribute to their children's biological composition, patrilineal blood relations are the ones considered to be the primary ones, because the man's sperm has great ideological significance in this society. It confers life and strength to the woman. Consequently, the value of the semen becomes the most important source of structure for kinship categories and it simultaneously regulates the ranking of the kin. This interpretation of semen first lays down a clear rule for which type of kinship bond is the most important, and, second, the man reinforces the legitimacy of his dominant position. When one asks Zaza-speaking Kurds whom they count as relatives, as a rule, one gets three categories of relations. In order of importance, these are:

1   *Eqrebĕ evzĕl* is the first category of kinship group and is patrilineal. They describe themselves as related through men. Here, only men can carry the kin further. These blood relations are perceived as the natural, genuine or legitimate relatives. The category extends from nephews through cousins to second cousins who are perceived as 'natural kin', sharing genetic material. Kinship solidarity through this line is extremely strong. Members have great obligations towards their uncles, cousins, aunts and so forth.

2   *Dezĕ* is the second category of kinship group. This fellowship consists of somehow more distant paternal relatives who do not share genetic material. The designation is valid from third cousins onwards. Although feelings of relatedness are somehow weaker through this line, there are, all the same, good reasons for designating them as tribal relatives.

3   *Khal/warzĕ* is the third type of kinship group. This category consists of matrilineal blood relations. Although they share a certain portion of genetic material, they are treated as somehow external relations. Moreover, the last category is not counted as part of the symbolic fellowship because matrilineal relations do not form the primary foundation for kinship.

Such a categorization of kinship groups confers variable rights, opportunities and memberships, and, further, has different significance for the members' social identity and continuity. Let us expound this further. I take the three categories in the Meneshkut region as my starting point. Each category represents different degrees of affiliation. There are different rights, opportunities and affiliations connected with the three categories. These affiliations again bind the members to different feelings and allegiances. But there exist certain principles of kinship that determine to what extent one has access to rights and opportunities, to what extent one belongs to a category, etc.

Generally, there are certain rights and opportunities connected with the kinship systems in Meneshkut that cause the system to be maintained. These rights and opportunities constitute the existential basis for the kinship systems. As a member of a descent group, one has certain rights and opportunities. Acquisition of the most important rights and opportunities, and their transference to the coming generations may, without ranking them, be listed as follows:

1 The right to membership in the group that confers belonging.
2 The right to settle at the same place with the group members.
3 The right to cultivate land. (This right is incorporated patrilineally.)
4 The opportunity to contract marriage with group members. (This type of right can be perceived as a priority right with respect to people external to the group. It is not an automatic right but as a group member one is favoured to some extent.)
5 The right to protection by group members.
6 The right to convey one's views through decision-making processes within the group.
7 The right to demand solidarity, for instance, during economic difficulties.
8 Access to confidential information within the group.
9 Possibilities for extended kinship through circumcision of boys.
10 Opportunities for close friendships.
11 Opportunities for external support.
12 Strict demands of loyalty.
13 Strict demands of family commitment.
14 Tight emotional attachments.
15 Looser emotional attachments.

Beyond this, members have rights to grazing land, common grounds and access to a series of collective goods. Such privileges lead to

developing emotional bonds between members, but opposite interests may also often arise.

We will take a closer look at how rights and opportunities are distributed, and which principles are at the heart of such a distribution.
It is precisely the principles of distribution that determine the formation of the three types of kinship relations in this society. I want to
draw the reader's attention to the fact that the boundaries between the
three categories are not always clear. In many situations, they overlap.
They also vary from time to time and from case to case. In some cases,
the principles are given nearly equal status. But there are also many
cases where there are clear-cut boundaries. Nevertheless, I will
attempt to concretize to which categories these rights, obligations and
opportunities belong. Let us arrange them as shown in Table 2.1.

Table 2.1 An overview of various rights, obligations and opportunities connected
with kinship categories

Eqrebĕ evzĕl (close patrilineal relations)	Dezĕ (further patrilineal relations)	Khal/warzĕ (close matrilineal relations)
The right to group membership.	The right to convey one's views through decision-making processes within the group.	The opportunity to contract marriage with group members.
The right to settle at the same place as other group members. The right to cultivate land.	The right to demand solidarity, e.g. during economic difficulties.	The right to demand solidarity, e.g. during economic difficulties.
	Access to confidential information within the group.	Tight emotional attachments.
The opportunity to contract marriage with group members.	Possibilities for extended kinship through circumcision of boys.	Access to confidential information within the group.
The right to protection by group members.	Opportunities for close friendships.	Opportunities for close friendships.
The right to convey one's views through decision-making processes within the group.	Opportunities for external support.	
The right to demand solidarity, e.g. during economic difficulties.	Looser emotional attachments.	
Access to confidential information within the group. Strict demands of loyalty. Strict demands of family commitment. Tight emotional attachments. Opportunities for close friendships.		

Most of the rights, obligations and opportunities classified under kinship category 1 are transferred from father to son(s). This is applicable especially to 'the right of membership in the group', 'the right to cultivate land', 'the right to settle at the same place as other group members', 'the right to protection by group members', 'demands of loyalty', 'demands of family commitment' and 'tight emotional attachments', all of which follow paternal lineage. Consequently, we are dealing with an exclusively patrilineal system in which property, right of inheritance and political leadership follow paternal lineage. The patrilineal system seems to be favourable first and foremost to men, who control the most important resources. The system allows men to make the formal decisions within the family and the kinship group. In this system, women are defined as irrelevant or outsiders, without property or inheritance rights. In this system, one will be a member of the same kinship group as one's father, paternal grandfather, paternal uncle, paternal cousins and so forth. Yet loyalty and obligations towards members within the Zaza Kurdish patrilineal system decreases with increasing genealogical distance. Distance reduces the magnitude of power, but it does not prevent members from influencing each other. They consult each other when they make important decisions.

The same principle, for instance, paternal lineage is applicable to kinship category 2, concerning transference of rights, but here my primary discussion will be a comparison of kinship categories 1 and 3. There is a big difference between being a member of a kinship group based on paternal lineage and being a member of a kinship group based on maternal lineage. A distinctive feature of kinship groups based on paternal lineage is that favours, recognition, loyalty and trust bind people within the group closer to each other.

In Table 2.1, we see that kinship category 3, which consists of blood relations connected to maternal lineage, lacks quite a few fundamental rights of transference, compared to kinship category 1. There are no situations in which rights are transferred from father to daughter or from mother to daughter and to granddaughter. Yet membership in this group varies for some people. Some families, for example those who exchange girls, have developed close ties to each other. Often, they enter commitments in order to strengthen the bonds.

The kinship categories also have some rights of transference common to all. But according to the dominant view prevalent in the Zaza society, these features are considered as unimportant compared to the rights of transference in kinship group 1. A concrete example is the opportunity to contract marriage with group members, which is a kind of transference of rights and common to both kinship categories 1 and 3. This transference of rights is perceived to be insignificant, due to the totally subordinate position of women in the society. Consequently, contracting marriages that follow the maternal lineage will not be a sufficient foundation for a powerful symbolic kinship group. The same can be said about the emotional attachment based on maternal lineage. My impression concerning 'the right of the individual to demand solidarity during economic difficulties', 'access to confidential information within the group' and 'opportunities for close friendships' is that these are somehow weaker in category 3 than they are in category 1, apparently because transference of rights based on maternal lineage is either not inherited or is quite modest.

Although membership in a category determines the content of the relations, there are common obligations and opinions with respect to which kinsfolk act independently of the category to which they belong. In difficult situations, they have a common moral responsibility towards each other and they stand together, so to speak, and they often demonstrate this. For example, they are obliged to hide relatives who are political activists when the Turkish authorities search for them. When the gendarmerie sets out to find the person in question, the relatives use many methods to protect that person. They know where the person is but they withhold information so that the person will not be arrested.

Kinship groups underline the mutual dependence between kinsfolk; they mark the social system and contribute to forming the characteristic Middle Eastern mosaic in which people are categorized or identified through kinship or occupation (see also Skogseid 1997). It can be said that kinship categories belong to a subculture with its own fellowship rules and acquisition forms. Clearly defined property rights and access to common goods, concerning either individual or collective rights to resources, are often dependent on an authority that is capable of regulating the system of rights or imposing sanctions. In the Zaza area, the Turkish state is physically present through its military power yet it is weak in regulating the system of rights. Access to rights and administration like these are often dependent on the ability of the kinship groups or tribes to mobilize physical strength in the form of manpower towards each other. Therefore, there is a need for strong kinship-based fellowships that regulate the system of rights, which, in its own turn, creates a kind of stability with which the kinship groups are apparently content.

Is the kinship group based only on the right to cultivate land?

Until recently, people in the Zaza society believed that the right to cultivate land was the fundamental basis for developing close ties between kinsfolk because the tight relations including political positions, rank and hierarchy, power and hegemony, religious and ritual leadership, and the right to command are directly derived from the land (Leach 1961; Smedal 2000). Those who have property and own most land have more say. Those who do not have property and do not own land have less say. According to Leach, kinship first and foremost has to do with property and land. In the Zaza society, in some contexts, those who do not own land – not an insignificant number – are still not represented at village-level meetings at which important decisions are made. This applies especially when the leading figures in the village discuss how grazing lands, other common areas and collective goods, shall be dispensed the following year. Those participating in such meetings are those who have rights by virtue of their being landowners. Their power and influence lie more or less in their owning land.

To cultivate land does not seem to be the fundamental basis for close relations between kinsfolk in the Zaza society. Due to the high birth rate, there are not many who live by cultivating the land anymore. This population growth has led to more than half the population becoming landless. The population growth in this portion of the Zaza society is about 4 per cent yearly. Each woman gives birth to, on average, six to eight children. This natural increase of the population creates a net surplus of 80–90 per cent with respect to what the agricultural economy of the region can absorb. This means that only about 15 per cent on average work in agriculture. The rest are either unemployed or have become seasonal workers in other parts of Turkey or in the Gulf States.

What is remarkable is that, although more than half the population has become landless, the close relations between kinsfolk in the Zaza society have not changed. Marriage contracts between close relatives still occur frequently. Kinsfolk still have strong bonds with each other; among other things, they help each other financially to start new businesses where group members are employed. When the landless journey to other parts of Turkey in order to work, they are also helpful in getting employment for close relatives. Some work in the Gulf States and they send for more relatives to join them. Through my field work among Zaza-speaking immigrants in Oslo, I know that many contribute economically to their relations in the home country. This help is given not only to the closest relatives but also to distant ones, such as second cousins. Those who are well off still contribute economically to their relatives. They are still loyal to their relatives and have close emotional ties to them. They still consider themselves as members of kinship groups. Although many Zaza commute to work, the majority still live at the same place as the group members. Finally, they are obedient to their authorities, view them as sacrosanct and perceive them to be legitimate whether they are feudal lords, sheikhs, mullahs or patriarchs, although they are not dependent on these power structures economically.

The observations so far indicate that membership of the kinship groups is not primarily based on cultivation of land. It is not cultivation of land that holds the kinship group together. It no longer forms the essential basis for a close bond of fellowship between kinsfolk in the Zaza society, either. The communality has neither been weakened nor dissolved after many, maybe up to half, of the members of the kinship group have ceased to make a living from agriculture. Values such as respect, obedience, solidarity and care, which have been central to kinship groups, have not been weakened as a consequence, either. Kinship relations, conservation of group belonging, group solidarity, rights and obligations, and the behavioural and emotional content of the relations are still expressed and conform to the kinship system. In other words, the kinship system still constitutes the totality of the social system. But this is grounded in a fundamental idea, namely the sexually determined substance as a result of the patrilineal ideology. This ideology rests on bonds of consanguinity with the paternal lineage, members of which are considered to be primary blood relations. From a sociocultural understanding of genetic relations among the Zaza people, one may say that the universal adage 'blood is thicker than water' has some substance, without implying that the biological is more important than the social because kinship is something else and something more than biology.

An essential reason why kinship still functions as organizing principle in the Zaza society is that this society has not yet had the opportunity to build its own political, social, economic, juridical and cultural institutions. From modern societies, for example from Scandinavia, we know that a quite large portion of the social life is regulated by the aforementioned institutions. A closer explanation of why the Zaza people have not yet had the opportunity to build their own modern institutions will be given in the next chapters.

Descent groups

How do relations function within descent groups? How do social relations, social interaction and cooperation proceed within descent groups? How are social control, power and dominance exercised to maintain cohesion in the groups? Here the focus is on the relationship between the individual and the descent group.

Descent groups regard themselves as homogeneous. They view themselves as a homogeneous group with respect to other groups. They have mutual obligations towards each other by virtue of their membership of the group. They stay together in relation to external groups. External groups also view them as more or less homogeneous groups. Internally the groups are marked by disputes although mostly this is hidden from the external world. This is because they do not wish to give an impression of discord to the external world, because this would be interpreted as a sign that the group is weakened. However, external groups are aware that the group will stand united on the surface.

Descent groups are homogenous first and foremost on the kinship level. The group members are highly aware of what group belonging entails and what is demanded from them in order to comply with rules of belonging. It is legitimate for the behaviour of group members to be controlled by the other members. Breaking rules leads to ostracizing, which is costly for the ostracized person.

Group membership appears to be intact through generations. First and foremost, this is because the descent group has protected itself and its members against abuse from without. Moreover, the groups have developed strong internal ties because the members have become dependent on each other.

But homogeneity has its limitations. They are seldom homogeneous at the economic level, although they have certain obligations towards their next of kin in case some of them need economic help. Yet they need not cooperate with group members if they engage in commerce or carry out other types of economic transactions. In such situations, one prefers to cooperate with a person from another group. Such interests, however, do not mean that one has resigned from the group. One can be a member of only one descent group.

As a preliminary conclusion, it can be established that the kinship relations in the Zaza society with the accompanying rituals function as integrating principles for descent groups based on paternal and maternal lineages. Family relations are close and kin solidarity is powerful. A person's social identity is mainly connected with kinship. Under most circumstances, this limits their contact with the outside world. Personal network is to a large extent bound to kinship and neighbourhood, where most needs are cared for. Often one gets a spouse through kinship, an abode to live in, land to cultivate and also work through kinship. One gets economic support from kinsfolk and so forth. These conditions bind them together and create a kind of stability with which they are apparently satisfied. In this fashion, kinship in the Zaza society acquires a legitimacy that often governs contracting marriages, political power or religious hegemony. In the next two chapters, we take up related topics such as tribal relations, patriarchal traditions and contracting marriages, which all have to do with kinship.

Chapter 3

A tribal society

Tribal society still manifests itself as a social arrangement in the Zaza region where powerful tribal men direct most of the everyday life, especially in the villages. In order to maintain itself, the tribal society must necessarily have functions and statuses that integrate kinship groups, because kinship generates power. Therefore, the tribesmen's most important tasks are connected to internal affairs of the tribe. Then to analyse the questions about who does what, with whom and why, and, not least, how tribal leaders obtain their powerful positions becomes technically important. In this chapter, to answer these questions I will take a closer look at tribal structures and relations, the origin of the tribes, lineage structures, partitions and internal tensions, and at the end of the chapter I will discuss dissolution tendencies in the tribal structure.

Tribal structures and relations

Tribal structures are very hierarchical and consist of a fixed pattern of traditional rules, customs, statuses and roles where members act obediently and predictably within the framework of the structure. Further the pattern incorporates rights, obligations, division of labour, norms, social control, and so forth, which aim at maintaining the tribal society. Seen technically, it is the internal context and the social relations that are interesting, because these, according to tribal members' own notions, create fellowship and solidarity; they promote stability and secure tribal continuity. It is important to answer the following questions in order to understand this: how are the tribes organized in the Zaza society? What is it to be tribally related? What does it comprise and how is it organized?

Here, the central common denominator is that members of the tribe view themselves as direct descendants of an ancestor and that they have the same blood. Blood is the most important common substance that imparts feelings of common group identity. When the common denominator exists, the social construction of identity will take shape. It is constructed through the values expressed during upbringing. For example, children learn norms for how relatives are to behave towards each other, for instance, values such as discipline, child rearing, life style, prescriptions and proscriptions, and so forth, which integrate the person into the descent group and aim at strengthening the feelings of fellowship. Consequently, descent functions as an ideology.

In the Kurdish society generally, the idea of tribal formation is very old. It belongs to civilizations that are several thousand years old. The tribal tradition probably originates from ancient Mesopotamian social structure. But it was further developed after the Kurds had been exposed to Persian, Roman, Arabic, Mongolian and Turkish intruders after the first part of the past millennium. To this day, the brutality of these intruders has been the subject of conversation. This is an oral tradition that has lived through several tens of generations. Even today, people call these intruders 'plunderers, ruthless and brutal occupants'. These intruders were so brutal that the Kurds probably had to create their own loyal forces in order to resist them. This happened through organizing in tribes based on kinship bonds. Only strong tribes were able to defend themselves to a certain extent against foreign powers.

Also among Zaza-speaking Kurds, it has been necessary to organize in descent groups. This is justified with reference to one's own relatives being the right ones to offer the necessary protection. In other words, for protection, one trusts his next of kin more than any state apparatus or any other forms.

Three of the three large tribes that dominate in the Solhan region are called Solaxan, Umeran and Tavzi. They live in their respective territories. Their core areas are relatively far apart but often they border each other. In addition, there exist more than ten small tribes. These are Bilikon, Chomergij, Xelbij, Guevij, Zikti, Begler, Ki melĕ Kal, Ki mele Azin, Hezarshayij and some others. The three large tribes mentioned above have always formed the powerbase in the whole Solhan region. Their power also made it necessary for the sheikh – the religious leader in the area – to cooperate closely with them. The sheikh could not have total power without their support. How are these tribes organized? How do the intra-tribal relations function? I will discuss these questions in this chapter.

The origin of the tribes, lineage structure and partitions

According to tribal leaders tribal kinship consists of kinship bonds and feelings of kinship and moral responsibility that presuppose close contact, protection of life, property and services. This is the driving force behind the formation of tribal fellowships based on equality between the members, cohesion and feelings of solidarity. This fellowship is called *Merdumati*, which has two meanings. The first is a wider meaning used for a neighbour, a fellow villager, a member of the tribe, a Zaza-speaking Kurd, a Muslim and so forth while the other meaning is confined to the fellowship between close relatives, *Merdumati a evzel* (compare kinship categories *Eqrebĕ evzĕl, Dezĕ* and *Khal/warzĕ* in the previous chapter).

Organization of tribes is based on lineages or common ancestry. Members of the tribe accomplish this by tracing their descent by means of the names of their forefathers. Among the Kurds it is a generally established duty for every family to know seven forefathers at all times. Identification of tribal belonging is actually simple; if you can know who your seven forefathers are then you know to which tribe you belong. Tribe leaders consider themselves to share a common substance with a forefather. Because of their patrilineal ideology, Kurds value kinship through paternal lineage, and maternal lineage is excluded. In Northern Europe, uncles, cousins and second cousins on both sides are referred to by the same terms. Among the Zaza people, this is not the case. The term 'uncle' is *ap* in Zaza and includes only the paternal lineage. Uncles through the maternal lineage are called *xal*, which means the mother's brothers (maternal uncles) and do not have the same status as the paternal uncles. Paternal uncles are regarded to be closer and more genuine kinsfolk. Maternal uncles are, on the contrary, viewed as somehow 'more distant' and have a relatively lower status and are treated accordingly.

The patrilineal principle also prevails further through the kin, for instance, cousins, second cousins, third cousins and so forth, and pervades the whole patrilineal society. Those who try to connect themselves by use of maternal lineage to the genealogy of a tribe they wish to be members of are not considered to be genuine members. Only those who can trace their connection through paternal lineage are considered to be genuine members of the tribe.

The explanation for this probably lies in the totally subordinate position of women. In the Zaza society, there are strongly patriarchal power structures legitimized by Islam. These structures have assigned a subordinate position to women. But women are treated according to patriarchal principles, not only in the Zaza society but also all over the Islamic world, especially in the rural societies strongly dominated by men. Uneven distribution of privileges and rights has resulted in the total discrimination of women. (Women's situations will be described more closely in Chapter 10 on gender and family.)

Consequently, descent from a forefather is established through male links. The forefather may be the seventh and upwards, and indeed up to the 13th or 15th in the chain. The large tribes usually identify themselves with a forefather who had lived at least 13–15 generations earlier.

The three tribes in the Solhan region mentioned above are approximately of equal size, concerning both their numbers and relative strength. Each has between 2,000 and 3,000 members. Equal size and strength results in the tribes keeping each other in check and creates a kind of balance and eases tensions.

The names of the tribes both in the Zaza region and in the rest of the Kurdish area are inherited from a forefather. An example can be useful for explaining how tribes develop. I take as my example the Solaxan tribe. Solax was the forefather of this tribe. He had six sons. One of the brothers moved to another part of the country and, gradually, contact with him was lost. One of the sons was childless or did not have a son to carry the kin further. The other four brothers were Osman, Shemsxon, Hasen and Hamed. It is not sure when these men lived but it is believed to be 10–12 generations back in time. The probability that this number tallies with reality is large considering the number of forefathers in each separate chain, from top to subgroups, and the relative numbers of the subgroups. These subgroups are of equal size and can be linked to the forefather Solax by a quantifiable time period. Simultaneously, we see that the genealogy is a construction: Kurds who were contemporary with Solax are not included in the genealogy.

The number of descendants of the four sons of Solax increased and gradually aggregated into four main units. These main units take their names from the each of the four sons of Solax. The increase in numbers of the four main units continued. Gradually, one or more subgroups emerged and they were called after their respective forefathers. The subgroups are called Wesmonon, Hamedon, Wĕlion, Ĕmiron, Muson and Qason. It was at this level that segmentation arose and was followed by further segmentations, which formed into a pattern resembling a pyramid.

Figure 3.1 shows the tribe as a pyramid, with the originating man at the top, some main units at upper levels, some lineage groups at intermediate levels and a number of 'small' and distinct lineage groups at the bottom. Figure 3.2 shows the relation between tribal units and the unit leaders at different levels. This partition at the same time forms the basis for the distribution of power between the units.

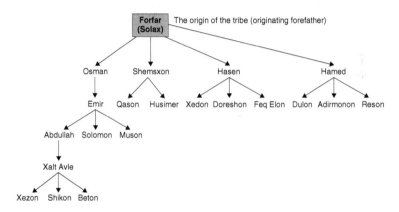

Figure 3.1 The origin of the tribe, lineage structure and the partition into levels
Source: Based on oral sources. Nihat Karadag and elderly members of the Solaxan tribe have been the primary sources for designing the figure.

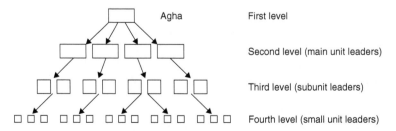

Figure 3.2 The relation between tribal units and unit leaders at different levels

Political power and position in the tribal hierarchy

The tribal organization provides positions of leadership and makes coordinating political, social and economic activities possible. But as the above model demonstrates, kinship relations between tribal units take place at varying levels. At the first level of partition, the relations take place on an almost macro plane. At this level each main unit has its acknowledged chieftain. When conflicts arise, the supreme tribal leader (*agha*) gathers all the main unit leaders. These act as his closest advisors.

The uppermost structure in the pyramid can be described as a network consisting of the most important decision-makers in the tribe. They make the most important decisions concerning the security and cohesion of the tribe. They debate the state of the tribe and possible measures to avert external threats to the tribal unity.

The closest collaborators of the main unit leaders are the leaders of the subunits. At the bottom level we find small units that also have their petty chiefs. Petty chiefs function as a link between their subjects and leaders at the middle level. In this way, a tribal hierarchy is formed in which the boundaries between the units are clear and distribution of duties and responsibilities is well defined. What we see is an unambiguously socially constructed phenomenon.

Tribe leaders, also called clan chiefs, usually view themselves as bearers of tradition. They believe it is their moral duty to transmit the tradition they have inherited from forefathers to future generations. If one does not behave or act within the traditional framework, it will be regarded as a 'forbidden' or 'illegal' action and forbidden actions are morally condemned.

So the tribal hierarchy is pyramid shaped. The tribe is vertically organized, partitioned into segments. From top to bottom, it is organized into various subordinate and superior relations between main and secondary units. At all levels, whether it is top, intermediate or bottom level, a significant social hierarchy is formed, for instance, leaders, intermediate leaders, subordinate leaders and rank and file. It is not personal qualities or prestige that decides the position of a small, middle or top chief, but an inherited tradition that prescribes that the position is left from father to son or to a brother. The same pattern is seen also in the sheikhdom, which will be described later.

Yet, although tribes often appear to be unitary, there are considerable differences between the various levels. We see that the tribes consist of several descent groups down in the model. As said, these groups have different ranks. Hierarchical constructions in the tribes also structure the power relations between the descent groups. Until few years ago, the higher a chief was placed in the tribal hierarchy, the more power he had. But in the last years it seems that the petty chiefs at bottom level have constantly acquired more power. During the last 5–10 years, tribal relations appear to be restructuring themselves. This happens through the main and subunits becoming less compact. The bonds between them have become weaker. There has been a tendency towards tribal disintegration. Subunits are becoming more and more important, because the kinship bonds at this level are closer. For example, closer contact and cooperation is taking place within small groups at the bottom level. There is a larger distance between the bottom units and the top level. It can be said that general guidelines are formulated at the top level, but mutual relations, which are more significant for most people, take place at bottom level. Therefore, the leaders at bottom level have a large influence on peoples' daily lives. The relations are more intense, practical and controlling at this level.

Power is unevenly distributed between the units; those representing the upper units have had greater power and influence than group leaders placed at bottom level, and this uneven distribution of power is possibly the reason that mutual relations at bottom level have more significance.

At the lowest level, power is exercised by petty chiefs on other group members. This is somehow necessary to keep the group together or prevent fractures within the group. Moreover, without such an exercise of power, they cannot protect their common interests.

Organizational structure of the three mentioned tribes in the Solhan region, as well as in all the Zaza Kurdish society, is identical. They are based on kinship, consist of segmented units and are hierarchically organized. This leads to tribes being less centralized and having a weak political leadership. The tribes are not governed from above at all times, although formally they have acknowledged chiefs. Among the most important tasks at top level are maintenance of the unity within the tribe in order to stay stronger in relation to hostile tribes, to deal with moral questions, for instance, to fight moral dissoluteness, to prevent adultery, to prevent women obtaining more rights, etc. Some of these questions, especially the moral ones, are solved often in consultation with the sheikhdom, with which the tribes have a close relation. I will return to this point later.

Throughout the tribe, the power is delegated downwards so that the tribe is ruled by several subordinate chiefs. But the tribe can mobilize fully when it is attacked from without or is in conflict with other tribes or is threatened, especially when a member is killed. Then the tribe must seek revenge, otherwise it will lose its honour and place itself in a weak position in relation to competing tribes, and this is a costly situation, something every tribe wants to avoid. Such conditions necessitate that the whole tribe stands together, both to defend its position and to resist the declared enemy. Meanwhile, some tribes cannot manage to activate the lineage principles wholly in situations of conflict. Activation acts more in a fictive manner because, often, it has been seen that some tribes, because of internal discord, could not manage to take revenge. All the same, in many ways, the tribes appear to be decentralized and at the same time rather integrated. Integration is particularly visible and expressive at the segmentary lineage level. At this level, segment members meet more often, discuss common issues and direct mutual relations.

As a conclusion to this section, one can say that the tribal society in the Zaza region is primarily integrated through kinship. It maintains the unity both through kinship and through cooperation between the superiors and the subordinates, between main and subunits and between lineages and clans. Yet it must be added that not all issues are such that tribal members agree on them. There are issues that create profound divisions among the tribal members. I will discuss this subject in the next section.

Disintegration tendencies in the tribal structure

Although the tribes have a series of good reasons and a set of criteria they muster in a nearly stateless society, such as feelings of kinship, group solidarity, protection of group members, among others, it would be an exaggeration to claim that the tribes can be mobilized in all cases. There are certain areas around which the tribes cannot mobilize fully, at least not all the tribes manage to do so. Politics is one such controversial area, causing intense discussions and discord among tribal members. Until the 1990s, nearly all tribe members voted for the candidate whom the tribal chief wished to be elected. But today, not all obey the tribal chief. The most important reason is an increasing national awareness among the Kurds. The unstable political situation that marked the country in the 1980s and 1990s, during which Kurds led by the Kurdish liberation movement, the PKK, declared war onto the Turkish state, has divided almost all the tribes. PKK cadres do not cooperate with the tribal chiefs; they organize people at the grassroots level while the tribal chiefs, to a large extent, have allied themselves with the Turkish state and its political parties.

Disintegration tendencies within the Zaza tribes became more vivid at the last parliamentary elections in November 2002 when most of the large tribes were divided about whom they should vote for. While, on average, half of the tribes supported the Kurdish sympathizing party, DEHAP (People's Democratic Party), the other half led by the chiefs, voted for different Turkish parties.

But there are other circumstances that affect the disintegration of the tribal structure. A slow but secure transition from traditional to somewhat more modern societies is taking place in the Zaza areas. The tribal structure reminds one of pre-modern times. The form of orientation or the social formation is deeply anchored in religious and traditional principles and it seems to be quite static. People acquire the prevalent view of life through religious socialization. Yet, one can observe certain cautious breaches with the tribal society among some educated young people. These people think more rationally and defend secular views. Increased education can entail a change from kinship to other principles as the groundwork for social organization. Education affects social relations and can be a driving force in this context. Increasingly higher numbers of Zaza families wish their children to get an education. From European studies, we know that there is a causal relation between the level of education and individual independence. Increased education among the Zaza people can also promote individualization and lead to increased liberation with respect to religion, culture and tradition, structures that the tribes are deeply anchored in. The problem is that the Zaza receive poor education at the Turkish institutions. Turkish educational institutions, particularly those in the Kurdish regions, do not promote such ideas.

When people belonging to different tribes live together

Kinship relations appear to be the core for unity in the Zaza society. Yet, not all kinship groups with tribal ties necessarily live in the same village or settlement, although the majority may do so. Many who consider themselves to be close relatives, for instance, at least second cousins, usually live spread over several villages and settlements without their contact being influenced by this. Distance only seems to strengthen the feelings of kinship. Some small groups connected with these large tribes live side by side in certain villages, but they keep close contact with all the levels in the tribe. A description of the village of Xirbizun is an example to illuminate how people with different tribal connections live together. The example can in many ways be representative for the rest of the Zaza society. Four smaller groups of different tribes and some other families without tribal connections live in the village of Xirbizun. Three of the four tribal groups are of somewhat equal size, with about 200 members each, while the fourth group is slightly larger in terms of numbers. Each of them in turn belongs to larger tribes in the surrounding area. The settlement plan is such that each group lives in its own village quarter. The idea behind is that the tribal members should live physically close to each other. The Shexon, the largest group in terms of numbers but the weakest physically and politically, live in the lower part of Xirbizun. The Bilikon, the third in terms of numbers but having greater influence than the first group, due to being wiser tacticians, live in the upper part of Xirbizun. In between them is the smallest, Hushajion. The Xezon live in the uppermost part of the village, Keshkon, which is a distinct settlement area. And finally there are families without any tribal connections who live spread all over the village.

Continuity with the past is important and all lineages point out a distant forefather who founded their settlement. The political power in Xirbizun follows lineages so that each lineage has its own prominent leaders who participate in the decision-making process at village level. In many ways, the tribal groups in this village function as local branches or departments for their respective tribes. This is a consequence of the fact that each group must obtain external power in order to protect itself or its members. Without power, the tribe is insignificant. As an individual without tribal connections, one does not have possibilities to defend one's interests and life. Therefore, it is important to know how these small tribal groups relate to each other. Some families within these groups have exchanged girls, but those are not regarded as the most 'suitable' girls. Girls are first and foremost married into their respective groups. Exchange of girls between groups has had the consequence that quite a portion of the inhabitants have already become kinsfolk. This situation contributes to the groups having moral obligations towards each other.

Disagreements and less serious conflicts between groups arise often. At those times, they follow the paternal lineage and display a cold attitude towards the contending group. So the lineage principle makes the group stand together against other groups. All the same, when the conflicts become more serious now and then, they do not seek external help from their respective tribes, but they think over the case and often express that they have to live together because they inhabit the same place and share the same territory. The consideration about continuity is important. Therefore, they must display solidarity with each other, not the least with those they are related to through marriage. Exchange of girls and the fact that they share territory create a sort of stability between the groups.

Families without tribal connections have come to the village often as a result of being recruited by their own relatives living in the village. Such families are to be found in all the villages in the Zaza society. They move to a new village often as tenants, servants of affluent families, shepherds or as exiles from other villages as a consequence of unacceptable behaviour. They do not own land but have obtained gratis building sites from prominent village persons. The village inhabitants define these families as the absolute lowest status group. They are called 'foreign immigrants' by the natives for a long period, usually 40–50 years. To get accepted they strive hard to gain entry to the groups in the village. They must behave as the natives do, at times perform free services for the natives, at all times display humility and gratefulness towards the natives, be good neighbours and so forth. In this way, they can achieve a kind of local belonging or membership, but without any particular rights and opportunities such as the descent groups have (see Table 2.1). It also takes a long time, often several generations, before these families reach a level at which they are accepted as equal members in the local society and some natives can consider contracting marriages with them. Until now, there have been few marriages between these families and the natives. The pattern has been such that these immigrants have rather been the 'providers of girls' for the natives. So there has not been reciprocal exchange of girls between 'foreign immigrants' and natives. Members of the first group often marry their relatives living in villages further away. But even after marriages between 'foreign immigrants' and the natives, these groups are not included in the decision-making process at village level.

Internal tensions

So the relations within the tribal group are very dense. Mechanisms regulating social behaviour are both visible and invisible. The secretive aspects of the inner processes are not always easy to observe, because we are talking about an extremely closed society. Only certain mechanisms governing social behaviour are perceivable. What is visible is that people within each group watch each others' behaviours closely. One is followed by others round the clock. People look at others' acts thoroughly. The elderly especially think that they are morally entitled to know all about everything. This is a consequence of their having many common interests and obligations. Yet we should not believe that such societies are free from conflicts. The source for internal antagonisms, tensions and conflicts lies at the foundation of such societies. Let us take a closer look at how the traditional Kurdish authorities mentioned earlier are formed and function.

The Zaza society is very densely built, both physically and socially. The houses lean closely towards each other. An important reason for this is that the inhabitants have many common interests, and are materially and socially dependent on each other. Such a closeness of relations also forms the basis for internal tensions and conflicts. Often, milder disputes arise between individuals, families and kinship groups. There are many and insignificant causes of conflicts. Typical disputes arise usually due to settlements of inheritance, disagreement about distribution of water to gardens, fields or pastures, usage rights to agricultural or grazing lands, disagreement about the boundaries between real estate or fields, some one borrowing an article from the neighbour without the asking the owner for permission, suspicions of theft, quarrels about the neighbour's cow or sheep having grazed on one's fields or pastures, quarrels about children being beaten by the neighbour's children, rumours about the girl next door's behaviour or flirting with boys, gossip or suspicion of infidelity about the neighbour's wife, conflicts with the neighbouring villages and so forth. They may quarrel endlessly about such issues; they can fight repeatedly and avoid communicating with each other for many years. Often, these conflicts between two people also involve more than one family and kinship group on both sides. Painfully malicious envy is to be blamed for many of the disputes. At times, this envy actually constitutes a more serious threat to the social order. So, how do they solve their conflicts?

There is a central arbitration authority (police force, public prosecution, state administration, military garrison and so forth) in Solhan. But the population will not call on the arbitration authority to solve their conflicts. Moreover, the arbitration authority is regarded as consisting of foreign institutions or arrangements. The Zaza society has an old but well-established system for resolving conflicts. Their own arrangement for resolving their conflicts seems to be an extension of the idea at the basis of tribal formation as a means of self-protection against foreign powers, as I claimed at the beginning of this chapter. Somehow, depending on the nature and extension of the conflict, the resolution is obtained at three different levels. The first level is at which close kinship groups reach a settlement with one or more independent persons from without acting as arbitrators. The second level covers local conflicts that are not very serious. These are resolved at the village level, for example, influential persons from the village, the mullah and possibly prominent persons from neighbouring villages take the initiative or they are called upon for a solution. A solution at this level is respected by the disputing parties because those who take the initiative have acknowledged status in the local community. At the third level, more serious conflicts are resolved. The village does not have sufficient number of authorities who can resolve serious conflicts. Therefore, one appeals to external higher authorities, such as the sheikhdom, prominent tribal chiefs and other prominent persons in the area. Such spiritual- or kinship-based authorities still function in the Zaza society because as long as the population does not wish to resolve their conflicts through the Turkish arbitration authority ('the judiciary system'), there are ever more tasks that can be accomplished by its own authorities. Also, as long as the people do not change their attitude, the arrangement will continue to function. This brings us further to a closer observation of the Zaza Kurds' own authorities. One of them is the institution of patriarchy, which will be the subject of the next chapter.

Chapter 4

A patriarchal society

It is often difficult to differentiate between tribal and patriarchal ideologies, since both of these power structures are built upon a patrilineal ideology and they both legitimize their powerbase by referring to their being the rightful authority to provide the necessary protection and the sense of belonging which their members are entitled to. What differentiates these two unities is their size. As we have seen, a tribal society is larger and usually contains several lineages, while a patriarchal community is much smaller and more tightly integrated.

The Zaza society is strongly dominated by patriarchal traditions. Here patriarchy is perceived as a power structure confined to small units such as family and close relatives. Traditionally, patriarchy expresses a power formation where the power in the unit is connected with men, age and paternity. In the Zaza society, the patriarchy is regarded as the inviolable dominion of the paterfamilias and the head of the kin. This is the purest form of customary hegemony and it has long traditions.

In Europe, a patriarch is associated with nobility, clergy and royal traditions. On the contrary, in the Islamic world, this custom is practised by nearly everyone. All the families or kinship groups have their important and less important patriarchs, so to speak. The patriarch in the Zaza society has a very dominant position, both in the family, the neighbourhood and the local community. But first, a closer description of who the patriarchs are, should be given.

The typical hallmark of the patriarchs in the Zaza society is their being all men. They are regarded as venerable family heads and have predominant power and authority, both within the family and among kinsfolk. What characterizes them most is their being both very authoritarian and dominating. They act as self-conscious and determined lords. They are somewhat milder and nicer outside the group but towards insiders they are very authoritarian and strict. Within the family and among kinsfolk, they communicate with their adult or older sons and nephews often. The communication with wives, sisters, daughters, daughters-in-law and so forth is limited and also not mutual, especially when important decisions concerning the family and the kin are to be made.

The patriarchs follow paternal lineages. Many of them function patrilocally, that is, they govern what we would describe as several families according to western concepts, which is however defined as an extended family by the Zaza society, for instance, a large family dwelling in one place under the control of a male head of the family. This is a typical example of a patriarch. This extended family includes at least three generations plus some brothers, paternal uncles and nephews, together with their spouses and children. When some women not belonging to any large family are widowed, either the eldest brother or the paternal uncle of the deceased husband will act as the patriarch for the widow and her children, without necessarily marrying the widow.

The most essential issue in such an extended patrilocal family is how it is to be kept together and governed. The principles of government are informal and concrete. Here the relations of authority are based on personal dependence and tradition. The patriarch's words of command are clear. He determines who decides what, how the family members are to behave, and he has decisive influence on who will marry whom. Even the names for newly born children must be approved by him. All requests directed to the family are evaluated by the patriarch. Further, he functions as the family spokesman externally and when resolutions at the village or district level are to be formed, he represents the family. And finally there are clear rules for succession. He often appoints one of his favourite sons, whom he considers to be the most talented in the family, as his successor. Here personal considerations and favours play a more important role than competence. Consequently, patriarchal structure functions as a set of relations with a material basis, between powerful men. But, despite the fact that the structure is hierarchical, these relations manage to create dependence and solidarity between men. This makes oppression of women possible for them. But the patriarch is not always the formal owner of land and other property. If he is, the ownership does not mean anything other than his being responsible for the running of the property in the best way. All the same there is a definite 'alliance' between powerful men that has legalized a traditional hegemonic relation between the genders.

In other words, patriarchal relations have become hegemonic and work as an established institution with long historical traditions. The patriarchy expresses itself politically by disregarding the fundamental rights of women, among other things. Women, especially those in villages, are subjected to extensive control and monitoring. But also in small and medium-sized towns, there is more control than in large cities. Education plays a certain role here. The patriarchs have a certain degree of respect for educated women, because these women know their rights. They also now and again venture to demonstrate their rights against patriarchal praxis.

Yet the number of educated women in the Zaza society is so small that education still cannot be considered as a means to oppose patriarchal oppression. Men who are educated do not use this possibility to forward equality between the genders, either. On the contrary it seems as if well-educated men contribute to maintaining the extensive oppression of women. Looked at in this way, education can be considered as an equality-creating mechanism.

An example may illustrate this reasoning. Most of the Zaza people do not send their daughters to school after they have completed primary school. There is no tradition about this. The girls are not encouraged to do so, either. They are brought up to be married off. Often, only one or two favourite sons get the opportunity for further schooling. The most usual explanation I was given was that the duty to support parents, when they were no longer able to do so themselves, was not imposed on girls, although they get an education. Anyway, if the girls are educated, this benefits the husbands. The boys, usually son number 2 or 3, get an offer of education. It is seldom that the eldest son gets an offer of education, because he is obliged to support his parents and, in addition, he will inherit the property for further operation.

Most patriarchs are tradition oriented. They do not realize the necessity of binding the old in the form of tradition with the new and modern to create a coherent continuity for their members. Instead they invest unilaterally in inherited customs or conventional notions based on moral, religious and cultural traditions and values. The patriarchy transmits these values to girls and women through socialization. By this, they learn to believe in the traditions and to be obedient. In addition, they are continuously urged to build upon what is thought to be familiar, typical, stable and traditionally persistent.

The patriarchal culture is not characterized by openness to change, diversity, self-realization and equality between the genders, to mention some of the circumstances. The girls do not learn to be independent and modern. They are not given the opportunity to develop their own views about the world, about their lives or about alternative ways of thought and diverse ways of life. They are raised mainly to be married off, sometimes against their will, because they are defined as subjects or devoted individuals who are bound to the established traditions and hierarchies uncritically. As of today, the girls do not have the potential to break free of these conventional views.

Additionally, girls are not relied on as resources for the family. My impression was that if the girls got an education, this would lead to changes in the family pattern. People were afraid of this. They had certainly heard that educated people cohabit without getting married, that some of them have children out of wedlock, that divorces are increasing among people with higher education, and about 'the sexual liberation' and so forth. All of this threatens the stable family institution that they defend at all costs. They have judged the developments in the modern society that have led to the dissolution of the family institution to be hostile features. Consequently their family patterns became even more important. In addition, they regarded their own family pattern as a social heritage. Therefore, it was important to transmit it further. But from a modern perspective, this tradition appears to be quite inimical to development and a hindrance to the modernization of the society. In the future, it will act divisively between groups, between men and women to begin with. The relation between the patriarchy and women consists of latent conflicts and is connected with power and interests, because the patriarchy refuses to acknowledge women's rights and interests. It will also influence the relations between the older and younger generations, between better educated and poorly educated and so forth, and will necessarily create social changes.

The patriarchs do not think rationally, their actions are not legitimized by the belief in reasonable thought either, but rather they use holy scripts as a reference for their views. Moreover, they refer to the lifelong experience that they possess. They legitimize their actions by divine scripts, that is to say a belief in the inviolability of the authority, which, moreover, resembles Weber's typology of authorities. In addition, the subjects expect that the attitudes, stance and actions of the patriarch shall be anchored to religious scripts or justified religiously. This confers on him social power and a considerable devotion from subjects.

The power and the authority of the patriarchs are conceived as legitimate by the family and the kin. Their power and authority is not necessarily built upon personal qualities as is the case in European societies, but upon inherited family tradition, for example, congenital rank and status. Also their power, authority and prestige increases with age but decreases somewhat when they become very old, somewhere around 70 to 80 years old. Then they are perceived of as senile, which results in that they are not taken seriously by the family and the kin any longer.

Consequently, one of the foremost tasks of the patriarch is to keep the family as a moral unity. After that comes the contribution to the cohesion within the kin. This is done by the patriarch by monitoring the behaviour and movements of the family members and the kinsfolk closely. Rules of conduct in the patriarchal Zaza society are very strict. But, in certain cases related to kinship, the praxis is more flexible than what is prescribed by the rules. However, this does not imply that the rules provide a space for action.

Let us consider the principle of virginity as an example. This rule entails that in all the patrilineal families in the Islamic world the girls who get married should be virgins (as brides). This means pride for the girls: they must demonstrate their credibility to the men they marry. For the men, this means a confirmation of the fidelity of the women they are marrying. When the girl gets married, the man's family wants to know if the girl has been a virgin or not. To determine this, white bed linen is used for the mattress and the quilt cover on the wedding night. The bed is tidied up by other female members of the family, preferably the mother or a sister of the bridegroom, the following morning and these report further to the head of the family, other relatives and neighbours. This tradition has been widespread up to now. But there is a lot that points to a change in the tradition. In the villages where I conducted field work, I was told that not all families undertake such a control of the bride's virginity. It seems that people are no longer so scrupulous about it. My impression was that most people have acquired an understanding that it was a matter that should be between the bride and the bridegroom.

Another example of flexible praxis is connected with contracting marriages. A usual rule prescribes that a boy and girl must be acquainted before they get married. That somebody from the girl's family, most usually a sister or a cousin, must be present at the first meeting has been the tradition. This tradition has been changing lately. Many families let the two parties meet without the presence of a chaperone.

Patriarchs are to be found in all social strata. Most heads of the family more or less try to play the role of a patriarch but not all have the ability to play this powerful position. Some families have weak patriarchs. They lack the characteristics of the patriarchy, are by nature not authoritarian enough or have a such weak position in the family that they cannot tackle their role. Some also disagree fundamentally with the patriarchal traditions as the ideal form of government. Those who really manage to function as patriarchs are the economically affluent ones, for example tribal chiefs, sheikhs or religious figures. Naturally, the majority of the patriarchs are found among this stratum.

If something positive has to be said about patriarchal traditions, it must be that the patriarchs, by use of the old-fashioned morals, have prevented the commercial exploitation of the female body. This they accomplish very effectively. On the other hand, they favour men by referring to their being better qualified, both physically and intellectually. This is the reason that men generally have more freedom of movement than women in all patriarchal societies. This freedom has a social function and they make maximum use of this freedom. Otherwise, the patriarchs refer to women in a condescending way and they refuse equal property rights to them. This will be amplified in Chapter 10 on family and relations between the genders.

Kinship and marriage

Descent and marriage have been important components of kinship relations in the Zaza society. As in most other Islamic societies, the Zaza also have clear rules for who can marry whom. In this section, I will describe the types of marriage relations developed by the Zaza society. I will not describe everything that has to do with the gender relations here. Instead, an entire chapter is dedicated to this purpose (see Chapter 10). Therefore, in this chapter, I will limit myself first and foremost to the gender relations that have to do with kinship.

There are two types of rules that regulate contracting marriages in the Zaza society. One is the *prescriptive* system or principle, which has created the FBD marriage (marriage with father's brother's daughter). This involves cousins marrying each other, for instance, one marries father's brother's daughter or father's sister's daughter. This is allowed both religiously and legally in all Islamic societies, but this custom is practised more frequently in West Asia and North Africa. The prescriptive marriage is still dominant among large portions of the Zaza society. According to studies carried out by the Dicle University in Diyarbekir in 2002, prescriptive marriage makes up 42–46 per cent of marriages. In certain areas, such as remote villages, this number is even higher as people have generally limited contact with the outside world in such villages.

Contracting a marriage of the prescriptive type is decided by the respective kinship groups. This does not necessarily imply that biological kinship is attributed precedence over classificatory kinship.[1] In the Solhan region, it is usual that two lineages, for example, two lineages related distantly through the paternal line, exchange women among themselves for longer periods. Descent groups that exchange women simultaneously form close *symmetrical alliances*. This implies equivalence between the groups, because both belong to the same tribe, both have somewhat similar social and economic status, both are donors and receivers, and there is no particular difference of rank between the groups. This tradition is quite widespread within more than one subgroup in the tribes.

An important reason for a group member's preference to marry a near relative – endogamy[2] – is first and foremost a wish to strengthen or consolidate bonds of kinship within groups. They see the advantages in forming an alliance. Another reason is the necessity of maintaining the most important values of the kinship group at the time of contracting marriages. Such marriages also contribute to the stability of the group over longer periods. Consequently, consideration of stable unities between groups leads to many marriages between cousins or second cousins. If some members in the same descent group have not married each other during one or two generations and kinship ties are becoming weaker, the families feel almost disturbed. Then they commit themselves to having some members marry each other to tie the bonds of kinship more closely. The groups arrange marriages with an eye to strengthening the bonds of lineage between themselves. Reinforcing their close relations is considered to be safe. Therefore, it is usual that contracting a marriage is regarded primarily as being about the relation between groups and only secondarily between two individuals.

The ideal of marrying someone from the vicinity of one's family in the same village or a neighbouring village still exists among young girls, because being near their families confers them a series of practical advantages, not least the opportunity of close contact with their families. A woman living close by can often move back to her family if she feels mistreated.

A more important justification for marriages within the descent group is security: the parties know each other better. They are familiar with the obligations related to kinship. These obligations make them more considerate towards each other and treat each other with more respect. In case problems between the spouses arise, they can, by virtue of kinship, appeal to other members in the family or in the kinship group for help. A woman marrying within her own descent group often fares better than a woman from without. Naturally, there are many exceptions here as well. But the main pattern is that women marrying within the same descent group display greater respect and consideration, close feelings, responsibility and so forth for family members. To be brief, they feel they are one of the ranks, and are accepted more easily by the kinship group than those coming from without.

An example comes from the many small and big quarrels I witnessed between women. When they quarrel, they are in the habit of swearing in the same way as men, although their swearing is not always as malicious as men's. Men's swearing has the characteristics of assaulting the person and is directed to the opponent's sexual organs in order to insult both the individual and his kin. Two women quarrelled occasionally in the house next to where I lived. The two were married to two brothers who lived together in the same house. They were not happy with this situation. They wanted to move into separate homes but could not convince their husbands. Quarrelling was a way to realize their plans, with the hope of making their spouses grasp that it was unbearable to continue to live together. One of the women was related to her husband through the paternal lineage, while the other woman was from outside the lineage. When they accused each other, they used to swear, as well. The outsider acted quite inconsiderately. She used obscenities primarily to strike the other woman but this was insulting to her husband and children, as well. The result was that the second woman had to defend her husband, who was a cousin. This made her popular both in the family and among the kinsfolk. She acquired greater sympathy and influence.

The outsider gradually became unpopular with the family and was socially excluded in many ways. The family members distanced themselves from her because they thought she did not respect the family members and did not behave responsibly. The result was that she felt lonely in the family.

The point of this example is that women who marry within their own descent group are held responsible more easily, due to feelings of kinship, and this provides them with advantages in the form of popularity, acceptance, acknowledgement and influence. Prescriptive marriage is still widely practised as a result of such advantages, particularly in the remote mountain villages. All the same, there is much that points to prescriptive marriage losing ground, particularly in the densely inhabited districts. The picture of prescriptive marriage is about to change in these areas.

The other type of principle that regulates contracting marriages is *preferential*. This principle is not regarded to be as absolute as the first one, but is more flexible. Preferential marriage involves marrying somebody who is not closely related biologically. Many people marry someone who is not related biologically but who belongs all the same to the Zaza population. Although this type of marriage is becoming more widespread, it should be noted that only a few people married someone from outside the central Zaza areas.

The most usual marriage pattern in the Zaza society is that people marry within their own social class and cultural milieu. Often, people with high prestige or privileges prefer to marry someone with a similar background, while those with low status or the underprivileged marry each other. This principle is applied more often to people not belonging to the same descent group than to those within the same kinship group.

Contracting marriages based on preferential rules are perhaps becoming more dominating in the Zaza society, but all the same this has obvious limits. One attitude that dominates is that one cannot marry a stranger. Practising this type of marriage is regarded as complex, because a series of conditions are imposed. More familiarity with the stranger, making a survey of his/her family background, religious affiliation and, in some cases, ethnic affiliation are among the most important conditions that must be clarified before one's mind is made up and the procedures for contracting a marriage are initiated. In the case of a girl being married off, the economic situation of the future husband must also be investigated.

It appears that the newer generations prefer spouses from without the descent group more often than from within. This is partly due to their being less affected by traditions and the past than their parents are. That they are bound less to traditions has led them to seek spouses from other categories than their own descent group. But this is not wholly unproblematic. In the patriarchal Zaza society, the 'adult–youngster' relation is organized along a strict 'senior–junior' axis, on which women are assigned an everlasting junior position within the kinship group. Choice of spouses outside the descent group breaks with this tradition and, therefore, often creates problems with respect to the cultural norms that the parents have transmitted. Parents perceive changes in this social pattern and cultural notions in relation to choosing a spouse. They also discover conflicts between the generations with respect to preferential rules and they interpret this process of change as a cultural rebellion against stability.

An important obstacle arises if the partners, including the families, have a different social status. It is not usual that somebody with a middle-class background marries someone with lower social status. A certain equilibrium is expected with respect to status, income, education, occupation and, not least, the family prestige and esteem. It is totally inconceivable that a girl from a prosperous family would marry a shepherd or a servant of the family. It is nearly as unusual as a noble woman marrying 'a man of lowly birth'. The same rules apply also when boys choose their partners. A topical question often asked is, how are partners to be chosen based on preferential rules?

People marrying according to preferential rules meet stricter additional criteria when they choose partners, criteria that would be ignored if they both had belonged to the same descent group. Usually, some importance is attached to personal attraction and family background, but attention to social class, status or education, employment, economic situation, common interests and so forth pays off more in choosing a partner. Such demands are made, particularly by the girls. Girls often choose partners with a secure future with respect to work, education and economy, not on the basis of having similar social positions that produce people similar enough to thrive together in a marriage, but rather because the position of women in the society is so much weaker than that of men; therefore, they are forced to choose a secure future.

In principle, partner selection based on preferential rules in the Zaza society does not differ that much from the so-called 'free selection of partners' practiced in western societies. But because of deficient opportunities and limitations connected with women's weak social standing in the Zaza society, partner selection becomes nearly totally different compared to partner selection in the west. In western societies, there are certain criteria on which a choice of a partner is based. In North Europe, there is a well-known rule which expresses these criteria: 'Similar children play best.' (Birds of a feather flock together.) The adage clearly and distinctly expresses what is thought about partner selection. To play best or to thrive together, it is expected that the partners should have somewhat similar social position with respect to employment, occupation, education, economic background, tastes, common interests or personal attraction, and so forth. Such additional criteria are relevant also in the Zaza society. The difference is that while in western societies additional criteria in partner selection are used in order to thrive together, in the Zaza society they are used so that the women can achieve a safer future. Women in western societies have more freedom of choice. They are not dependent on the man's income. The woman and the man may have a relationship for a considerable time before they finally reach a decision concerning marriage. This is justified by reference to getting to know each other better. This possibility does not exist in the Zaza society. Partners must get married before they really get to know each other. This creates problems for some people, while others put up with it.

Meanwhile, the greatest obstacle is connected to situations in which the partners belong to different religions or opposing denominations within Islam. Contracting a marriage would be unthinkable if one of the partners is a Muslim and the other is a Christian. The same problem would arise if one is a Sunni Muslim and the other is an Alevi. In such cases, both the family and all the kinsfolk would intervene to prevent the marriage.

The rule that marriage should take place within the ethnic group – endogamy – has been widespread until recently. Marriages between people with different ethnic backgrounds, for example, between Kurds and Turks, has not been usual. There are few people with Zaza background married to Turks. First of all, the large geographical distances between these groups of people has resulted in very little contact between them. Second, there are still significant reservations against it and these reservations are mutual. Zaza people, especially the politically conscious ones, justify their reservations by referring to their being oppressed by the Turks. 'One does not marry an enemy', is a dictum heard often. The reservations of the Turks are connected with attitudes of the dominant people. The Kurds are generally regarded as subordinate, inferior and, above all, as enemies, because they constitute a constant threat to the Turks. It is legitimate to look down on them. Therefore few marriages are contracted between the Zaza population and ethnic Turks.

Consequently, kinship relations with the accompanying rituals in the Zaza society function in relation to contracting marriages, tribal society and patriarchal unity. Often, these relations operate as totally fundamental and integrating principles for the groups.

Chapter 5

A society with its own authorities

Large portions of the Zaza society de facto lie outside the Turkish state organization. The population itself has very little to do with the Turkish state. For them, it is fine that they live outside the Turkish state's control as state authorities do not attempt to protect them, but instead act as brutal oppressors. In the villages there are no kindergartens, health care or other public services. The primary school is the only institution that symbolizes the Turkish state. On average, three out of four children have attended school. Each school has 150 pupils on average. The school usually has only one teacher and very few have two. The teaching is in Turkish. However, the educational activities proceed in an unsystematic manner, because the teachers may be absent for weeks, either due to alleged illness or as a result of threats from the Kurdish guerrilla movement, the PKK, which demands that education should be conducted in Kurdish, something that is strictly forbidden.

Large portions of the Zaza population clearly understand why they are abandoned to their own devices. They know that the Turkish state does not represent them either ethnically or culturally. They also know that they are not regarded as part of the administrative or political power of the Turkish state. They realize that their ethnic background is the main reason that the Turkish state has for decades consciously enacted policies that aim at keeping their area as underdeveloped as possible. This situation has resulted in the organization of the population in a nearly stateless society. While the state does not wish to come to their aid, Zaza-speaking Kurds strive to achieve their own form of arrangements. Many other population groups in the Middle East live in orderly societies without any state organization.

In such a situation, one asks many questions: how does the Zaza population manage to live in a society without state institutions? How is the society integrated? How can this society maintain loyalty when it does not surrender itself completely to the 'formal authority', that is the state apparatus? How do they resolve conflicts without recourse to courts and a judiciary system, which are totally foreign to them? Why does such a society not disintegrate? How can such a society be governed and why is it not integrated into the Turkish society? Many people ask why the Zaza population lives as it does, today in the twenty-first century. The Zaza live as they do *not* because they are not familiar with the outside world. Meanwhile, that the Zaza population is organized in a *stateless-like* society does not mean that they regard themselves as rootless, as many human rights organizations have claimed. Let me illustrate this with an example to show how they achieve their moral rights or struggle for them, which are at least as effective as legal protection by the state.

Memo was a relatively young boy from a comparably prosperous family in a mountain village to the north-west of Solhan. He had a university education and a good job. Memo fell in love with a girl from the neighbouring village. The girl's family were tenants and ranked at the bottom of the social scale. Memo's family staunchly opposed a marriage with the girl because her family were held in low esteem. On the contrary, for Memo the girl and her family were humans with equal value. But above all, he wanted the girl because he loved her, and everything else was insignificant. Memo could not persuade his family. They would not accept him marrying her. So Memo had to find another solution. He decided to abduct the girl. The abduction happened willingly, that is to say both Memo and the girl wanted such a solution. Abduction of girls is a widespread tradition in the Zaza society and it happens when the parents of the boys or the girls do not accept the opposite partner as equals.

Yet abductions of girls without their consent also happen, that is, girls being abducted against their wish by use of physical force. Fortunately, such marriages occur much more seldom now than in previous times.

What kind of solution did this, the abduction, achieve? Although the abduction was an escape that Memo and the girl took, this does not mean that the issue is resolved as a matter of course. An abduction can lead to a marriage only if the girl's parents accede to it. Although this case is not perceived as a forcible abduction, it is still quite serious, because the boy's family had insulted the girl's family by declaring them to be inferior. Ironically enough, once the abduction happens, the boy's family is forced to take the initiative for a conciliation of the involved parties according to the tradition. This must happen if the boy and the girl are to get married. A solution must be affected under the auspices of an authority and there are two choices in such a case. Either the case is brought before the court in Solhan for a decision or it is solved in the traditional way.

The first alternative is of very little interest. The Zaza society generally has very little contact with the Turkish state. It has even less contact with the local police or the judicial administration. The few occasions when they have come into contact with the police or the judiciary have ended with rough treatment and corruption. They are harassed and looked down on and get a clear impression that they must put up with the Turkish arrangement, although this can be perceived as an occupational power. Nor do they identify with the decisions reached by the Turkish courts. There is hardly anything more humiliating than being subdued by foreigners, in both significant and insignificant cases. To the Zaza people's consciousness, the Turkish military and political hegemony is an unbearable situation. They have been humiliated time and again in the worst thinkable manner, and humiliated human beings can become very sensitive, which is exactly what characterizes this people. Therefore, they have good reasons not to involve the police or the judiciary to resolve conflicts. Moreover, they are very wary of letting the foreigners solve what they term private conflicts or internal affairs. Such considerations make the people in Solhan region resort to their own solutions, and in this manner they keep the Turkish authorities at a distance.

To save the family honour and esteem is the most important consideration in such situations. The concept of honour is absolutely the most important guideline for the Zaza population. According to Fredrik Barth (1991), to act honourably in Islamic societies is to control oneself rather than one's surroundings; it is the capability to display decent and courteous behaviour under all circumstances and towards all fellow human beings. Such an ideal of humanity among the Zaza people leads them to regard it nearly as a holy duty to solve their own conflicts without government interference. They also know through experience that intervention by the state results in more traps and provocations. So they know how to protect themselves against foreign interference. There are many conditions for not wishing to involve the state authorities. Even the awareness of the need to keep state power at arm's length is enough to mobilize the local population to resolve the conflict that Memo and the girl created.

Since the Zaza population keeps the state power consciously at arm's length and is not interested in solutions coming from without, this void is handed over to internal forces so they may mobilize for a solution. Following the tradition, Memo's father initiated a process with a view to a solution. He invited sheikhs, the mullah in the village and several prominent powerful persons from the neighbouring villages to find a solution to the abduction of the girl. They went to the girl's father and obtained his permission for a marriage between Memo and the girl. This was a conciliation supported by all the population in the area.

According to the local population, the abduction case ended in a just and respectable solution. The legitimacy in the case lies in the fact that the elderly, with Memo's father at the head, intervened and conciliated the families, leading to permission for a marriage between Memo and the girl. This is a solution that the local population received with satisfaction. They want to define their own events and find solutions for their own conflicts. The alternative would be submission to the brutal resolution of the police and the court, a forcible solution that would damage the esteem of the local community, first because it would be considered as a defeat for the Zaza society. It would mean that they were not able to find their own solutions. Second, it would mean accepting interference on internal issues as a matter of course.

Moreover, a decision issued by a Turkish court will not be respected. In some respects, it will not be regarded as a proper decision, because it will not have been based on their moral grounds. Their morals prescribe that when members violate established rules of conduct, it will be natural that the local society itself takes action and accommodates itself to its own solutions. Keeping the state at a distance gives them the possibility to express their wish for peace and to escape oppression. The Zaza demonstrate by this that people in a society without state control can in many ways have greater freedom contrary to being completely brought under state control.

When, in addition, the state acts oppressively, people in this region are forced to avoid establishing any form of relations with the state and its institutions. They try to become as independent of the state as possible. Meanwhile, this does not lead to freedom for the individual. He must just accommodate himself to the existing systems, for instance, the sheikhdom, feudal systems and kinship systems that we will describe in the coming chapters.

The sheikhdom in the Solhan region

In a society without the rule of law and police protection, other arrangements are required to keep the order. Here, by arrangements I mean customs, a set of rules for human behaviour that persists for a long time or a typical praxis for resolving conflicts. In Memo's and certainly in many other cases, the Zaza people's own solutions worked very well and quite effectively. But a system outside of state control does not function on its own. What makes this system function? Which motives drive this system? How and why can the system be so effective?

A sheikhdom built on faith in authorities and demands of loyalty, and well organized to some extent, reigns in the Solhan region. In the Zaza language, this sheikhdom is called *Shexi Melon*. I will give a short description of this sheikhdom in order to explain how the social organization functions in this area.

The sheikhdom manifests itself as an order over the entire Solhan region and its environs with the present sheikh, Wahdedin, as its supreme leader. He owns half of the three large villages Melon, Yekmal and Beruej. In addition to the villages, he also owns large tracts of land such as mountain pastures and highlands, which are very productive, especially for sheep farming. Every year, he rents out the land for several tens of thousands of American dollars, and by Turkish standards this is a lot of money. Melon has been this family's permanent residence for many generations, but in the last 30 years the sheikh has lived in Bingöl in the winter and in the village in the summer. The sheikh's paternal relatives are also among the richest in the area, owning large tracts of land and pastures.

The institution of sheikhdom in the Zaza area must not be confused with the Arabic sheikhdoms, despite many signs of similarity. The sheikhdom in this area is somehow different. Its legitimacy builds on religious myths that go back well over 100 years. The myth relates that Sheikh Wahdedin's great-great-grandfather, Abdullah, gained his esteem through another famous man, Sheikh Ali of Palu. In that time, Palu was a neighbouring province of Bingöl. Today it is converted to a district and subordinated to the Xarput (Elazig in Turkish) province. It is said that during a visit, Sheikh Ali granted Abdullah apocalyptic powers. Consequently, Abdullah could prophesy correctly, have presentiments of the invisible and, therefore, could maintain that he was indispensable for the presence of God (Allah) among the believers. Abdullah gained recognition from this and was chosen to be the spiritual guide of the people in the Solhan region, with the village of Melon as the religious centre. His authority was legitimized by his alleged apocalyptic powers and he was accepted as legitimate by his subjects. This was received with enthusiasm by the people. It was said: 'Finally, the people in the Solhan region have got their religious leader.' Since then, the sheikh's power and authority have been inviolable.

There are no written documents that can explain why Sheikh Ali of Palu appointed the relatively poor and unknown Abdullah as the spiritual leader of the Solhan region. Sheikh Ali was a spiritual leader, but was established in Palu and the surrounding areas. Sheikh Ali was a member of the Nakshibendi movement, a religious order that had established itself in Kurdistan at the beginning of the eighteenth century as a counterweight to the Ottoman rule in Istanbul. There is much indicating that Sheikh Ali wanted to extend the Nakshibendi movement's territorial boundaries to include Solhan and the surroundings, with Abdullah as his closest ally.[1] Later cooperation between them, political as well as spiritual, and mutual marriages shows this theory is probable.

But the sheikhdom in the Zaza area must be set in a wider context. Many wonder why sheikhdoms have arisen at all, not only in the Zaza region but also throughout Kurdistan and the Middle East. As an institution, the sheikhdom has played a dominant role in the social life, especially in the last couple of centuries. Indeed, the Nakshibendi Order had existed in Kurdistan in the 1400s but until the beginning of the 1800s it did not have any real influence. The Nakshibendi Order began to be organized in earnest from 1811 onwards, with Mewlana Khalid as spearhead. The most probable explanation for the appearance of the sheikhdom is the reforms introduced by the Ottoman Empire at the beginning of the 1800s. Until 1830s, the Kurdish areas were administered by local Kurdish feudal princes (*Mir* in Kurdish), often with local private militias financed by the Ottoman Empire. The principalities were quite autonomous and had considerable support among the people. But Sultan Mahmud II (1808–39) put an end to principalities as an administrative arrangement in his lifetime. He introduced the rule through governors appointed from Istanbul, who were largely Turks. They were not familiar with the Kurdish culture, did not have sufficient knowledge about the local conditions, tribal relations and so forth, resulting in not being regarded as legitimate authorities by the population. Some governors also used 'divide and rule' methods. Introduction of rule by governors also led to increased tension between the tribes. Due to their lack of knowledge about Kurdish culture, they could not play the role of arbitrator between disputing tribes, either. Consequently, the appointed governors enjoyed neither natural authority nor legitimacy among the population to reduce the conflicts. The Nakshibendi Order saw this power vacuum and the discontent of the population. Therefore, they began to organize. During the turbulent time in the wake of organizing of governorships, the Nakshibendi sheikhs were fully aware of the great need to re-establish the social order among the population. In the course of a few years, the organizer, Mewlana Khalid, sent out a large number of sheikhs to all of Kurdistan (see Figure 5.1). They were authorized to

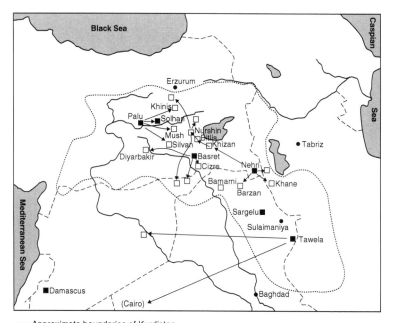

······ Approximate boundaries of Kurdistan
■ Residences of Mewlana Khalid's khalifas
□ Residences of other Nakshibendi sheikhs (khalifa of khalifa, etc.)
→ sheikh-khalifa relationships

Figure 5.1 Important centres of propagation of the Nakshibendi Order
Source: Adapted from Martin van Bruinessen (1992).

arbitrate between disputing tribes without consulting the governors. Their first priority was to reduce the conflicts between the tribes and among the population and this led to their becoming very popular in the course of a short time. It was not long before the sheikhal clergy became an institutionalized powerbase in all Kurdistan. Later, many of these Nakshibendi men appointed by Mewlana Khalid played very central roles in the Kurdish liberation struggles, in particular Sheikh Ubeydullah of Nehri, Sheikh Said of Palu and Mullah Mustafa of Barzan. All three of these families have a highly respected place in Kurdistan.

The appointment of Abdullah and others as sheikhs initiated a long process full of wealth, gross exploitation and abuse of power, and harassment and discrimination of the population on religious grounds. Yet when all is said, it must be added that the sheikhdom in Melon has also played a positive role; one example was in 1920s when Sheikh Abdullah (Junior) led a major popular rebellion against Turkish oppression, which we will describe in more detail later. However, the legendary Kurdish leader Sheikh Said had this to say about the Nakshibendi Order: 'The Nakshibendi movement has formed a gangster band in Kurdistan' (van Bruinessen 1992: 312). Until the end of 1800s, the Nakshibendi movement had resisted attacks by the state, but gradually it was infiltrated and used as an instrument of oppression against the Kurds.

Because the newly appointed Abdullah was a poor man, he acquired property without payment. The villagers in the neighbourhood handed three villages and large areas on the plateau over to him, which are owned by Wahdedin today. Consequently, the sheikh suddenly became rich, overnight so to speak. Acquisition of apocalyptic powers and large, rich lands formed further grounds for Abdullah's moral authority and influence in large portions of the Zaza society. These powers at the same time became a source of hope for poor people.

Quva, a holy grave where the sheikh's forefathers are buried, is one of the more important sources of hope. At the *Quva*, people, especially the destitute, seek help and comfort, and protection against evil forces. People ask for their wishes to be fulfilled, for example, recovering from crises such as illness or marrying the person one wants. People have expectations regarding the sheikh's greatness. Those who ask for help at the holy grave feel they are spiritually not mature, while the sheikh is close to God. So they are totally devoted to him.

At least 200 landless people make a living in the three villages owned by the sheikh today. They work both for the sheikh and for themselves. These peasants are completely subjected to the sheikh and a large portion of his enormous income is from the surplus production of these peasants. But he has assumed a series of other roles and duties beyond this. The sheikh has acquired enormous power and authority due to religious myths and alleged apocalyptic abilities, to the extent that he is nearly deified. Many are willing to die for the sheikh and what he stands for, and he can mobilize the population politically and religiously around local issues and in other situations. This is the background for his being able to assume many roles. His task is to act as an arbitrator, for example, to resolve conflicts in agreement about the holy Islamic law. There are many who turn to him to act as a counsellor in religious and political issues. In short, he is a religious leader with the might to hold sway over large parts of the Solhan region and surroundings, giving both his blessings and condemnations. He is respected and his advice followed. But many of his most important tasks have been of a political nature. He exercises his power mainly in three areas:

- the economic,
- the political,
- the religious and the moral.

The sheikh's economic authority

In the economic area, the sheikh manipulates the people's religious feelings and exploits these to enrich himself. For example, he makes people work for him without payment. This contribution usually happens as follows: a few years ago, the sheikh had some 800 sheep, including lambs, which were part of his wealth. But these sheep are tended nearly for five months in the winter by the people of the Solhan region, of course, gratis. When winter approached at the end of the harvest, the sheikh's servants took the flock of sheep to many villages, where each family felt obliged to receive one, two or three sheep, depending on the family's economic circumstances. Most of them are so poor that they struggle to get their daily bread but, all the same, feel it to be a religious duty to take care of the sheikh's sheep.

Once I witnessed the sheikh's servants distributing the sheep to the inhabitants of a mountain village. It was the middle of the day when three of the sheikh's servants arrived with a large flock of sheep.

They stopped in the middle of the village and began calling out: 'Come forward quickly and take His Eminence's sheep. Hurry up, it is a religious duty, you owe this to God', and so forth. The call appeared as a clear religious order that hit home with all the inhabitants. At least one person from each family showed up within a few minutes. When each one received 'his' sheep, the servants said, 'May God bless you and your children', and he went away with 'his' sheep. I saw that some of them who received the sheikh's sheep actually could not afford to take care of it, but they dared not refuse. A friend of mine asked, 'Cannot the sheikh himself afford to keep these sheep? After all, he is the richest man in this region'. The oldest servant turned towards my friend, cast a severe look at him and said, 'Who are you to oppose God's will? Watch out or the sheikh will put a curse on you'. After threats from the servant, some men strongly tried to persuade my friend to be cautious with the sheikh. He should not ask critical questions, otherwise the sheikh would wish his death.

Another example is that the sheikh uses his moral authority to summon people for different tasks connected with agriculture. Here the labour is also provided for free. These people must even bring their own victuals, which is unusual because, according to tradition, one either works for wages or gets free food from the host. In return for all these services, the sheikh reciprocates by arbitrating serious conflicts, such as vendettas, forcible abduction of girls, property disputes, tribal conflicts and so forth. The poor's misfortune becomes in many ways the sheikh's happiness and success. He acts on it with an eye to his personal gain and, according to his critics, without any feelings of conscience.

The sheikh's political authority

In the political area, the sheikh uses his moral power and prestige for, among other things, mobilizing people to vote for the candidate he himself supports. The sheikh has been active in all elections, especially the parliamentary elections. The candidate has often been his son, his close relative or supporter. His son has had a seat in the parliament in Ankara for two periods. He has also had a hand in the outcome of other elections, be it elections for the municipality or the county council. But the sheikh's influence at the grassroots level has been considerably weakened in the last decades. Doubts about his political credibility have been raised by portions of the people, especially after he changed his party several times in the period after 1980.

Many people think that the sheikh has not displayed any political consistency in his attitude towards the political parties. The sheikh committed himself strongly to the party for which his son was a parliamentary candidate. He went to the extent of expressly announcing that those who would vote for the other parties must recognize that they were committing a sin; they must realize that they were infidels and repent. When in the next elections his son ran for another party, the sheikh encouraged people to vote for this party, again in order to avoid a sinful act. The sheikh justifies his threats by claiming that people must submit to God's will by complying with the holy law, which he himself interprets. But there is nothing in the holy law that says people must vote for the party the sheikh demands. It seems that, according to the usual democratic principles about political responsibility and participation, the people in the Solhan region are relinquishing their democratic rights and duties.

The sheikh's attitude towards the Kurdish question has also contributed to the decline in the support for him. There has been a 15-year armed conflict between Kurds and the Turkish state that does not recognize the Kurds as a people. Over this period, 37,000 people have been killed as a result of the conflict. Two-thirds were Kurds. Sections of the people in the Solhan region have also supported what they regard as a liberation struggle against Turkish hegemony and oppression. Many young men from this region have become guerrilla soldiers and many have been killed by the Turkish security forces.

The sheikh has been silent on this subject and this does not conform to people's expectations. A portion of the people I have talked to are deeply disappointed over the sheikh's (lack of) political judgement. Many are of the opinion that the sheikh's political strategy is incompatible with what the sheikhdom has stood for. The sheikh's grandfather, Sheikh Abdullah (Junior), was a prominent Kurdish politician in the 1920s. He was one of the leaders of the 1925 insurrection. The great insurrection, named after Sheikh Said, was led specifically by the Zaza population and received almost full support in the entire Zaza region and some of the neighbouring Kurmanji-dominated regions such as Varto, Mush, Diyarbekir, Elazig (formerly Xarput) and Karakocan. The background for the rebellion was that the rights promised to the Kurds during the liberation of Turkey in the 1920s were not granted. The rebellion was suppressed brutally and the leaders including the legendary leader Sheikh Said, Sheikh Abdullah and many more from the Solhan region were executed by the Turkish authorities in June 1925.

The Turkish state has had a strategy for incorporating the Zaza Kurds into the state since Atatürk's time. The strategy was based on the idea that the people could be connected more tightly to the state via the landowners, especially the sheikhs and the tribal leaders. So the tribal leaders and the sheikhs would play the major role in the assimilation strategy. According to this strategy, the tribal leaders were assigned the task of using tribal relations to strengthen the authority of the state. Seen from the Turkish side, this strategy has been partially successful.

The sheikh's cooperation with the state has been one of the most important circumstances that led to his defeat in the 1998 elections and his son's failure to be elected to the Turkish National Assembly. Those who oppose the sheikhdom believe that the sheikh's interests generally do not oppose those of the state. Therefore, he cooperates with the state. The idea behind this opposition to the sheikhdom is the demand that the state should expropriate the sheikh's enormous land and distribute it to the landless poor. But the state rejects such a demand because of its alliance with the sheikh. People think that the sheikh has allied himself with the state to prevent demands for land reform and that he resists the Kurdish liberation movement in return. Many think that as long as the state does not start a process of land reform, its interests coincide with those of the sheikhdom.

This is not the only case. Nearly all the influential sheikhs in the Kurdish region have allied themselves with the state. Many of them have had seats in the Turkish parliament for years and some of them have been also in the cabinet, among others members of the Sheikh Ali of Palu's kin, the sheikh who appointed Abdullah as the spiritual leader of the Solhan region. One of them was Ali Riza Septioglu, a minister in the Turkish government for a period in the 1970s. Septioglu was a member of the parliament for about 30 years before he died a few years ago. Yet not all tribal chiefs, sheikhs or mullahs were given lucrative offers to cooperate with the state. Some families that had participated actively in the 1925 insurrection have never been invited to cooperate. Neither have these families shown any interest in cooperating with the state against their own people.

Meanwhile, after the Kurdish liberation movement, the PKK, established itself in the 1990s, the Turkish state felt a greater need to invest in the idea of acquiring more supporters in the Solhan region. Many were invited to cooperate with the state in the fight against the PKK. Those who turned to a close cooperation with the state were rewarded with different political offices and positions in the local administration. Yet the state power felt a greater need to expand its activities on more fronts. The need to split the unity of the tribes received a higher priority because the state feared that the tribes would support the PKK. Therefore, they had to be divided. In order to achieve this, the military authorities engaged the MHP in the fight against the PKK. The MHP stands ideologically very close to the military and the party has armed paramilitary militias, which the state used in the fight against the left-oriented activists in the 1970s. Political experts think that the military regards the MHP as its closest ally. In the police corps, among officers and in the National Investigation Organization (MIT), the MHP has the most supporters compared with the other parties. The Turkish paramilitary units were allowed to use means provided by the state to divide the tribes. They have succeeded in carrying out their task to a certain degree. They have split first and foremost the Solaxan tribe. About half of the tribe's members support this party. The MHP has managed to recruit some unemployed and poor people, badly educated youths from economically poor families. MHP supporters among the Kurds function exactly as the Norwegian supporters of the Nazis, for example, Quisling's and the Rinnan Gang's crimes against Norwegians during the Second World War. These people are indoctrinated with a false racial ideology which propagates that the Kurds belong to the *superior Turkish race* and this propaganda influences some naive people, often poor and illiterate ones without self-confidence who allow their ignorance to be exploited. There are many of this kind of people in Turkey, since the state has seen to it that people do not have the opportunity to access other sources of information to educate themselves.

The MHP has also functioned as a recruiting ground for two secret military organizations, the Gendarmerie Intelligence Organization (JITEM) and the Turkish Revenge Brigades (TIT). Up to 4,500 people were executed, mostly in the 1990s, by these two paramilitary units, without trial or conviction. This was admitted by the then-prime minister, Mesut Yilmaz, in late 1990s.[2] There is a general consensus that the JITEM and TIT has been behind thousands of political murders and disappearances in Turkey. The TIT attempted to assassinate Akin Birdal who was both the leader of the human rights organization Insan Haklari Dernegi (IHD) and the deputy leader of Amnesty International of Turkey in 1998. He survived but was left physically disabled. These two competing organizations have recruited executioners, also from the Zaza population via the MHP. Mahmut Yildirim from the Solaxan tribe in the Solhan region, better known by his alias 'Yesil', has been behind more than 500 political murders in the 1990s, according to a report by the prime minister's office. Many of the JITEM members who have committed these murders have been exposed. Yet these executioners are at large because the military protects them; therefore, the authorities dare not put them on trial.

The sheikh's religious and moral authority

The religious and the moral field is the third area in which the sheikh exercises his authority. It is in this area that the sheikh has built up his enormous power and influence, and it is here that the sheikh asserts himself most. However, politics has previously prevented the sheikh from devoting time to this area. After yet another defeat in the parliamentary elections in which his son did not manage to be elected, the sheikh has tried increasingly to move his focus from the political to the religious area. He would from then on concentrate more on religious and moral questions in the region.

Moreover, he sees to it that ritualistic forms of social intercourse such as marriage and gender-dependent division of labour are maintained. He manipulates religious feelings in a masterly fashion and demands loyalty in return. His interpretation of traditions and beliefs constitutes a set of guidelines for daily life. Meanwhile, this interpretation does not aim at tying the present social order with the new, modern one, but refers to the preservation of a well-established social heritage in which belief in solidarity is considered to be a highly regarded value. The sheikh knows that people are strongly tradition oriented and resist every attempt at modernization. Consequently, he maintains his powerful position as spiritual leader by appealing to traditional values.

The critics of the sheikh, that is, people who have close relations with the PKK, think that his interpretation of traditions and beliefs do not aim to strengthen the awareness of the Zaza population but to create more oppression in order to reinforce his position of power. Fear of God is his most important weapon in this context and it is deeply rooted in people's consciousness. There is a widespread belief that if one says something against the sheikh, he will be excommunicated by the sheikh himself, because this is against God's wishes. Therefore, people are terrified of expressing anything that could be perceived as disloyal or critical towards the sheikhdom. An example illustrating this is given below.

One day the sheikh's cousin, Sheikh Mustafa from the village of Yekmal, was in Solhan to recruit some men to carry out some work for him. A tribal chief from the village of Gelbĕ adjacent to Solhan was there together with his fellow villagers when the sheikh asked for help. For some reason or another, the chief did not encourage his fellow villagers to follow the sheikh. The sheikh was provoked by this. He was so angry that he rode away on his horse and left the place quickly. On the way, he stopped at the village of Keshkon. He sat down and asked for some water to drink. The people who received the sheikh realized quickly that he was angry but they dared not ask him what had happened. While they were trying to find out why the sheikh was so disturbed, he raised his hands and head towards the sky and cried wrathfully: 'Allah, curse him, punish him who defies you'. When the sheikh pronounced the curse, he mentioned the chief by his full name. Then the people understood who the curse would strike. Several people entreated the sheikh to forgive the chief by saying that he is a respected chief, but to no avail. The sheikh did not withdraw the curse. A couple of hours later, news arrived that the chief had died suddenly. The time of death was in the middle of the day when the temperature was around 40 degrees centigrade. The chief probably died of a heart attack because he was both very old and physically weak, therefore could not tolerate the heat. Although his death was most probably a coincidence, it was all the same interpreted to be a direct consequence of the curse pronounced by the sheikh. Therefore, the incident became a useful basis for myths about the sheikh as God's ambassador. One further consequence of this incident was that the sheikhdom managed to create an extreme fear of God. The result was that people dare not do anything that could be thought to be against the sheikh's wishes. As one critic of the sheikhdom said: 'Curses are an effective means of creating fear in people's hearts'. The sheikhdom also strengthened its position further as a moral institution in the society. However, nobody dares to think or reflect on the fact that to pronounce a curse with the intention of harming another person is a punishable act.

Due to fear of God among other reasons, the sheikh is often referred to in daily conversations. I witnessed many such conversations. Even when people are discussing daily issues, one is often reminded about what the sheikh has said on different matters. His statements and advice are brought into various subjects of conversation and they are used as a guideline for nearly every discussion that did not have morals as its starting point. But what was most disturbing from my point of view was the sheikh's influence on how people, especially the poor, organized their future, particularly with reference to their children. Once I witnessed a family discussing whether they should allow their 12-year-old daughter to begin secondary school. The girl had just completed five years at primary school. She had been so successful that the teacher advised her to continue her education. But the parents were in great doubt because the sheikh had advised people against sending their daughters to school. He meant that by sending children to secular schools one commits a sin, but this happened when the sheikh's own granddaughter was studying at a university in Ankara.

Another example is as follows. One day I was invited to a meeting. There were about 15 middle-aged men who had come together to discuss whether they should rent out the village common land to a rich man who was an outsider. The rich man had proposed to cultivate rice on common ground about 10,000 acres in size. These men discussed to and fro for hours without reaching an agreement. The disagreement involved whether they could rent out land without consulting the sheikh. I wanted to ask: 'Can you not decide for yourselves? The sheikh is after all not a co-owner. Consequently, he cannot interfere in this case'. One of the oldest men replied as follows: 'We know that the sheikh is not a co-owner, and maybe it does not concern him, but all the same we must consult him. It is just like this and such it shall be'. My impression from the way they discussed this matter and from the arguments they used was that this was due to their basic expectations of the sheikh. I believe the most important reason is that they do not want the sheikh to distance himself from their realities. They want to involve the sheikh to maintain a close relation with him. They want the sheikh still to be their protector. He will continue to be a guarantor for their culture, religion and lifestyle. There is much in their lifestyle that they can maintain through him.

Culture, religion and tradition are fundamental values of the Zaza society. These values confer a sense of belonging to a historic continuity, and the sheikh is aware of it. He knows that the people in the Solhan region have a strong wish to preserve their own values as a basis for stability and continuity. Portions of the population, particularly the adults and the elderly, still want the sheikh to solve their conflicts and to act as an alternative to the Turkish institutions. His advice is followed by the people and fills the vacuum that the Turkish authorities have not managed to fill, in such cases as abduction of

girls, tribal disputes and other local conflicts. This type of arrangement aims at solving conflicts between people. In this way, the conflicts are prevented from being brought before the Turkish
authorities. This manner of proceeding keeps a certain distance from
the Turkish institutions and gives a certain feeling of belonging to
one's own culture and not to the Turkish culture, which is foreign to
most people. One can also say with good reason that the sheikh as an
arbitrator has prevented many serious conflicts between tribes and
families, which probably could have produced catastrophic results
as has been the case in large parts of Kurdistan.

Questioning the sheikhdom

The sheikh is not particularly authoritarian but appears to be somewhat arrogant in his actions. He does not communicate with everyone and socializes preferably with persons from higher strata, for
example, religious figures as mullahs, tribal chiefs and persons with
high social regard. He speaks in a condescending manner to people
from lower strata. Very often, he also questions people's integrity by
condemning unwanted actions, actions that conflict with tradition
or fail to conform to religious commandments. The condemnation is
expressed on a religious/moral basis.

But the sheikh's reputation has weakened recently. An increasing
number of people are cautiously questioning the background of the
sheikhdom. Some want to have scientific explanations about how
and why the sheikhdom came into existence. Others want to know
why many people in this area became sheiks at about the same time.

There are no scientific explanations for these questions and there
is very little knowledge at all about the sheikhdom. First and foremost, it has been a taboo to research the sheikhdom in this area.
Furthermore, perhaps the sheikhs in this area were uninteresting as
research subjects. All the same, it is not difficult to find explanations
for the aforementioned questions from a cultural anthropological
perspective. In a time when science was totally foreign and all the
population in the Zaza area was illiterate, it was probably easier for
certain cunning people to acquire the positions of a sheikh and many
have done so.

Another explanation is connected with psychology. If one has an
attack of nerves, one does not recognize any boundaries. One may
speak out loud all one thinks and feels, have tremendous fantasies
and present a series of prophecies without inhibition. When someone

from this area is stricken by intense psychological problems, he begins talking as if he is seeing right into hell and heaven. He talks about his being able to see who is a true Muslim and who is an infidel. He speaks about everything between the heavens and the earth. When some of the prophecies expressed by this sick person are realized coincidentally, he is declared as a sheikh because he has proven that he has apocalyptic powers.

Today, no one dares to act so theatrically. After the schools were established and many especially in the towns and the cities were educated, the sheikhs also began restricting their activities by distancing themselves from these milieus. When they are in an intellectual milieu, they act more cautiously than when they are in the villages. Among the intellectuals they will not give the impression that they have apocalyptic powers. Yet in the villages they still give such false impressions.

The rule of mullahs

Mullah means a Muslim cleric (*Mela* in Zaza). Mullaharchy is another religious institution besides the sheikhdom. Contrary to the sheikhdom, mullaharchy is not hierarchical. In principle, all mullahs are equal. However, there are some who are more knowledgeable than others and who are ranked by themselves and others to be several degrees above the rest, a situation that is also to be found in most professions in modern societies. Some mullahs, particularly those with better training and those who are well established, are considered to belong to the uppermost stratum in the Zaza society. They all are men. There are no female mullahs, because Islam forbids women in religious positions. The word of a mullah has great importance outside the political area and most people heed what the mullahs say. The mullaharchy contributes to maintaining large portions of the social order that are not controlled by the state.

The mullahs administer the religious and moral issues. They have more duties than does the sheikh, often in the form of practical tasks. They lead the five daily prayers, communicate the holy texts from the Koran, interpret the Islamic law, Sharia, and administer it. Based on the principles of Sharia, the mullahs present the people with lines of guidance in the form of rules and norms for what is allowed and what is forbidden. Most people relate actively to the norms and sanctions administered by the mullahs because these are perceived as a set of stable and clear rules. The mullahs lead all the religious rites, teach

the Koran to the children, see to it that the ritual forms of social intercourse such as marriage ceremonies and gender-based labour division are maintained. The mullah directs funerals and, in some cases,
also acts as a spiritual counsellor in connection with deaths.
Furthermore, they conduct the mass for the soul of the deceased
(*Molud* in Zaza). The mullahs also issue *fatwas*[3] or edicts, and give
religious advice when someone asks for it on an individual basis. The
mullahs prepare amulets as magical protections against evil eyes,
sorcery, sickness or accidents. These often contain shreds of paper
with magical signs and formulas that are ascribed magical powers.
The amulets are said to protect from people with an evil eye that can
harm or kill a child, household animals, homes and valuable property. Then the amulet will reflect the evil cast back to the sender.
They also prepare talismans that they claim bring good luck and
impart good qualities. The mullahs also get involved in cases that do
not concern religion. For example, they often are involved in resolving local conflicts. But the mullah's greatest and most frequent activity is to spread the fear of God, which dominates every conversation
concerning people, both individually and in social gatherings.

The mullahs communicate messages with intense religious content
at all ceremonies by clearly expressing that Allah's will decides everything. They try to connect the religious rules, norms and rituals to
peoples' daily lives in their messages and they aim at strengthening
peoples' belief in divine forces and their loyalty to the current social
order. The religious interpretations prevent people from thinking for
themselves or finding alternative interpretations. Even if someone
dares try it, this is interpreted as an attempt to undermine the legitimacy of the religion and is reacted to accordingly. Most people are
passive receivers. The messages are taken as a matter of course. The
religious rules and norms especially are perceived as so natural that
nobody dares even question them. The divine rules are not a subject
of discussion and consequently one does not dare think about their
validity. It seems that it may take a long time before people here will
suspect that life can no longer be explained with religious concepts.

The sheikh and mullah network

A network consisting of the sheikhdom including small sheikhs, mullahs and other interpreters of the religion in all the villages and
towns, and other influential figures such as large landowners, feudal
lords or tribal leaders is at work to maintain this type of social order

or collective unity. The relations between them are close. They cooperate in many areas, particularly those concerning moral issues. They aim at preventing social norms from being violated and if necessary they can mobilize force to implement sanctions in case such a violation takes place.

Yet the religious authority is distributed hierarchically among them, especially between the sheikh and the mullahs. The sheikhs deal with the primary and important social tasks while the mullahs' tasks are confined to the local issues. The sheikhdom in the Solhan region is ranked as the superior of the mullah institution. An example will be illuminating: When a mullah issues a *fatwa* concerning a problematic marriage, it can be appealed to the sheikh. It is the sheikh's advice that is decisive for the consequence of the *fatwa*. It must be pointed out that the senior role is not applicable to all sheikhs but only to the great sheikh in the Solhan region. Each region in Kurdistan has its great sheikh. These great sheikhs are taken seriously. Otherwise there are many (small) sheikhs, both in the Zaza society and the rest of Kurdistan who are not taken as seriously by the people.

The sheikh can express himself on important religious issues because in addition to his position he is trained and versed in the scriptures. The sheikhs and the mullahs as his closest collaborators act within a religious sphere with its own logic. They refer to a sincere attitude towards life, making promises for the hereafter. Often they cite the prophet Muhammad: 'An act for God's sake is better than any thing else in the world'. They are promised eternal paradise if they display a true fear of God and act according to God's will.

However, it must also be said that the sheikh's advice always has a shade of uncontemplated habitual thinking. His statements are so obviously routinized that they are perceived as the opposite of any rational thinking. His statements often refer to the established customs, which are often not deliberated upon. These statements are taken to be true and natural guidelines for living one's life. This has influenced the fact that the Solhan society constantly repeats itself. People, particularly the older generation, refuse and nearly fear thinking about or heeding new ideas, changing their life patterns, adapting to new conditions, etc. They believe their lives are preordained and predictable. They have subjected themselves to a standardized and norm-bound life form with which they are content. People follow a deeply rooted pattern that dictates how they should act, how they should meet, how and about what they will converse and how they should cooperate among themselves and with other people etc. In general most people display loyalty to this pattern of life in all areas. I believe this loyalty is partly an expression of a desire to not be incorporated into the Turkish state. My impression is that people are now increasingly beginning to regard the sheikhdom as problematic. The scepticism is spreading, especially among the younger generations and the politically aware. Particularly great is the dissatisfaction felt for the sheikh's flirtation with the Turkish state, which is hostile to the Kurds, and the political parties that are supportive of the state. The sheikh also makes use of a *divide and rule* method. He often manipulates the religious antagonisms within the Zaza society. I will expound this in the chapter on culture and identity (Chapter 9). The mullah institution is regarded as less problematic. This is probably a result of not many mullahs being involved in politics, as the sheikhs are and fewer of them sympathizing with the parties that have directly inimical policies towards the Kurds. My impression is that people still want to keep this type of social order despite increasing scepticism towards the sheikhs, mainly due to two considerations. Although the sheikhdom and the mullah institution are very old-fashioned, conservative, traditional and in many ways incapable of meeting peoples' increasing needs for solutions coinciding with contemporary reality, they are, after all, perceived as their own authorities. These institutions perform an integrating function holding the Zaza society together. Second, people hope that these arrangements will make them less dependent on the Turkish authorities, which they perceive as largely foreign, both culturally and politically. These considerations result in peoples' apparent desire to keep their own authorities and it is highly understandable with respect to the comprehensive oppression that this population has been subjected to. I will return to the sheikhs and mullahs in the chapter on religion (Chapter 11).

Social structure in the Zaza society

Spiritual leaders (sheikhs), tribal leaders (*agha*) and mullahs (clerics) are traditionally considered to have high status in the Zaza society. They still enjoy a high esteem. Yet their status and prestige is not a result of education, occupation or talent, as it is in modern societies. Neither the sheikhs, nor the tribal leaders, nor mullahs have formal higher educations. Many of them, especially those who were born before the 1950s, have never been to school. A few of the younger generation are schooled relatively better than their parents. The social prestige of the sheikhs and tribal leaders is a result of a hereditary tradition, for instance, the position is passed from father to son, while the social prestige of the mullahs is based on religious schooling or denominational belonging. For example, the status of the sheikhs is based on alleged apocalyptic powers such as presentiment, prophecies, divination and miracles, which accord them high prestige. The prestige of the mullahs is connected with communicating and interpreting the religious texts, while the prestige of the tribal leaders is based on the physical strength of the tribe.

All the three components, the sheikhdom, the priesthood and the tribes, as shown in Figure 5.2, together form a social structure with different functions and tasks. By social structure I mean a more or less clear arrangement of mutually dependent institutions and the institutional organization of social arrangements. The common aim of all the three bodies is to maintain the most important social rules and values, that is, to keep the people together. The purpose is precisely not to liberate people from the coercive and routine social structure.

Moreover, this social structure or social formation is both horizontally and vertically ordered. The horizontal dimension consists of different social networks that contain the families of the sheikhs, the mullahs, tribes and other religious groups. The vertical dimension

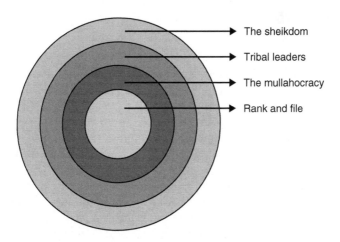

Figure 5.2 Types of authorities or institutions in Zaza society

consists of superior and subordinate groups such as descent groups within the tribes, lesser sheikhs, mullahs, religious figures and groups of various ranks that exercise power and influence at different levels. These social constructions function as a complementary structure, that is, the different components complement the functions of each other. For example, the functions of the sheikhs are connected with the primary tasks of the society because of their apocalyptic powers. The mullahs see to it that each action is anchored in Islam and the tribe will mobilize its physical power if it becomes necessary. Another example is that when the sheikh supports certain candidates in the elections, he seeks support from both the tribal leaders and the clerics who mobilize the population.

This social structure based on spiritual and tribal leaders of kinship groups has apparently been successful until now because social rules and common values have been transmitted first and foremost by firmly rooted religion and tradition. However, religion is gradually losing its position (see Chapter 11). It does not correspond to peoples' needs any longer. This results in some people breaking the religious rules, making exceptions, interpreting the norms differently and so forth. Infidelity, which occurs in the Zaza society, is a good example of norm violation. But norm violation happens more often in other contexts such as settlement, inheritance, rights to water usage, fields and grazing lands, theft, and buying and selling of goods and products, etc.

The practice of justice

This chapter will close by describing how the Zaza people's perception of justice is administered. This is connected to the spiritual authorities described above. The perceptions of justice are not built on legal rules and principles. People do not use these rules and principles for their own judgements or actions. In the Zaza society, perceptions of justice are often based on moral principles, religious rules and injunctions, and cultural and traditional attitudes. This is because the Zaza-speaking Kurdish culture is an overwhelmingly oral one. In this context, an oral tradition means that it is not anchored in a judicial system or written culture. Being tradition oriented, experience and memory are central in oral cultures, while in literate cultures, perceptions of justice are based on knowledge and interpretation. We will come back to oral culture in Chapter 9.

Perceptions of justice among the Zaza-speaking Kurds are interpreted, justified and administered by two aspects: religious norms
and principles, and power relations. Moral interpretations are made
by the mullahs, that is, those versed in the scriptures, but also the
sheikhs often interfere and point an admonishing finger at the people. The mullahs and the sheikhs administer justice through interpretation of religious rules and norms and have acquired
considerable power and influence by this process. Mullahs, sheikhs
and tribal leaders are all close allies. These persons are further allied
with other powerful men, families and groups.

Power provides rights in a stateless society as Barth (1991) had discovered in Lower Swat between Afghanistan and Pakistan. Such a
perception also dominates in the Zaza society. Unfortunately, the
powerful nearly always prove to be right because they can mobilize
force, in contrast to their counterparts, especially when the counterparts are weak and cannot mobilize force. It is a typical and recurring
theme that the powerful people involved in a controversial issue
resort to violence in order to secure their rights, although the Islamic
rules can be interpreted differently. An example that illustrates this
practice is as follows. A large farm called Zimi lies between the villages Xirbizun and Guele Quling to the west of Solhan. Zimi, which
covers several hundred acres, is considered to be one of the most productive farms in the Solhan region. The farm is on the Xirbizun side
but half of it is owned by a kinship group from the neighbouring village of Guele Quling, and the rest is owned by a kinship group from
Xirbizun. The owners from Guele Quling belong to a large and powerful tribe, while the owners from Xirbizun belong to a small and
weak tribe. Until 35 years ago, each kinship group had the right to
use half of the farm, but this situation then came to an end. The owners from Guele Quling refused the other owners the right of use by
physical force. This created great shock in the area. There was no
doubt about who was right. Most people in the region thought that
the kinship group from Guele Quling had committed a particularly
gross injustice by refusing the owners from Xirbizun their right of
use, and appealed directly to their humanitarian conviction of justice, but to no avail. Public opinion could not protect the weaker
party even when they were felt to be right. The weaker party
appealed to the spiritual authorities, that is, the sheikh and the mullahs, repeatedly for arbitration when public opinion had been of no
help. The sheikh and the mullahs dared not expressly condemn the
injustice the stronger party had committed. Instead they appealed to

their veracity but this was also not accepted by the stronger party. So the weaker party brought the case to the public prosecutor's office in Solhan. The stronger party managed to postpone a division of the farm indefinitely through bribery. Meanwhile, the authorities prevented a solution by trickery and deception. Judicially, the weaker party has the right of use until the case is finally resolved, that is, the farm is divided, but they are still prevented from exercising their right by the stronger party through use of physical power.

This minor example demonstrates that the weaker parties are the losers. Weaker people do not have 'property rights' to which they can have recourse in solving their conflicts. Neither the sheikh nor the mullah clergy nor the state apparatus will protect the weaker party. As the example shows, those who can deploy physical force will be proved right as a rule. In other words, might secures the powerful one's right.

Many such cases are experienced in the Zaza society and this has made people realize that religion does not function as a source of legal protection any longer. Many figures also use religion to advance their own interests. Some people directly say that religion is exploited or misused, but they are not willing to discuss why religion acts against honesty and truthfulness. The worst that can happen is that religion loses its position, that is, it is not regarded as the source of perceptions of justice or objective morals any longer. In such a situation, subjective perceptions of justice and morals are not sufficient to resolve their conflicts. Then what objective justice must they have to resolve their conflicts or to reduce the evil feelings and interests of human beings? What can the solution be for weaker people such as the kinship group from Xirbizun or what solution can the weak seek in such situations? Will it become more acceptable for the powerful to coerce the weak to implement their wishes as the above example demonstrated?

People in traditional societies always find their own solutions, although these may not always be the best. My impression was that the weaker sections did not particularly believe any longer that the religious authorities were capable of protecting them. This leads to the appearance of another pattern that itself is traditional. In order to protect themselves against the powerful, the weak seek to establish alliances with families or tribal groups who are stronger. This is a way of avoiding injustice or correcting an injustice when they are not willing to seek protection from the police or the courts. In other words, instead of becoming dependent on the community of the state, which is corrupt, they choose to adapt in ways that make them more dependent on each other.

In this way, sometimes based on Islamic moral norms but more often on power relations or physical strength, a kind of praxis is established for sense of justice. When this praxis is constantly realized, it reproduces itself and then it amounts to a form of judicial system. When, additionally, it is regarded as morally right and is supported, a basis of legitimacy is also established. It is precisely through such a perception of justice that they have managed to establish a relatively stable social order and communality that often is based on the unhappy 'marriage' of the two dominating ideologies characterized by the brilliant absence of democratic institutions.

The reason for traditional solutions is that people do not want to publicize their social lives in courts. When their lifeworld is confronted by juridical laws or principles, they defend their life patterns fully. This is justified by reference to juridical laws being extremely foreign and, therefore, their being perceived as juridical colonizing.

The Zaza population usually strongly doubts that the laws and rules prepared by the central state power in Ankara are just or good enough to regulate their conduct or to resolve their conflicts. Therefore, people care little about the so called 'temporal sovereignty'. They perceive Turkish laws as very unjust because they do not regulate the citizens' relation to the state by individual rights such as freedom of expression, religious freedom, political freedom, cultural belonging, etc. Zaza Kurds feel that they are not given equal status with the Turks, nor are they given equal status with the other officially recognized minorities in Turkey, such as the Armenians, Jews and Greeks. This results in their lack of fundamental rights such as legal protection, legal opportunities and status.

Therefore, they perceive the Turkish state as a despotic power apparatus through which the authorities treat them arbitrarily. They constantly experience the authorities interfering with the citizens without legal basis. Turkey rules by force of imposing the formal rules on people. The state expounds its hegemony over the Kurds as something 'just and deserved', and the Kurds are portrayed as somehow guilty because they do not obey the Turkish laws and rules. When the Kurds do not identify with the Turkish laws, a crisis of legitimacy arises. Therefore, they are compelled to cultivate their own tradition, which they think provides the basis for their continued existence. They have a strong belief in the inviolability of tradition and display great respect and devotion to the rules and norms based on tradition, which form their lives. They fear that their society will disintegrate into chaos without the concord derived from practising their traditions and customs in peace.

I believe Zaza-speaking Kurds would accept the judicial principles if they are freed from what they regard as Turkish coercion and foreign domination. Only after this would worldly principles dominate their actions in the social life.

Chapter 6

Reciprocity among the Zaza population

Reciprocity means mutuality. In kinship research, the reciprocity concept describes any relation that refers to exchange, barter or other social acts between at least two parties. In social anthropological literature, reciprocity is considered to be a fundamental feature of all social life (see, for example, Mauss 1995; Sahlins 1972; Eriksen 2003). Mutual exchange and dependence is a necessary premise for social interaction in every society. In this context, reciprocity refers more to mutual change, exchange and dependence among the Zaza-population. This type of interpersonal relations is widespread among the Zaza-speaking Kurds. Such relations are part of the daily life. Therefore, it is important to elaborate the concept in this chapter.

Mutuality and dependence

The Zaza population has a proverb: 'Only the despots think of themselves'. One feature characterizing the Zaza people's relations to each other is the ability to share and exchange. Although all people in traditional societies exchange things now and then, what characterizes mutuality among the Zaza people is their helping each other continually and being very conscious of their responsibilities towards their close relatives and neighbours. Mutuality is based on norms of reciprocation that are understood and accepted by all. This type of mutuality functions as a basis for communality.

I stayed in a mountain village to the north-west of Solhan for a period of four weeks during my first field work. One of the families was building their cowshed at this time. The walls were completed and only the roof remained. The family had gathered timber, twigs and other building materials. They would put the collected material in place and then set earth on it. There were two adult sons in addition to the head of the family. They would be able to construct the roof in two weeks. Since I lived with them, I wanted to contribute to the work, although I had limited knowledge about how it was built.

The head of the family, the two sons and I got up for the work early on a September morning. We started after the family head described briefly how the work was to be executed. In the course of the first hour, 17 able-bodied men from the tiny village of about the same number of families had showed up. It meant that each family had provided a man. It was almost like a voluntary community work that is also widespread in North Europe, and it reminded me of the phrase: Take care of your closest.

While I was contributing my small amount of work, I was thinking about why one man from each family turns up without being asked in advance. I asked questions and was answered by the head of the family that it is like that when one builds or repairs a house, cuts grass for this purpose or executes other tasks based on bodily labour. One feels a kind of moral obligation towards one's neighbours.

They displayed considerateness and willingness to help each other; they smiled encouragingly and paid attention to the others while working. I was gradually impressed by how all this characterized the cooperation among them. They created fervour and harmony, gave expression of having a good conscience because of their contribution and displayed warm feelings at the opportunity to help a neighbour. However, there were also scenes that I thought were negative in relation to the common task. While we were carrying on with the work, two men of about 75 years came to the building site and sat down. They wanted just to talk without any effort to contribute. I did not like such behaviour because it was only distracting. I felt slightly provoked. I said to one of them: 'Can you come and help a bit instead of talking rubbish'. I expressed this with a humorous tone. The man took it like a cold shower, cast a serious glance at me but said nothing. Suddenly it was all quiet. I realized that I had committed a blunder. From his thoughtful looks, I believe he thought: 'Yes, he is a stranger and obviously does not know about our culture and traditions. He committed a blunder but I do not need to reciprocate'. In the stillness, I heard someone mumbling and a young man came up to me and said, 'You insulted the man. Be careful. The man has sent his son to help. He himself is here to entertain us and himself'. Gradually, I understood that the man had assumed the duty to contribute to the team spirit, to keep the workers' morale high and to create a positive atmosphere so that the work would continue in a happy spirit. This way of proceeding proved to be a clear expression of loyalty to teamwork and communality, a very widespread attitude in the Zaza society.

The Zaza people generally display mutual attention, consideration and tactfulness towards each other. They stand for continuing tradition. The contribution to the building of the cowshed demonstrates a collectivity that marks a 'local society' characterized by close and dense relations where feelings of communality between people are of a durable type. This type of solidarity functions and it motivates people to cooperate and create a unique fellowship. However, I gradually discovered that the families in this mountain village also had considerable conflicts of interest among themselves. Such conflicts are quite usual in the Zaza society. All the same, they could stand together for certain common interests.

Circumcision of boys

Reciprocity is an important form of social integration that keeps the Zaza society together. Some Zaza people stressed reciprocity as one of the strongest bonds established to hold the society together. *Kerwa* tradition (circumcision of boys) in the Zaza society can be an illustrating example for the social integration between large and small families. Circumcision of boys is a very widespread ritual tradition and a highly respected occasion both in the Zaza society and in other Islamic cultures. In fact, it is an old Jewish tradition advised for Muslims by the prophet Muhammad. But circumcision among the Zaza differs somewhat from the rest of the Islamic societies. When a boy is to be circumcised, the feast with the family is often more important than the religious significance of the ritual. I will describe an example of the Zaza variant of circumcision from the Solhan district.

The circumcision itself entails two male persons, one godfather called *kerwa* and the boy to be circumcised. Although the *kerwa* and the boy are central to the ritual, they are considered to be links between their respective families. The decision to become a *kerwa* and for whom is often made by the respective families wanting to establish close ties to each other. It is further expected that the boy's *kerwa* is a kind, helpful and preferably rich man so that he can fulfil the economic expectations connected with this type of relationship. It is an established cultural rule that the *kerwa* will give many presents, some very expensive if he is a relatively well-off person. There are two forms of giving presents, described below.

One form of giving presents is based on reciprocation. This form is particularly common among affluent families. Many rich people are invited to the ritual and they contribute expensive presents. These people get presents in return next time it is their sons' turn to be circumcised. Poor people cannot afford to arrange large feasts and will have a limited ritual.

The other form of exchanging presents is connected with the relationship between the *kerwa* and the boy to be circumcised. It is the *kerwa* who is obliged to give the circumcised boy presents, and this relationship is not considered to be a one-off situation but a lasting kinship relationship.

A further example of reciprocity involving *kerwa* from the Zaza society is connected with business activities and demonstrates the deep feelings of fellowship and solidarity the partners have towards each other. This is an ancient tradition but is still alive particularly in the villages. For example, when a person starts a business he will borrow interest-free money from the *kerwa*, a friend, a relative or a fellow villager. The donors feel obliged to contribute, especially in starting up a business. The obligation is as if one is helping his own brother. That the money is given free of interest is due to the status and esteem this provides for the donor. There is also an implicit expectation that the donor might end up in a similar situation and need help from the receiver. This transaction of money may seem to be purely economic but it also involves other humanitarian considerations such as compassion, conscience, sense of duty, avoiding a loss of honour, etc. Such contributions are also made when a business is failing such as when the stock breeding of sheep is in trouble. 'Saving actions' in which near relatives, friends, the *kerwa* or the neighbours each give a sheep or a lamb free of charge are organized so that the stricken family will be able to survive. Much of this concerns saving one's honour because bankruptcy is considered as a defeat that strikes not only the person involved but also the local society around him.

Exchange of presents is perceived as a prototype or a model of human communication (see, for example, Mauss 1995). In most societies, giving presents is seen as a universal phenomenon and considered to be fundamental for social integration. Among the Zaza population, the gift is also considered to contain the following elements: the duty to give, the duty to receive and the duty to reciprocate with a countergift. But not all can or are willing to reciprocate.

The poor or the economically weak cannot always reciprocate and, consequently, must stay in a debt of gratefulness and naturally not all want to end up in this situation. They make presents themselves when they are not able to or do not want to buy them, often handmade articles such as sweaters, socks and similar things. Such articles are especially valued in Europe because handicraft is highly esteemed, but not among the Zaza people. They think it is the poor peoples' way of making up for a debt. The tradition of giving presents is more widely distributed among people with a middle-class background. They buy presents from modern stores such as a jeweller's shop. Donors with a higher social status do not expect to be reciprocated in the form of material things, particularly when the gift is made to poor people. But they then expect to be honoured, spoken well of or praised.

In many other countries, particularly in the modern western societies, this function is taken over by the state, social institutions, organizations, trade, the market and so forth, which means that exchange of presents has lost its original significance because it lacks an essential element, namely the humanitarian considerateness in its original or personal sense.

Exchange of girls

In the Zaza society, it can be easily observed that the gift tradition is upheld with its original meaning and it is prevalent in many areas. It also functions under different social circumstances in addition to circumcision of boys and business activities, especially in connection with weddings and exchange of girls when presents are exchanged frequently. All contribute with presents, both the rich and the poor. Exchange of girls, which is called *bedel*, appears first and foremost among kinship groups. They exchange unmarried girls with the aim of marriage. The theory of kinship considers marriage generally, and exchange of girls particularly, to be an important form of reciprocity relations (see, for example, Levi-Strauss 1969). Exchange of girls is also considered to be an important form of reciprocity relations among the Zaza people. But this type of exchange of girls arises most frequently among people of reduced means, who are poor and have limited resources, and are not related to each other. I have not witnessed or heard that exchange of girls takes place among affluent families. Rich people, it seems, do not exchange girls.

There are no certain statistics of how widely the practice of the exchange of girls is distributed in the Zaza society. It is generally supposed that about 5 per cent of all marriages are contracted in this way. This figure is even higher in remote villages. 'Exchange of girls' can have unfortunate consequences because if one of the exchanged girls is treated badly by her new family this leads, nearly automatically, to the other girl receiving the same treatment.

It is seldom that a girl from an affluent family marries a boy with a lower social rank than hers. When it happens, the man and his family must stay in a debt of gratefulness to his in-laws for a long time. However it often happens that a poor man who cannot afford to marry gives a daughter or a sister to someone in the same situation with the same needs. In this exchange, both parties avoid large expenses and difficulties connected with their economic situation.

Another explanation for exchange of girls is connected with the bride price and other expenses connected to the wedding feast. The tradition of bride price still exists in the Zaza society but it is not so widespread and inclusive any longer as it was until recently. Some poorer families demand a bride price when they marry off their daughters. The bride price is preferably taken from people not belonging to the same descent group. This can vary from a symbolic amount such as 200 American dollars to a genuine amount of several thousand American dollars, depending on the bridegroom's economic situation. Yet, in contrast with many other traditional societies, the bridegroom and his family group do not commit themselves to paying the debt over a long time or to work for the in-laws for many years after the marriage takes place.

To North Europeans, the bride price can sound like an arrangement that is oppressive to women, reducing them to commodities. The bride price is part of a social relation. It may be meaningless to say the bride price reduces human beings to commodities when something as alive and personal as another human being is experienced as part of a social relation. My impression is that those receiving bride price did not think of it as an economic exploit but rather as an amendment and reaction to events. The parents of a girl set the bride price as a prerequisite for a bridegroom with whom the girl has eloped or who has forcibly abducted the girl. Many girls elope with another boy when the parents press her to marry someone they recommend instead. When the girl does not want an arranged marriage, elopement with another boy becomes the only way out. The parents set a bride price as a revenge for this. They call it revenge but it may be more of a form of exclusion for the boy, his family, but first and foremost, their own daughter. In one of the villages where I did field work, 11 of around 30 marriages in the course of one year happened in this way.

In other societies, especially parts of South Asia and societies of the Pacific Ocean, men play the main role when exchange of girls is effected, which means that women are not involved in the decision. This process runs somewhat differently in the Zaza society. Often men play the main role when families exchange girls, in any case during the first exchange. In other words, the men take the initiative and start the process. But the process does not stop there. In many cases, the bonds between the two families become so strong that the women married into the respective families take the initiative for further exchange of girls. Often, the newly married woman wants her brother-in-law, that is, her husband's brother, to marry her own sister, who is single. If she does have an unmarried sister, she suggests a girl in her close family who is available for this purpose. It may be a niece, cousin, aunt or second cousin. This results in men from one family marrying women from another one mutually. It is known that one has difficulties in finding a spouse if one lacks relatives on the mother's side in the local society. An example illustrating the pattern of exchange between two families follows.

I lived with a family in a distant mountain village for a short period of time in connection with my field work. The mother, Sabiha, was the eldest woman in the family and she had married as an exchange girl for the husband's sister, Gule, who had married Sabiha's brother. Sabiha had five sons and three daughters, while Gule had three sons and three daughters. One of Gule's sons married one of Sabiha's daughters when they grew up. Another of Gule's sons married a daughter of Sabiha's husband's brother.

Many people in the Zaza society operate according to this principle of exchange. Therefore, very often one meets families where a woman is the aunt, sister, niece, cousin, second cousin to a new bride. It seems to be clearly systematic. The women are very active at this stage and participate in the decision-making because of their efforts. Although it is the women who persuade the concerned girl, men often control the process. Women's effort and participation cannot be interpreted to mean that they are the ones who exchange men, but it is a sign that the families as a whole take part in the process. This is also the case with dowry, a tradition also known from Europe.

When families within the same descent group or from different groups exchange girls systematically, it is an expression of deep and lasting relations of reciprocity and commitments. One more example illustrating relations of reciprocity is the following. When Gule gave birth, she decided in consultation with her new family that her eldest son should bear the same name as her eldest brother while two of Sabiha's children have names from her original family. This means that a married sister's son shall bear either his name or his brother's name. The fact that the girls move in both directions in an exchange has a certain result. The exchange of girls creates particular forms of alliances, relations based on marriage and in-law relationships, in which the parties are obliged to support each other in difficult situations. This happens although alliances deriving from the maternal lineage are not as stable as the ones deriving from the paternal lineage (compare the example of Fatma in Chapter 2, pp. 18–20).

As said before, exchange of girls is not mutual in all social strata. When girls from the sheikhdom or other higher strata marry men defined to be of lower status, it is not given that the girls from the so-called lower families marry men from the sheikhdom. In other words, if the sheikh's daughter marries the son of a tribal chief, something that happened in the Solhan district, where the chief is defined to have a lower social status than the great sheikhs, this does not mean that the sheikh's son does the same. The reason for this is that the sheikh's sons are of a higher social rank, according to perceptions of the sheikhdom, and therefore cannot condescend to a marriage with a girl with a lower rank. His dignity will be lowered and people will question his judgement if he marries beneath him. Therefore, he must marry a girl from the higher strata of the sheikhdom where the parties are in equilibrium in relation to each other. It is an ideal of all the social strata to strive for a marriage where the female belongs to a higher rank than oneself because one acquires high prestige and recognition from his surroundings as a consequence. There are deeply rooted and ancient traditions for this in the Zaza society. A principle that the Zaza people often refer to and is valid for all types of groups must be stressed in this context. It is the principle that each group reserves the right not to give nubile girls away. These should preferably marry within the descent group. Those given away are those whom no one within the group wants to marry.

It is an acknowledged principle or ideal in the Zaza society that a man should marry a woman from a higher social stratum than himself. This has resulted in particular constellations of groups as an institutionalized fact in which there are 'wife givers' who 'export' girls to another group called 'wife receivers', following the terminology of Levi-Strauss.[1] But that form of alliance, as we understand it, is not based on a mutual exchange of girls, but is one-sided. Consequently, the parties are not obliged to support each other. This type of alliance is not considered to be stable and the ties between the groups are much weaker than they are in case of a mutual exchange of girls (described above).

Giving presents in the neighbourhood

Giving presents takes place also in many other areas in the life of the society, apart from social gatherings and exchange of girls. Neighbourhood is such an area in which giving of presents occurs frequently, and in certain cases nearly daily. Some examples are given here.

According to a long-established Zaza tradition, it is a duty to provide support when a neighbour needs it. One of the most common forms of care is to breastfeed infants whose mother cannot produce milk. When a baby is born and the mother lacks milk, either one or several neighbouring women are appealed to for help, but often come forward without being asked because this is considered to be a matter of duty towards the neighbour. For some babies, this care will last only a few days until the mother produces milk and for some it may last considerably longer, up to one year or even more, especially if the family cannot afford alternative foodstuffs for the baby. In such cases, the infant's needs are covered by several neighbouring women rather than only one.

To breastfeed a neighbour's child is not only regarded as an acute need. This type of caregiving has both biological and social consequences. The biological consequences are expressed through rules of marriage, conduct and morals. For example, when the child grows up, he or she cannot marry children of the neighbouring women who had breastfed her or him. This is because the child is regarded as a foster child or sibling to the children of the neighbouring woman and it is treated accordingly. It is expected that the child will develop feelings of loyalty and duty towards the neighbouring women who had nursed him or her. The social consequences are expressed as continuity in the concord of the neighbourhood. This practice strengthens the social bonds and the significance of the relations between the neighbours.

The close bonds between the neighbours do not stop there. They have also other mutual duties to each other. The neighbours must be provided for when a person slaughters a sheep, a lamb or a cow. This does not mean that the slaughtered animal will be shared equally with the neighbours, but it means that they get to taste it. They will be criticized openly, often in social gatherings, if the neighbours do not receive their share of the meat and many seek to avoid this kind of criticism. Another form of sanction is that they do not receive their share of the meat when the neighbour next slaughters an animal. This type of giving presents is a mutual duty among the neighbours rather than a donation of free will and through it mutual expectations are created and this is a prerequisite for the functioning of the social interaction between the neighbours.

Another example is connected with people from the Zaza society residing abroad, and there are many who work in Western Europe, the Gulf States and in Western Turkey. It is expected that they distribute presents among family members, close relatives and the neighbours when they are taking holidays in their country of birth. If they do not do this, they are not received warmly and they do not feel particularly welcome.

A further example of mutual dependence in the Zaza society recurs quite often within politics. A person elected to a political office such as the parliament often has a background from the sheikhdom, a large tribe, a rich or land-owning family or he would be an imam. He must ally himself with certain groups, often influential persons such as sheikhs, tribal leaders, the wealthy, landowners and imams, in order to be elected. The politician must negotiate with these people for the votes of their subjects. To some he gives money in exchange for votes, while others get promises of jobs, positions or different contracts, such as construction projects for roads or buildings and the like. The politician starts delivering his promises as soon as he is elected to the parliament. It is easier to realize the promises if his party is in the government. Those who were promised jobs get their people appointed to offices within the public sector and those who were promised lucrative contracts realize their dreams. The supporters of the politician must continue to support him at the future elections in order to keep their privileges. Therefore, the parties assume that they are loyal towards each other.

Another example at the local level is given here. Local elections were carried out in Turkey while I was doing field work early in the spring of 2004. One cannot say that the elections were either democratic or fair, compared to what we are used to in Europe. Many parties stood for the elections with lists of candidates to the office of the mayor or the municipal council. I will not describe the nomination process, which was everything but democratic, but I will describe how the mayor won his office in this municipality. The future mayor had presented himself as a conscious Kurd until the beginning of the campaigning period. Yet after the Kurdish-friendly party, Democratic People Party (DEHAP), had refused him as its candidate he was placed in first place on the DYP (The Right Way) party's list. DYP has an extremely aggressive Turkish nationalistic ideology and it is utterly hostile to the Kurds, even denying categorically that the Kurds exist at all.

The DYP mayoral candidate won the elections in Solhan, mainly due to three reasons. He established an alliance with the Solaxan tribe, which is one of the largest in the area. He called most of the prominent leaders and influential persons of the tribe to a meeting at the home of the tribal leader. The candidate slaughtered 35 sheep for the benefit of the participants of the meeting. It was decided that the Solaxan tribe should vote for the DYP candidate unanimously. According to my sources, the candidate does not descend from the Solaxan tribe but he has linked himself to this relatively powerful tribe by claiming that his family originally descended from the Solaxan. There are many who do not belong to a tribe in this area but try to connect their line of descent with one or another tribe in order to strengthen their position. Lineage represents equality with those of the same lineage and equality is tied with kinship. Through such a manoeuvre, they attain influence and protection both within the tribe and with respect to other tribes.

The other reason for his electoral victory was that he struck a secret deal with the sheikhs. The sheikhs would support him and, in return, the Solaxan tribe would vote for the sheikh's son, who wanted to be re-elected to parliament in 2007.

And finally, the third reason for the DYP candidate's victory was the use of mafia methods. The candidate purchased many votes from the poor. According to sources close to him, about $150,000 US were distributed. In addition, people could have free tea at six coffee houses for a period of six weeks. The results of the election showed that he was supported largely in the poorer districts of the town of Solhan.

The electoral results did not demonstrate an unambiguous correlation between the objective conditions of the residents and their subjective national consciousness. There is no correlation between the people's ethnic belonging and political voting patterns. One asks why the objective interests of the Zaza people do not unambiguously transform into political awareness. The results of the elections would be seen as tragicomic by any European. That the Zaza people who are oppressed because of their ethnicity all the same vote for a Turkish nationalist party that does not acknowledge their existence or respect them as a people is not based on rationality.

These examples of the social relations, social exchange and mutual dependence say something about the Zaza society as a whole. Yet it must be stressed that reciprocity is not the only principle that moves the Zaza society forward. There are also certain corrective forces or reservations that regulate the exchange of gifts. Many Zaza-speaking Kurds told me that there was a limit to which one could simply exchange or give presents. There are certain things in the Zaza society that are not shared with others. These may be certain personal effects, valuables, secret plans about investments or business activities, expertise, inventions or discoveries, secret knowledge, secret rites, unsanctioned actions and so forth. Such things are not to be shared with others but kept to oneself. Only a few people from the close family may know about them. The surrounding neighbours should not know what is considered sensitive information. These thoughts are not foreign to other societies, either. In many other societies, as here in North Europe, certain things and certain knowledge are kept hidden from others. These are regarded as private and, consequently, may not be shared with outsiders.

There are also restrictions connected with interpersonal relations in the Zaza society, as in many other societies. For example, buying or selling sexual services is considered to be morally reprehensible. Such behaviour is regulated by extremely strict rules. Having a sweetheart, a quite common phenomenon here in the west, appears in a very limited form in the Zaza society. All the same, such relations arise, but then they unfold under controlled conditions. The sweethearts may not meet alone before they are married. They cannot go to a cinema or some other public place without being accompanied by someone from the close family. The relations concerning men and women will be described in more detail in the chapter on gender and family (Chapter 10).

There are also similarities between the Zaza society and the European societies concerning giving presents. One is not supposed to give the same thing as he has received. A present is not given again as a present to others. In such a case, it would be thought that the receiver had not considered the present valuable. But the similarities between the Zaza society and the European societies concerning presents end here. In Europe, the intention tied to the act of giving is important. When someone buys a present for another person, its value is not considered particularly but appreciation of the person is the dominating motive independent of the quality of the present. However, in the Zaza society, the economic value of the present should correspond to how much the receiving person is valued and with the nature of the relationship. If the receiving person is a highly regarded person and the relationship to him is considered to be close and friendly, the present must be expensive. Otherwise, the receiving person will feel offended. If the person is not highly respected, the present should be of lower quality. In other words, the value of the gift becomes a measure of the quality of the relations between people in the Zaza society.

The limits of giving

Many people have wondered why certain things cannot be shared or exchanged with other people. I have strived for an explanation but have not yet reached any concrete answers. Some have tried to explain it by the concept of honour, by claiming that not everything can be shared with others because it would be at the cost of one's honour. If one shares all, in the end one will be left with nothing with which to defend oneself. Therefore, certain private matters must be kept to oneself and remain untouched. The surrounding people consequently cannot have a claim to it and must respect the owner. Mauss (1995) and Eriksen (2003) among others have explained this by the inner-most essence of the thing. I also believe that the explanation is related to the innermost essence of the thing. There is a boundary to rituals of exchanging presents, as mentioned above. In the Zaza society, this boundary is found at the point where individual and collective inter-ests meet or collide with each other. The picture becomes clearer here and makes it possible to deal with the question of what is to be kept to oneself and what can be shared with the collectivity. Meanwhile, it must be stressed that this boundary concerns only certain rituals of exchanging presents and not all areas. The self-sacrificing feeling of belonging to the respective groups is so powerful in contexts of iden-tification that often it is difficult to draw the boundary between the individual and the collective. The individual's existence is intensely interwoven with that of the group the person belongs to, because the individual is included in the identity of the collectivity and expresses this. This relation is examined in Chapter 9.

Different forms of exchanging presents are kept alive probably because modern institutions are lacking in the Zaza society, as mentioned earlier. But the most important explanations are likely to be connected with economic conditions and moral obligations. Humans will do any and all kinds of strange things to survive. People in this area establish bonds with each other mainly on two grounds. These can be termed morally obliging reciprocity and expectations connected with relations of exchange. Morally obliging reciprocity characterizes the Zaza society as a moral collectivity with common moral perceptions in the sense of Durkheim. Everyone basically has the same perceptions of what is right or wrong, good or bad. These perceptions are quite immutable and have a superior role regulating peoples' conduct. In case someone violates the established moral rules, customs and habits, they are excluded socially and this is experienced as a great burden.

Many of the economic relations of exchange are also governed by moral norms and rules because the modern market economy is rather inadequate or has not yet established itself in this area. There is a lack of economic institutions with a rational initiative. Shopping centres are being established in towns and cities but these are so feeble that they are not able to stand against the traditional religious and feudal institutions. These traditional structures interfere with people and limit their freedom. The area can be compared to the conditions prevalent in Europe before the advent of mercantile capitalism in the 1600s, when it started growing up in Holland and England and paved the way for modern capitalism. Non-economic phenomena such as religion, culture, tradition, kinship relations, etc., still influence the economic sphere in this society. Daily economic intercourse and ties are still based on obliging personal relations because the market economy with its written laws is absent. This means that personal obligations not the written laws provide a guarantee. This has formed the basis for extensive trickery, lies, fraud, hard haggling over the price, bribery, cunning and so forth, where one tries to harvest gains without paying the price. Characteristics such as cunning, slyness, lying and haggling have become the most important cultural capital for a significant number of people. This type of culture has become widespread in all social strata, not only in the Zaza society, but also all over Turkey. Especially in difficult times, this type of activity becomes very marked. It is clearly seen that people use such methods and many have been successful. This type of thinking also influences other types of interpersonal relations. One is received with enormous friendliness, respect, openness and other positive attitudes when one meets a new person. But as soon as the person understands that you do not fulfil his expectations, you are shoved aside and regarded nearly as null and nothing. Seen thus, it can be said that the relations of exchange have become strongly materialistic through actions connected with low morals.

As a conclusion, it can be said that reciprocity functions as a fundamental characteristic of all social life in the Zaza society. Reciprocity is a basic quality of their existence through thick and thin for many people in the Zaza society. As we saw earlier in Chapters 2, 3 and 4, Zaza Kurds have strong kinship organizations and deeply rooted obligations towards their relatives. The ideal of kinship unity is strong and reciprocity is to be upheld first and foremost within the closest families of the kin. The population also has morals of loyalty and obligations towards their spiritual leaders, as seen in Chapter 5. This system of relations functions quite differently in the Zaza society, lacking written rules within other societies. Reciprocity was based on trust and mutual obligations and created lasting social bonds in the Zaza society until 1980s. Therefore, reciprocity was considered to be a fundamental characteristic of social life. But it is not the case today. Personal obligations have lost their value. People do not trust each other. This is due to a series of circumstances, first and foremost the struggle for life and the *survival of the fittest*, and also due to established moral obligations and the lack of modern institutions. This last condition contributes to the survival of reciprocity in the Zaza society. All these circumstances reproduce different forms of reciprocity and will contribute to maintaining the system of reciprocity through several generations in the future. In order to abolish the system of exchange, particularly the exchange of girls, the Zaza society must renounce the old morals, customs and habits, and develop new morals and new social institutions. This will take a long time. Much of the exchange and mutual dependence described in this chapter is undoubtedly a result of the economic conditions that are to be the subject of the next chapter.

Chapter 7

The economic system of the Zaza society

Economy can be understood as the production, circulation and consumption of concrete material services and goods. In other words, processes connected with production, trade, distribution and consumption of goods and services in a given society. These relations are central to a description of both the traditional and the modern, western economies. My description of the economic system of the Zaza society will not be the same as the description of the economy of a modern society, although I use the same conceptual apparatus. I focus on the established economical mentality, organization of economic activities and their modes of functioning in the Zaza society. While I try to describe the economic system in the Zaza society concisely, I will at the same time place this system in the wider context of the social and institutional system, of which economy is a part, because the economy is implanted in the society and certain non-economical phenomena influence the economic sphere in this society and, in turn, lead to consequences for individuals, families and groups. This has implications for understanding local arrangements, forms of conduct and agreements, and power relations all of which are institutionalized in different ways in the Zaza society.

The Kurdish population is considered to be one of the traditional ethnic groups in Western Asia and they have held on their cultural and socioeconomic traditions in many areas up until the present time. Large portions of the population still have relatively superficial contact with 'civilization'. The Zaza area can be described as mainly a village society. Household animals and agriculture constitute the main basis of the economy. Zaza society may be a typical example of a peasant society, with partial pastoral adaptations. Nearly all the society is based on a mode of production where the household is the most important unit of production. Consequently, peasant life is based on the household as the unit of production (see Shanin 1971; Helle-Valle 2000). What characterizes the peasant households in the Zaza area is their following a general subsistence strategy by which the household produces foodstuffs, cultivates the crops and keeps household animals of different sorts, mainly sheep, goats, cows, oxen or horses, primarily through its own workforce. Most people live off sheep farming but cows form the next important basis of economy. Zaza households use animal products mainly for their own consumption and bring a small surplus to a larger market. Most people live at a subsistence level by producing from year to year. Consequently, a luxurious life or consumption of luxury goods is still a foreign phenomenon.

Considerably more than half the population in the Zaza districts live off household animals and agriculture, often without any combination with other types of economy. They are mainly engaged in agriculture, both irrigated and precipitation-dependent wheat cultivation, which is combined with household animal husbandry. Therefore, the actors are dependent on their ability to exchange vital animals and agricultural products. A process of adaptation between humans, household animals, grazing lands and water is unfolding continuously. Their life is similar to pastoral nomads but it is also distinct from the life of other permanently pastoral societies such as the Beritan[1] tribe, which also shares grazing lands in Solhan region in summer. The pastoral adaptations of the Zaza population vary with the seasons and, consequently, can be divided into two phases: a life of wandering with the sheep flocks on the high plateaus in summer, and a settled life in the mountain villages in winter. These adaptations happens this: early in spring, for example, at the turn of the month April/May, the Zaza pastoralists move to the mountain areas on the Sherevdin high plateau to the north of Solhan. They follow the animal flocks to exploit the grazing lands and the water resources over a large area. There are good opportunities for grazing up in the highlands on the Sherevdin Plateau, which is an imposing and beautiful landscape lying 1,500–2,000 metres above sea level. The pastoralists have an idyllic life on the highlands. The nature appears to be nearly virginal, with fresh air and a healthy climate, the temperature being rather pleasant. The hygienic standards can be kept high, with plenty of cool and pure water available. Fortunately, the environment is still unpolluted due to the absence of the materialistic culture. They live here in black tents until late autumn (see Figure 7.1). Sheep breeding is the main economic basis of the semi-pastoralists. They tend

Figure 7.1 Summer camp of white and black tents in the Sherevdin landscape
Photo: Zozan Kaya Asphaug.

their flocks and prepare dairy products. The division of labour between the genders is clearly defined. The men's responsibilities are to provide the shepherds who tend the flock day and night, and to provide the means for covering the expenses of the sheep breeding. The women's responsibility is to milk the sheep twice daily and make this milk into dairy products, in addition to preparing food, doing the laundry and taking care of the children. There is a harmonious coexistence between humans, the flocks of animals and nature. Both the men and women have a close relationship to the animals, tending them with care and an eye to their wellbeing. They display consideration towards their needs and are careful not to destroy the grazing lands, forming lasting commonality, which makes life worth living. The fellowship among the pastoralists on the high plateaus is a unique phenomenon. Here they show more closeness, sensitivity and considerateness towards each other than they do in the villages.

In winter and early spring, the lowlands are exploited. Therefore, the Zaza pastoralism must not be confused with nomadic life, which is termed a permanent pastoral society. The Zaza pastoralists reside permanently in the villages, at least in winter. It is seldom that all the family follows the animals further to the south in winter. Only some members do it, usually taking turns every other month.

Adaptation to the environs

Animal husbandry must also relate to the environs, in addition to internal conditions such as tending and caring for the animals. The average Zaza family does not base its economic choices primarily on supply and demand, as it is the case in a modern market economy, but on how important the choice is with respect to the survival of the family. Maybe one-tenth of the families own more than 150–200 sheep and they take supply and demand into consideration more. Put more specifically, one can say that the Zaza family is a self-sustaining economic unit, which at the same time constitutes a unit of workforce. The average Zaza family owns 40–50 sheep, a few cows, a horse or a donkey used as pack animals or for riding and the family has a collective responsibility for taking care of the animals (see Figure 7.2). All family members work more or less to tend to the care of the animals all year round. Children begin contributing at the age of seven or eight. Sons will have the duty to work as a shepherd and

Figure 7.2 A hardworking farmer in Meneshkut. He is a father of eight children. The family lives off sheep breeding
Photo: Murat Van Ardelan.

tend the lambs, while daughters will assist their mother with daily chores. The average family consists of five to six children, plus parents and grandparents. Altogether, there are around eight to ten individuals under the same roof, making a living off the animals and as a general rule they have no other income.

In the course of a year, about 40–50 lambs and a couple of calves are born, so the number of the animals is doubled. The calves and the lambs are sold when they are about six months old, together with some surplus of animal products such as milk, meat, cheese, wool and skins. They sell these products to purchase the most elementary needs of the family such as food, clothes, flour, sugar, tea and so on. Out of this 'surplus' they must also pay any debts they may have acquired for the expenses in connection with the keeping of the animals during the year. They do not spend money on dairy products, which they produce themselves. Many families do not produce enough 'surplus' to cover the most elementary needs. They have to sell even more animals then, or they must borrow money from relatives and friends.

Consequently, the essential point is to maintain the status quo in which the struggle for survival and keeping the family alive is the most important. Also, due to population increase, there is a shortage of land. Quite simply, there is too little land in relation to the increase in population, which is the reason for an average family having only 40–50 sheep. Shortage of land limits their opportunities for greater production, reinvestment and expansion, which also has led to more poverty in the Zaza areas, particularly in the villages. Increasing numbers are turning to seasonal work in Western Turkey and workforce migration to the Gulf Countries to save their families, with no weakening of their bonds and loyalty towards their kin and local society.

The individual feels that he must take responsibility for himself because there are no social institutions to appeal to get economic help. There is, in fact, a poverty fund in Solhan where the poorest can seek economic relief. But the fund is administered by the military garrison and a condition of receiving help is to sign a declaration of loyalty by which one commits oneself to actively fighting the Kurdish separatism of the PKK. Second, seeking help at the poverty fund controlled by the military is perceived as an offence by the local population. It conflicts with their established tradition by which the population is more or less obliged to help the poor among their kin. It takes a lot to violate such an obligation of loyalty, which is deeply rooted in the culture. Third, a person who receives help from the military garrison is stamped as an agent, which is very stressful. To be perceived as an agent of the state in the Zaza society is nearly on par with the shame of committing suicide. The person marked as an agent is not only socially excluded but is also perceived as a traitor.

The bazaar economy

Solhan is a small town and the centre of Meneshkut and the surroundings. The district is administered from Solhan, as mentioned earlier. In Solhan and other densely populated areas, the main income sources are grocery stores, retail or wholesale trade, other kinds of shops, service sectors or trading in sheep.

An Islamic-oriented economic system, which is called *bazaar* (marketplace in Zaza), has come into existence in the area. Much of this economic system in the Zaza society functions in the same way as the Islamic-oriented Indonesian bazaar of Java, described by Clifford Geertz (1963). The economic system that has developed in the Zaza society is similar to the other economic systems all over the Middle East and therefore it is named bazaar in every language of the area, for instance, Kurdish, Arabic, Turkish, Persian, etc.

A bazaar does not entail all types of goods. It is segmented and hierarchic, divided into separate units according to the type of the goods. There is a bazaar for buying and selling different species of animals, another bazaar for harvest products, a third for jewellery, a fourth for clothes, and so forth. What is common to all types of bazaars is that the market mechanisms and the methods used are governed by informal principles, rules and arrangements. These rules and methods are so overpowering that they exceed all reasonable expectations. This type of transaction in which the merchant plays a central role is not similar to the western variant of free competition capitalism we are familiar with. It exists in its own world. There is no state authority to control the activity. The merchants deliberately oppose attempts to modernize the bazaar according to modern capitalistic principles. Many would characterize the bazaar as a pre-capitalistic economy.

The production of foodstuffs and crops, and buying and selling of animals or meat products is regulated partly through the aforementioned bazaar and partly by a growing number of merchants and middlemen who constitute a much feared group. In the Solhan district there are no organized bazaars apart from some small ones that arise spontaneously where certain animals are sold. Most of the merchandise and a great number of animals are often transported to the large Kurdish cities such as Erzurum, Diyarbekir and Antep, 200–400 kilometres distant.

The bazaar for different species of animals is located on the outskirts of the town. It covers a large, open space of several thousand square metres sectioned according to the species of the animals, for example sheep, lambs, cows, etc. At all times, hundreds, sometimes thousands, of people go around looking at the animals, wanting to know the state of the animals, enquiring into bartering conditions, possibilities for borrowing, prices and, finally, they start to haggle over the prices. There is not always a pleasant mood between the parties, especially when they are haggling. The buyer indicates the shortcomings of the animals, raising doubts about their qualities and uses all possible methods to lower the price.

Since the large bazaars are at a considerable distance from the Zaza areas, several groups of local wholesale buyers have arisen and these create a greater part of the economic activities in the area. This is connected with the fact that many producers cannot afford to transport their animals to the larger cities because the costs involved are too high.

Meanwhile, there is great dissatisfaction towards the local wholesale buyers. These people enrich themselves due to the extensive poverty and are perceived as inconsiderate and crass exploiters. The local wholesale buyers have capital that they lend as money to people who cannot afford to meet the most elementary needs of their families. Often, families with difficult living conditions appeal to the local wholesale buyers and ask for a loan. The buyers have a good overview of who needs a loan and they lie in wait. When the poor man takes the initiative for a loan because he has no other way out, an oral agreement is reached between the local buyer as the donor and the poor man as the receiver. It is usually a standard agreement. It involves the borrower repaying his debt by the animals he owns. This happens at the time that the animals are sold, that is either in spring or early autumn. The period for the loan is either six months or one year. The moneylender's aim is to double his capital during the course of the period, making the rate of interest 100 per cent, while the yearly rate of inflation is 18 per cent. On the other hand, the aim of the borrower is to save his family at all costs. The borrower is pawning his animals by agreeing through an oral agreement to sell them to the moneylender at the end of the loan period. The borrower owns 30–50 sheep on average and usually the outcome is bearable, but only just so. Many in the local society pity the borrower. Some expressly pronounce their concerns and think that the moneylenders line their pockets unfairly at the cost of the misery of others.

The unpleasant times begin when the period of loan expires, usually with the moneylender showing up and demanding to buy the animals, which he will select himself without considering the borrower's wishes about which animals he is willing to sell to repay his debt. The moneylender picks up the animals he wants as compensation, without consulting the owner. The transaction does not stop there. The moneylender wants to fix the price for the animals. This last condition often leads to disputes between the parties, which are resolved with the help of the local people.

This practice by what may be the majority of the local wholesale buyers is a new transgression of morality, if one is to call a spade a spade. Moral values of the local buyers are not based on assumptions of the ideal work ethics any longer but on inconsiderateness, lies and fraud. They can act a large repertoire of theatrical roles, which are possible only in a society without an apparatus for state control, and their interpretations are extremely profit oriented. I witnessed the following situation that I recount here as an illustration of inconsiderateness and gross exploitation of poor people.

One day, Baki, a man in his early forties from one of the villages of Meneshkut, travelled from the village to Solhan to buy a sack of flour for his family from a seller called Emin. The flour cost about 10 million Turkish liras, corresponding to four pounds sterling. Baki did not have money to pay in cash and had to buy on credit, whereby the flour would cost double the price. The seller and the buyer easily agreed on this condition. The seller also stipulated that the price would double for each extra month the payment was delayed. Baki had not paid after a month and the seller apparently had not heard from him. After seven months, the seller made serious threats to Baki. The seller belongs to a powerful tribe in the area, while Baki does not belong to a strong tribe. Baki took the threats seriously and went to the seller, who demanded 70 million liras, that is, 10 million liras for each month's delay, seven times more than what the sack of flour originally cost. Several people tried to mediate. They asked Emin to show compassion and appealed to his conscience to no avail. In the end, Baki had to pay seven times more.

This kind of example is not unique to the Zaza region but is to be found all over Turkey. If a state employee or an esteemed person had committed the same mistake, he would not have met with the same treatment as Baki. They would not take it. The function of the seller is particularly directed towards the weaker people and undermines the existing social order. The aggression of the seller may be a sign that the modern, liberal society, in which everyone should be judged similarly, not by their lack of economic status, not by being born into poverty but by what they can contribute, is making its appearance.

There are also other reasons that some people do not transport their goods to larger bazaars. Many dare not take the risk because they know too little about the rules of the game in the bazaar; they do not speak the language of the bazaar and they do not have a sufficient network of contacts, which can be of help in selling the goods to the right persons. Therefore, some of them prefer to sell their goods locally to wholesale buyers, who bring them further to the greater bazaars in the large cities through middlemen. There is always an opportunity to exploit these producers. In addition, there is lack of information concerning the bartering system of the bazaar. The producer is not totally aware of the production costs of the goods. The only thing he knows with certainty is that he must produce these goods to support his family and that production is done in a traditional manner. He has no premises beyond that to judge the further transaction and the process as a whole.

The wholesale buyers' systematic purchase and supplying goods and animals has led to the appearance of a significant group of middlemen and also forces a new form of market mechanism in the Zaza society. Therefore, buyers are not considered as units of production but are often called middlemen because they bring the goods further to the consumers. It is a concrete activity and a persistent process that takes a long time. In this process, the goods are exchanged between the parties going through different phases, and change owner time and again until they reach the consumer.

Middlemen are what can be termed as self-employed businessmen. They are thoroughly knowledgeable about the bazaar culture, which has its own special play rules, norms, skills and the mechanisms that govern the bazaar. They are used to wandering in the bazaar and they have acquired thorough knowledge about how it functions. The most important thing is to learn the art of negotiation, but hard haggling and compromising are also important. The more reliable they appear to be, the harder they can press down the prices. They comprise a specific occupational group with its distinct culture but act individually. The middlemen are not totally capable of thinking and choosing rationally in Weber's sense. According to Weber, to choose rationally means to act in accordance with reason. They do not make long-term plans but short-term ones. On average, the middlemen have little or no formal education. Very few of them have five years of school education. This is true not only in the Kurdish-speaking area, but is also the common characteristic of this occupational group all over the Middle East. Many of them have been pushed out of the labour market.

The middlemen buy the goods and sell them onto other middlemen. The goods change hands many times in their course. The middlemen often sell the goods to each other, due to their irresistible urge for manipulation in their quest for lucrative profits. The goods change hands so frequently that a product has at least ten owners before it reaches a consumer.

The middlemen also meet at the bazaar, in addition to supplying goods and trading animals among each other. Their role here is connected with providing goods. Profit is the motive behind their activity. Some of them have some capital but not enough to pay the entire amount when they buy wholesale. Therefore, they propose a little higher price for the opportunity to pay the rest later, often three to six months after the sale. Some others do not have capital and operate with credit in form of trust that they have acquired with respect to potential customers. They exert a lot of effort to appear loyal and trustworthy vis-à-vis customers. They use this also to get permanent customers. They are eager to gain short-term lucrative profits in the course of as short a time as possible. Therefore, they choose their own strategies independently of each other. Their strategies are marked by arbitrary choices, gambling and risk taking. They have strong beliefs in short-term choices and coincidences. Success is understood to be a result of luck and coincidence. Sometimes striving to have short-term gains succeeds, and sometimes it does not.

The selling and buying of goods to each other by the middlemen does not stop at the boundary of the bazaar. I mentioned that the bazaar is segmented and hierarchic. Actors of the segments are organized in a social rank order. The bazaar hierarchy mainly consists of three groups of actors: producers themselves who want to sell their goods, middlemen who buy the goods from the producers and sell them to each other, and the great merchants or owners of capital who buy all the goods in the end. The last-mentioned group are few but powerful in virtue of the economic means at their disposal. In the bazaar, the powerful merchants have their own representatives, consultants or some close collaborators. These act on behalf of their superiors. They get an overview of the activity in the bazaar by constantly touring it, looking at the merchandise, and making a good deal of preparations before going to their superiors and informing them about a possible barter.

This powerful group of rich merchants appears to be trustworthy also with respect to borrowing and credit, which means that the merchants can buy several thousand animals without paying in cash. They make maximum use of this opportunity. At the same time, this forms the basis of stable and mutually obliging relations and establishing social bonds between the parties, which leads to a few powerful merchants sitting at the top of the hierarchy and governing all the activity. There are fewer persons at each level up the hierarchy. In other words, the bazaar hierarchy is pyramidal and designates a power relation. The higher one is placed in the bazaar pyramid, the greater opportunities one has for obtaining lucrative profits.

Such a rank ordering comes into existence as an informal hierarchy because it is not directly formalized by legislature. In principle, the bazaar hierarchy is open to everyone. All the same, there are criteria. The entry ticket for becoming a serious trader in the bazaar is that one fulfils the demands of reliability, personal prestige, a wide network of contacts and a certain amount of capital. Also, a certain emphasis is put on how well established the actors are and if they have sufficient experience. The actors in the bazaar, the merchants and the middlemen are listed according to their rank, based on these criteria. Those who fulfil the aforementioned criteria are placed at the top. In this way, a few acquire the control of the bazaar and consequently receive the majority of the benefits. The greatest advantage is that they can purchase thousands of animals on credit only by oral promises, without any form of security and without signing any documents, because the seller trusts the dealer's words. This imparts to them nearly endless advantages, but the most important one is to acquire a monopoly in the bazaar. This is what decides the roles and the places of the actors in the bazaar hierarchy.

Much of the goal to become a serious, trustworthy and experienced dealer has marks of pure play, tactics and dishonest intentions. Some of them have a covert aim, namely making money for themselves. Often, some of the most trusted dealers have declared themselves bankrupt or have disappeared completely when they have made enough profits after making a deal on credit without signing any documents. They never pay their debts. Such a swindle strikes

The economic system of the Zaza society

both the middlemen and the producers because the middlemen also buy from many producers on credit, according to an oral agreement. In this game, the producer is affected the most because he is the one without any guarantees.

Consequently, the bazaar must be understood as an economic system with a certain mode of action and its own logic and an apparent rationality that is oriental in the regional sense of the word and, in fact, very un-capitalistic, a system that is doomed to fail. The system is apparently approved of but mostly feared for the many tragedies by which some have enriched themselves illegally while others have been hardly affected. The bazaar's magical power through extensive economic exploitation is inherited from the former generations. It has long-established traditions and these only repeat and reproduce themselves continuously. The oriental, or the regional system's mode of action, its logic and mentality makes changing the bazaar system in a capitalistic direction difficult. The well-known resilience of the conservatism in the Middle Eastern trade system and the bartering logics of the bazaar resist every change in the direction of a more liberal market economy. Understandably, many transactions that are not 'clean' also occur in the modern capitalistic market but this cannot be compared to what is taking place in the Middle Eastern bazaar system.

Population flight from rural districts

The Zaza region happens to be on the outskirts of the world market, so to speak. This society also has peripheral contact with the society at large. The population in this area is integrated to the administrative and the economic network of the larger society only to a very small degree in contrast with the comparable Turkish village societies further to the west. The Zaza society is also politically marginal. The population is typically a category with little or no political negotiating power and they still have an isolated way of life. It is a society that has lost its originally distinctive culture but that has not acquired modern ways of life.

Economically, the Zaza are mostly farmers with their adaptations typical of peasants, increasingly tied to the Turkish market and they have gradually become dependent on it. Simultaneously, the region is under a weak state apparatus, which has very little overview or control of the local development. As mentioned earlier, the Turkish state is present only by its physical force throughout Eastern Turkey.

Official administration and services are very weakly integrated to the local social system. The state apparatus is concentrated on mainly three things: controlling Kurdish separatism, collecting taxes and fees, and enforcing the cultural assimilation of the Zaza people. Turks have helped themselves to taxes and fees for many centuries without any investments worth mentioning in the area, apart from two things: constructing both an enormous number of military buildings and mosques. This colonization started with the Ottoman Empire in the 1500s. The area was administered by local autonomous feudal princes (*Mir*) until 1830s, often with local militia paid by the Ottoman Empire. These feudal princes were appointed by the Sultan in Istanbul and collected taxes from the local population on behalf of the Ottoman Empire.

The Zaza region and the rest of Turkey have dissimilar economic structures. The Zaza region is among the least developed areas in Turkey. The region is strongly characterized by less growth and development than other places in Turkey. What it lacks most is infrastructure. Because of this, no investments, which could have led to more industrialization, are being made. Industrialization in this area could mean a passage to a manufacturing system, increased productivity, urbanization and an increased use of scientific methods to rationalize the organization of production. This would lead in turn to social changes and, not least, to a new division of labour that the Zaza society needs badly.

There has been a large emigration from the Zaza areas in the last 20 years. Thousands of people, mostly young men but also many newly established families, have moved to the more urbanized and industrialized areas in South and West Turkey. Some of them work in small-scale industries, others are tied to the harvest season, so-called seasonal workers who function as a reserve workforce, that is, they are called into the production process when their labour is needed. Seasonal workers can be barred from the labour market when there is not a direct need for their labour. Many of these workers have moved to the Gulf Countries. Thousands of men from the Zaza areas work in Saudi Arabia and Kuwait.

Emigration from the Zaza region is not similar to emigration from other regions of Turkey in which a structural change towards mechanization of agriculture took place (Kaya 2000). This happened after the authorities introduced measures to make agriculture more profitable and competitive. The economic reforms entailed transition from a barter economy to a market economy, which again resulted in more freedom of mobility for some individuals. This transition also created high unemployment in rural areas and led to increased population flight from rural areas to large cities. In sociological literature, this pattern of population movement is described as a result of the industrial revolution that took place first in Europe and later in many developing countries. But these market economy reforms were not implemented in the Zaza region because the authorities did not want to carry out land reforms that would involve taking land from large landowners and distributing it to the landless. The authorities were not willing to do this because the landowners are their close allies in the fight against the Kurdish insurgents. Non-mechanization of agriculture in the Zaza area has been the reason that the economy is still run in a traditional way and the increase in productivity is small due to pre-modern methods, tools of production, and lack of knowledge and capital.

There are main two main reasons that have started population flight from the Zaza region: The first and perhaps the most important one is the population increase that has led to a shortage of land. As mentioned earlier, half of the population have become landless. Many of them want to move away from their homes. The second reason is forcible movement of the population. After the PKK started its armed struggle against the Turkish state in 1984, the Turkish authorities retaliated with scorched-earth tactics. During the 15-year-long civil war, about 3,400 Kurdish villages were burnt down. Inhabitants of the villages were given the choice between becoming village guards against the PKK or moving out of their villages. This policy also affected the Zaza area. The population in dozens of villages in districts of Solhan were forced to move from their homes in this way. Some villages were burnt down before the population had moved out, while the population in other villages were told to move out only one or two days before the military set fire to their houses and property and some people were executed by paramilitary units extrajudicially. These conditions made the situation unsafe. Many feared for their lives and fled to large cities or to countries in Europe, where they sought political asylum. About 1,000 people from the Solhan region have fled the country to places such as Germany, Great Britain, France, Sweden and Norway since 1980. In 1970s, about 50 people from Solhan and Bingöl had come to Europe in search of employment. Some years later their families arrived to establish themselves, mainly in Munich, London, Paris, Stockholm and Oslo. They proved to be enterprising in exile. Many of them have specialized as pizza bakers, restaurant owners and shopkeepers round Europe and have been successful with respect to economic adaptation. This must be understood based on the kinship relations that they also make use of abroad. The close social network they have in Europe provides solidarity, self-confidence, opportunities for credit and capital for the members and has made a decisive contribution to the establishment of individual persons and families in Europe.

The Zaza people of Solhan and the surroundings have all the same suffered from lack of real contact with other groups of people, especially in their relations with the Turks. Even those who have moved to the large cities in Western Turkey have little contact with the Turks. Here they come into contact with the Turks mainly through the labour market. In the private sphere, they have little in common and little contact with each other. An important reason for this is that the Zaza society regards the Turkish state as its enemy because it has been totalitarian for a long time. Consequently, they feel that it does not represent their interests. Turkey has had a hostile attitude towards the Kurdish demands about democracy, human rights and the right to cultural difference. In the next chapter we will see why Turkey has a hostile attitude towards the Kurdish demands.

Chapter 8

Turkey, a nationalist state in conflict

In the introduction, I asked how the Zaza population manages to maintain inner cohesion, how they can achieve integration and stability on their own and how they resolve their conflicts without a judicial system and courts. An essential explanation has to do with the attitude of the Turkish state, that is, how they treat the Zaza Kurds. The Kurds have an internal justice that leads to their solving the problems in their own way. In other words, they have their own social arrangements consisting of spiritual- and kinship-based authorities, resembling feudal domains and keeping the order by limiting and solving conflicts between people. These are authorities who provide their subjects with lines of guidance, giving them both joy and sorrow. But this chapter will not describe how the Kurds distance themselves from the Turkish state apparatus and state institutions. It will focus on how the Turkish state treats the Kurds. This has been totally decisive with respect to feelings of belonging the Kurds have developed, how they delimit themselves in relation to other groups, and the political and cultural consequences of their group formation.

Zaza Kurds live in Turkey, a country full of political and ethnic antagonism and contrasts that often lead to inner tensions and serious conflicts. Turkey has denied the existence of the Zaza Kurds since the foundation of the republic in 1923. Denial of a people presupposes intensive control and the culture of control has a long tradition in Turkey. The administrative power connected with the Turkish state is very systematic. The state has a direct control over 'its' populations and its first priority is to maintain such a control. It uses all it is capable of, from military control, a colossal surveillance apparatus to direct influence on the population as disciplined individuals. It is not the Turkish state that is perceived as their direct representative by most Turks. Contrary to this, the military, the bureaucracy and the police corps are what forms the basis of legitimacy of the state. The country has an exceedingly strong military that plays a decisive role in Turkish politics. In this chapter, we will first look at why Turkey's level of tolerance for the Zaza Kurdish demand for cultural freedom is low. Through the use of some examples, I will illuminate how the military undermines democracy and persecutes the Kurdish minority, human rights activists and other democratic powers. This can be coupled with the question of how nationalism becomes significant as an ideology for the state policies towards ethnic and cultural minorities in Turkey. Nationalism as an ideology is used by the authorities and military apparatus as a tool to prevent the minorities from developing their own independent organizations. But to understand the situation of the Zaza population we must first have familiarity with the Turkish state structure.

The structure of the Turkish state is relatively close to that of the Singhalese nationalistic state in Sri Lanka as analysed by Bruce Kapferer (1988). Seen ideologically, the Turkish state is an extension of a holistic cosmology in which the conception of the totality (the state) and its moral integrity has precedence over its individual parts (individuals or ethnic groups). The Turkish state is perceived as a holy entity. It is the state that is to be protected against individuals and not the opposite, as is the case with the modern western democracies. For example, when the Kurds demand fundamental democratic rights such as the right to use their own language and that their culture is respected within the Turkish state structure, it is perceived as a threat to the social order, that is to the Turkish state, or as activity hostile to the holy state. No such affront is tolerated. The affront is first labelled as terrorism or separatist activity and then followed with the harshest punishment. It is not the nation in the western sense of the word but the nationalist state that is celebrated in Turkey, in contrast to democratic countries. The state is nearly 'consecrated'. The state is the fellowship of those who define themselves as Turks and it represents their common spirit and mentality. This ideological construction is not relativistic but strongly ethnocentric because, seen morally, it is not anchored to absolute values such as cultural plurality, equality between ethnic groups and common human dignity but represents only one ethnic group, the Turks, by virtue of their equality as identical building blocks of the nation. Human beings who are not a part of this equality, that is to say the Kurds, who were called mountain Turks officially until recently, and other cultural minorities who do not deny their ethnic backgrounds are excluded and despised because they do not regard themselves as Turks and because they are considered sub-human by the state. They are often referred to as *animals*. This is perhaps the most important reason that the Turks always react negatively to the Kurds, often in clear ethnocentric tones because the wishes and the demands of the Kurds appear incomprehensible to them. Therefore, the Kurds are not considered in an inclusive way. They are kept out of the state administration and other state institutions, such as the army, the bureaucracy, universities, media and so forth. Some teachers with Kurdish backgrounds are found among the teaching staff in the school system but at low levels. These teachers are forced to deny their ethnic background as a matter of course. That the Kurds are denied participation in the political decision-making process is the most important factor.

The situation of the Kurds could be said to be worse than that of the Jews in Europe *before* the Second World War. As it is known, the Jews were barred from participating in politics but they were not, for example, prevented from working in academia. After the 1980 military *coup d'état*, Kurds and left-oriented Turks were banned from working in the public sector. Kurds and radical leftists were removed from important positions. According to Kurdish politicians, the Turkish authorities blacklisted around 860,000 Kurds and 500,000 left-oriented Turks after the military *coup d'état*. Based on ethnicity, Tansu Çiller's government removed the work ban on radical Turks in the 1990s. This renouncement of the ban did not include the Kurds. Kurds who are blacklisted cannot get a security clearance, a necessity to work in the public sector. The generals were afraid of Kurdish infiltration of the social system. Kurds are deliberately excluded from 'academic' institutions. (The universities in Turkey are not independent. Ideologically they are strongly directed by the state. Their task is to produce knowledge useful to the state. The opposite practice, production of knowledge which is not useful for the state, is defined as treason.[1]) In the Kurdish areas in Eastern Turkey, there are more than ten universities but the positions in these are filled by people with Turkish ethnic backgrounds. The economy is the only sector in which the Kurds can assert themselves. But also, here the Kurds are treated negatively and are accused of 'being fond of money', 'having a lot of money', 'dominating three-fourths of the economic life in Turkey' and so forth.

Only now it is possible to explore the identity of this population group for the first time in connection with negotiations about

European Union (EU) membership. Negotiations about EU membership have also made it possible to examine how the Zaza Kurds' identity has been formed in authoritarian Turkey. How the Turkish state treats them has been decisive for the feelings of belonging they have developed and for the prospective political and cultural consequences of their group formation.

The Kemalist state

The identity of the Zaza-speaking Kurds or, more correctly, their difficulties in maintaining their own identity cannot be understood independently of the political development in Turkey, and to understand today's political situation it is important to explain the official ideology of Kemalism, according to which the country is still governed. The Turkish republic was founded in 1923 and Atatürk launched the principles that still form the basis for the Turkish state and its internal conflicts. These principles are termed Kemalism as they are built on Mustafa Kemal Atatürk's political philosophy.[2] Officially, it is anticlerical and secular (see, for example, Heradsveit 1999), but politically it is closer to atheism, according to Islamic interpreters. The Turkish state is not secular in the western sense. It is true that officially religion is said to be kept out of the public sphere but the state controls the religious activity in the country with a gigantic official directorate (the Directorate for Religious Affairs). Practically, this so-called directorate functions at the ministerial level and its head is among the top official dignitaries. The tasks that the directorate carries out do not bear witness to the separation of state and religion, which has also been expressly demonstrated in an EU report (see Oostlander 2003). In Atatürk's time, the imams at all the mosques of the country received ready-made speeches that they would use for the Friday sermon. The speeches contained ideological and political propaganda. They also received detailed instructions about how they should conduct religious activities. This tradition is still actively practised by the Directorate for Religious Affairs.

Atatürk was an extreme nationalist. He created a national state in one of the most cosmopolitan and heterogeneous areas of the world, Asia Minor. But innumerable Kurdish rebellions, civil war between the Kurds and Turks, state oppression and so forth has demonstrated that it is impossible for groups of people to live within state boundaries that have been drawn across ethnic boundaries and strictly guarded by land mines and hundreds of thousands soldiers. Atatürk wanted to create a 'new Turk' who would be culturally Turkified and 'westernized'. He emphasized a Turkish nationalism inspired by the Pan-Turkic ideas of the Young Turks of the late Ottoman Empire. In Atatürk's Turkey there was no room for minorities without Turkish identity. All non-Turkish speaking groups of people (Kurds in the east, Arabs in the south, Laz, descendents of Pontus by the Black Sea, and Kartvelians, West Georgians, in the north and so forth) within Turkey's boundaries should become Turks. The histories of all these minorities were reinterpreted and directly falsified. When Turkish historians are writing, they only write about ethnic Turks, with the explicit aim of making all who live in Turkey regard themselves as Turks and feel obligations towards the state. That is to say, they must feel grateful to the state for letting them live and earn their daily bread. This propaganda is still created not only by all the historians but also by the whole state apparatus.

Further, Atatürk's nationalism was based on principles of forcible assimilation and homogenization. Soon after the foundation of the republic, Atatürk initiated forcible assimilation by prohibiting the Kurdish language. The forcible assimilation was comprehensive. Villages, streets, mountains, rivers and so forth were given Turkish names. Nothing would have a Kurdish name any longer. Parents were not allowed to give their children Kurdish names. All that was Kurdish was removed from history books and new books were confiscated immediately if they contained references to Kurds or the word 'Kurdish' was mentioned. All that was Kurdish was forbidden and even to call oneself a Kurd was banned. All art forms with Kurdish motives were either destroyed or removed from the museums. In all museums, one naturally does not find anything belonging to Kurds. The most tragicomic is when one visits the museums in the Kurdish areas. At these museums only artworks that are Turkish or from ancient Mesopotamian civilizations that have been dead for a very long time are displayed, but nothing that belongs to the Kurds who live there.

The assimilation laws were the strictest in the world. From then on everyone should perceive oneself as a Turk. No other ethnic or cultural characteristic and ideas than the Turkish ones would be tolerated. Turkish was defined more as an ethnic belonging (see also Heradsveit 1999) than a purely political or cultural phenomenon. To realize this it became necessary to cultivate the Turkish nature. In the 1930s, a theory (the Sun and Language Theory[3]) that claimed that Turkish was the mother of all world languages and all world languages descend from Turkish was launched. Further, the theory asserted the Turkish civilization was the model for all other civilizations and so forth. 'One Turk is worth all the world', 'Fortunate are the ones who call themselves Turks' are some of the perpetually quoted slogans that Atatürk used and are still used in school books. The slogans are also displayed as posters all over Turkey.

The Turkish-centred main element of Kemalism has created ethnic tensions. Ethnic minorities who do not allow themselves to be assimilated, first and foremost the Kurds, feel that they are alienated from the Kemalist state. It has in no way created social equilibrium but expresses and strengthens imbalance and conflicts. It has been impossible to eliminate the contradictions and inconsistencies, which have been fundamental. Turkey has been seen as a colonialist power, particularly after the Kurdish language and culture were forbidden following the foundation of the new republic. This was the background for the Kurdish rebellions a short time after the foundation of the republic. The insurgents demonstrated that they did not recognize the new republic. The first and the largest rebellion was in 1925. In a short time, the rebellion spread to many cities in the Kurdish area and the rebels captured several large cities, including Diyarbekir and Xarput. But because of poor organization the rebellion was suppressed and the leaders were executed. Five years later (1930), the Kurds started yet another rebellion around Mount Ararat. This rebellion lasted until 1932 before it was suppressed. In 1937, the Alevi Zaza population staged a greater and stronger rebellion in Dersim that lasted for two years and ended in a similar tragic defeat as the previous ones and the leaders were executed in the same way.[4] The well-known Turkish sociologist İsmail Beşikçi has this to say on the tragedy of the Kurds:

> The historical injustice committed against the Kurds is of such dimensions that it should create a conflict of conscience for all humanity. I will use all my life to remedy this injustice. The Western duplicity towards the Kurds is of such a character that I do not want to make use of the opportunity to try my case before the European Court of Human Rights.
>
> (See Steen 1999)[5]

The Kurds cast doubt on the legitimacy of the Kemalist republic because the so-called 'Kurdish representatives' then in the parliament who participated in the founding of the republic were not elected by the people in a democratic manner but appointed by Atatürk. Therefore, the very basis for the legitimacy of the state ceases to apply.

As an ideology, Kemalism was built as a construction from above in which the people are passive. Atatürk did not permit the people to participate in the political decision-making process. He was practically an elitist. The people had to be educated and 'civilized' first. Democracy and market economy could only be realized in long term. His recipe for education and civilization naturally applied to such groups of people as the Kurds and other non-Turks to an even greater extent. He saw them as underdeveloped lower races. In order to oppress the Kurds and other minorities and to maintain an unjust social order that benefited only the elite, it became necessary to be hard against one's own to be able to be even harder towards others. 'Perhaps Atatürk learned this from Balzac: *Un prince de la boheme*: The bohemian prince looks down to the citizens as boring and unfree; they have to live according to morals that deny them many pleasures and moreover these morals require hypocrisy' (Ōsterberg 1999).

An anti-modern republican project

Atatürk called his 'nation-building project' a 'modern republican project' and this would be exemplary for the rest of the world. Meanwhile, there are many who have questioned this and think that the project does not have anything to do with modernity. In this section we will discuss more closely whether the assertion about the 'nation-building project' can be defined as modern.

The concept of modernity denotes manifold tendencies within art, culture, politics and science and a prevalent western cultural pattern, which appeared in the nineteenth century in Europe and since then has become applicable to all the western social life. It appeared as a reaction to certain historic and contemporary aspects of the western societies. More generally, western modernity partly refers to a pronounced breaking down with respect to traditional social forms and their religious way of functioning and partly with respect to an elitist court culture and ideological and political views that emphasized the distance to what is daily and commonplace.

Concepts such as the free individual, reason or rationality as principle, differentiation of cultures, democratization, secularization, scientific orientation and progress have been fundamental

characteristics of modernity (Österberg 1999). These are the fundamental concepts of modernity; that is to say modernity is measured
or evaluated with reference to these concepts. The concepts at the
same time form the basis for daily life. It is by use of these concepts
that life is understood and explained in modernity. Lack of one or
more of these areas is connected with another existence or reality,
another way of understanding the world. This is precisely what happened with Atatürk and his Turkey.

Attempts to form a morality grounded in reason that corre-
sponded to the culture of the people was hindered by Atatürk. By
refusing to acknowledge the existence of the Kurds and other minorities and by preventing them from developing their identity, Atatürk
also hindered the development of a differentiated society in the political and cultural sense. The particular Turkish variant of secularism
that Atatürk stood for, and which is essentially different from the
western interpretation, was used to strengthen the Turkish nationalism that formed the groundwork of the republic. Atatürk also effectively prevented research institutions from producing knowledge or
making scientific progress. Knowledge should not serve people by
aiding them to attain more freedom and to liberate themselves
among other things from the state apparatus, nor should it lead to a
more humane society. Knowledge had precisely one purpose, namely
to serve Kemalism.

Finally, Atatürk's ideology has effectively prevented people from
thinking independently. The state is more important than and has
precedence over the nation. It requires that the individual defers to
the state and subordinates himself to the totality unconditionally.
The state shall not liberate individuals and groups but subdue them.
Furthermore, the state is entitled to prevent the members of society
from thinking differently; the state shall be the prevailing power and
see to it that people do not think freely and wish anything different
from what serves the interests of the state. Therefore, the Turkish
state constantly acts aggressively and violently towards individuals
and groups of people. This also becomes an expression of insult to
their human dignity and existence. So this runs like a connecting
thread to the 'Young Turks' times, the period when it was attempted
to destroy the Armenian ethnic minority.

Consequently, Atatürk's 'nation-building project' had nothing to
do with western modernity. Quite simply, this is because the project
did not move in a modern, democratic direction. Atatürk's thought
is anti-modern because it overrides the principle of equal rights and

freedom to all individuals and cultural minorities, in sharp contrast to the demand of the modern society for individual freedom and independence. The individual is free, as we understand from modern western societies, wants to be free and will not tolerate coercion and constraint. Liberation of the individual is directly connected with modern individualism and cultural freedom. The republican project was a very totalitarian system of government in the form of a nationalistic dictatorship based on military power.

Atatürk's 'nation-building project' did not allow any progress and it overruled important democratic procedures and administrative principles. Modern nation-building is a process which aims to give inhabitants a sense of deeper cultural fellowship and a stronger feeling of common national identity. A project that denies the existence of the non-Turkish minorities, something Atatürk's predecessors – the Ottoman Empire – did not deny, and that utilizes coercion to implement such denial cannot be described as modern. It is an expression for a false modernity. To deny the existence of or forbid the identity of other population groups contradicts the fundamental code of modernity. On the political plan, the code of modernity prescribes *equality* between groups of people, not total denial and subjugation, because in modernity there is no room for the holy whole (the Kemalist state). Therefore, Kemalism does not entail any progress but a backward step with respect to modernity. We can, with Charles Baudelaire's words, say that abuse of such concepts about progress in the name of freedom and reason are ridiculous in the best case.

Moreover, Atatürk's nationalism failed to break with the ultranationalist 'Young Turks' who ruled the Ottoman Empire from 1908 to its dissolution in 1918 and who committed the Armenian genocide in 1915–16. Atatürk incorporated the ultranationalists into his regime, which means he was equally as nationalistic as his predecessors. Both Atatürk and his successors denied and continue to deny the genocide. Lately, several documents in the state archive that indicate that Atatürk was a member of the 'Young Turks' have been publicized. This was also confirmed by the late sultan's son who lives in the USA.

A totalitarian dictatorship

According to western concepts, Atatürk's Turkey has clearly been a dictatorship. After the negotiations for EU membership started in

October 2005, the Turkish authorities opened the state archives. Historical documents demonstrate that both before and after the foundation of the republic, Atatürk supported the idea of founding a totalitarian regime. Kansu adds: '[W]e would like to believe that the republic in 1923 was liberal democratic but after 1923 we have not had a parliamentarian regime in Turkey' (*Radikal* 27 June 2005).

Atatürk ruled Turkey with an iron hand from 1923 until he died in 1938. He was a dictator.[6] His political opponents were purged and the country was ruled by a one-party system. He was the president of the country, who had all the power, and at the same time he was the commander in chief of the armed forces, president of the parliament and the chairman of the ruling party CHF (Cumhuriyet Halk Fırkası), which he himself established. He concentrated all power in his hands and ruled the country as a despot. The elderly describe Atatürk as a despot in the same class as Franco, Mussolini, Hitler and Stalin. When they harvested corn and other products they had to share them with the state. Atatürk demanded exactly half of the harvest. They say: 'We were the slaves of the state'.

Like the other dictators, Atatürk achieved a personal Führer cult, both while he was alive and after his death. His personality cult has been and is still enormous; Atatürk is nearly divine. It is difficult to find the like of the enormous personality cult of Atatürk taking place elsewhere. The opponents of the regime in Turkey say that even the personality cult of Saddam Hussein in his time does not compare with Atatürk. Atatürk is everywhere. A few examples can illuminate this enormous personality cult.

Portraits and statues of Atatürk can be seen everywhere (see Figure 8.1), in schools, public offices, private homes and shops. Roads, dams, city district, schools, universities and other higher education institutions, airports, bridges, football fields, sport arenas, parks, theatres and opera venues, cultural centres, business centres, conference halls, hospitals, cemeteries and so forth, are named after him. It is dictated that his portrait is to be hung not only in all official buildings and offices but also in the private sector such as restaurants, hotels and other workplaces. His portrait is to be found on all banknotes and coins. All school books, even those in a foreign language such as English, German or French, contain his portrait with text about how Turks should think, act and rule the future. As if this is not enough, Atatürk's political philosophy is obligatory in all education. Nobody can get a diploma or certificate if they do not pass the course 'Atatürk's revolutions' taught at all universities in the country.

Figure 8.1 A mountain top vis-à-vis the Kurdish city of Hakkari. On the top of the
mountain Atatürk's controversial slogan 'How happy he is who says he
is a Turk' can be read. The slogan is written with large white letters
that are legible from a distance of several kilometres. There are also
several flags that symbolize Turkish state power.
Photo: Memo Darez.

Atatürk's name must be pronounced on all formal occasions. Even
when members of the parliament take the obligatory oath, they do it
in his spirit and principles. School children must pronounce this oath
in Atatürk's spirit every morning before they start the first class: 'I
am a Turk. I am truthful and industrious. My existence is a present
to Turks.' The critics of the system think this is a Turkish nationalistic indoctrination with clear racialist undertones. However, any public indication of criticism towards Atatürk and his ideas and form of
government will not be tolerated and are met with many forms of
reaction and severe punishment because he is deified and criticism is
a taboo. Criticism towards him is also perceived as an affront to the
Turkish nation. For example, if one chews chewing gum near one of
Atatürk's statues, it will be perceived as insult. The concerned person
will therefore find himself imprisoned for this act. On 6 May 2006,
the *Economist* reported that the mayor of Fatsa, a little town on the
Black Sea coast, was imprisoned because he had chewing gum in his
mouth while he was laying down a wreath of flowers in front of an

Atatürk statue in the town.[7] The mayor belongs to the ruling Justice and Development Party (AKP). (For more on this case, see the *Economist* 6 May 2006.)

Atatürk's political philosophy and his model for state building brought another reality to that expressed by modernity: despotism, brutality, contempt for minorities and cultures, and a regression in humaneness that has dominated Turkish politics up to the present date. Oppression of minorities continued after Atatürk's death. It was strengthened after 1980 when the military grabbed the power with a *coup d'état*. This was the third coup in the course of a 20-year period. It will not be an exaggeration to assert that Atatürk's dictatorship is in the best health even today. After Atatürk, the military has positioned itself as the foremost spokesmen for his regime and as the central symbol of secularism. To understand the power and influence of the military in contemporary Turkish politics, it is important to look at the founder of the new republic himself, Atatürk. He had a background as a professional officer in the Ottoman army. He staged a *coup d'état* against the sultan and took large parts of the Ottoman army with the aim to reconquer the territories lost as a result of the First World War. The Ottoman Empire had to surrender territories because it was on Germany's side in the First World War. During the peace settlement, the Ottoman Empire signed the peace treaty (the Sevres Treaty) that conferred the Kurds the right to form their own state. But Atatürk reconquered and annexed the Kurdish area and formed his own republic from the geographical area that constitutes the present boundaries of Turkey. In other words, it was the military that had liberated the country and founded the Turkish republic because the participation by the masses in the liberation of the country was feeble. Because of this, Atatürk managed to implant an understanding that the military owns the state. Also Atatürk's successor, İsmet İnönü (also called National Leader), was a general and a close collaborator. Up until today, the military has had the opinion that it owns the republic. This is constantly demonstrated in Turkish political debates, recently by the previous prime minister and president for many years Süleyman Demirel, on 17 April 2005 in a live interview in one of the Turkish channels, CNN Türk, in which he said: 'The military are the founders of the republic Turkey. And they always fear that the state is heading towards its ruin'.[8]

The military portrays itself as the guardian of Atatürk's ideas, which will be lines of guidance for ruling the country, but in practice it functions as his inheritor. The military leads a fight in Atatürk's spirit with methods that effectively set democracy and civil society aside by referring, among others, to the statement Atatürk made on 7 March 1925 when he ordered the military forces to crush the Kurdish rebellion: 'The honour and the judgement of the republic's military forces, police corps and the gendarmerie units lie above all other points of view' (*Hürriyet* 21 March 2005). The military is consecrated by virtue of being the founder of the republic and, therefore, has precedence over the population. Its sanctity is expressed in many contexts. For example, it is politically resolved that military personnel will be referred to as martyrs when they die, irrespective of whether they die in a traffic accident or fighting the Kurdish insurgents. See, for example, the report of an incident in the Turkish media on 27 May 2005 that sanctifies the military.[9] In a clash between PKK terrorists and security forces in a village in Diyarbekir region, two soldiers were martyred and a tractor chauffeur who freighted food for the military died.

The military has carried out three *coups d'état* after Atatürk's death, all at times when the country tried to democratize the society by introducing a multi-party system. In addition, there have been several military interventions. The last intervention (called a 'soft' coup) happened in February 1997. The military ousted the coalition government of Necmettin Erbakan from the relatively moderate Islamic Welfare Party (IWP). The justification was that the party had transgressed the constitutional boundary between politics and religion. The democratic principles are set aside at every military coup or intervention. Military coups or interventions are justified by referring to the constitution from Atatürk's times. The military leaders think that they have a direct mandate from the constitution to intervene in the political order if they think the security of the country is threatened. It is their duty to interfere and carry out coercive measures. A flourishing of Kurdish culture or Islamic identity is perceived as a serious threat. The generals assert that the basis for national unity and identity of the secular republic is threatened by the political advent of the Kurds or the Islamists. According to opinion polls, most people are dissatisfied that the generals have given themselves more power by making use of a paragraph of the constitution that allows them to interfere with politics when they think the republic is threatened. In western societies, to allocate more power to oneself is a characteristic associated with dictatorships. But there is little the people in Turkey can do. They cannot criticize or demonstrate against the military, which has the political and military power.

The political system has developed from a totalitarian dictatorship to an authoritarian state under the supervision of the military. The country is still considered to be a strict authoritarian state that holds the general population, and particularly the Kurds, under tight control. The political elite in Turkey are to a great extent a product of the Kemalist era, which coincided with the period of the nation-building project. Even those who were born after Kemal Atatürk's death and do not share his vision of a common national identity define themselves and their values with reference to Kemalism. The somewhat western-oriented middle class and the bourgeoisie do not have political dominion yet. The bourgeoisie have access to economic activity, which presupposes certain individual freedoms in the market, but they do not have greater political power.

Despite the introduction of Kemalism and many other 'secularization' measures, Turkey has not left Islam and traditionalism behind. The Kemalist 'nation-building' project has met with hard criticism. Today, many intellectuals and reformist politicians see Kemalism as a historical error that undermined the normative order. Not everybody connects their identity with Atatürk's definition of the 'new Turk'. The Islamic movement has been Turkey's largest political movement since 1995. At the 1995 elections, the Islamic party REFAH (the Welfare Party) became the largest. After the party was banned in 1999, Recep Tayyip Erdoğan and his colleagues from the Welfare Party started a new moderate Islamic party, AKP. Today, the Islamists of AKP are Turkey's largest party and have the government power. This happened after the party won the 2002 parliamentary elections with a landslide victory and obtained two-thirds of the seats in the national assembly. These Islamists reject Atatürk's definition of 'new Turks'. They identify themselves as 'Muslim Turks'. For them, Islamic Turkish identity is more important than a cultivated ethnic identity as a 'new Turk'. Consequently, the Kemalist 'nation building project' has not succeeded in its goal of creating a new national identity and unifying the heterogeneous population of Turkey.

The general perception in Turkey is that the political landscape will not change however great a majority the Islamists get in the parliament. It is still the military that plays a central role in Turkish politics. In Turkey there is a widespread perception that the most important political discussions and political decisions are taking place outside of parliament. Today, the military is the prime mover of the political process to prevent the Kurds and the Islamists from developing their identities and it cannot stand to be contradicted.

Many people think that the policies the military subscribe to do not create national consensus or respect for different groups. It has led to greater polarization and tension between the groups. A recent example of how a thrust from the military increases the tension between groups of people follows.

The Kurds celebrated their national day, *Newroz*, on 21 March 2005. The Kurds arranged 56 large meetings all over Turkey. In the large Kurdish city of Diyarbekir, nearly one million people had gathered for the meeting. The meetings proceeded peacefully everywhere except in the Turkish city of Mersin by the Mediterranean coast. About 20,000 Kurds gathered. A couple of Kurdish youths of 12 and 14 years age, who were also participatants, were asked by a man in plain clothes if they could carry the Turkish flag. The arrangers of the meeting believe that the man was from the police intelligence and was aiming at provocation. But the youths refused to carry the flag. They threw it to one side. The incident was captured by cameras and shown by several Turkish TV stations. Meanwhile, there were no reactions to the incident until the chief of the general staff, Hilmi Özkök, made a written statement 48 hours after the incident. Özkök reacted hysterically and condemned the youths' rejection of the flag with strong words in his statement. He further criticized the Kurds for having trampled on the flag, which according to him is the very symbol of honour for the republic. The chief of the general staff used the expression 'so-called' Turkish citizens with reference to Kurds who did not respect the flag and the general characterized this as treason. The designation 'so-called Turkish citizens' was perceived as a serious accusation and expression that signals the Kurds must be stripped of their citizenship, an attitude that was reminiscent of previous military coups that were particularly oppressive against the Kurds. The statement was formulated in such a manner that it was perceived to be directed to all Kurds in the country. He depicted the Kurds as 'others' and encouraged people to react in order to defend the flag and the state because he believed it was a 'sacred duty' (compare Kapferer's interpretation of 'the holy state'). The statement also contained threats and signals for excluding the Kurds as usual. This triggered a hysterical demonstration of power by the Turks directed towards the Kurdish minority. The military and the police authorities demanded that each and every individual and family, party and organization should hang the flag over everything: on cars, in homes, official buildings, at workplaces, on TV screens, football stadiums, neckties and jackets, dining tables and so forth.

The flag hysteria triggered massive demonstrations among ethnic Turks. These did not get any support in the Kurdish areas but Kurdish school children were compelled to participate in the protest parades. A group of Kurdish children were flown to the Atatürk mausoleum in Ankara. In the political propaganda they were portrayed as evidence of Kurdish children loving Atatürk. The flag hysteria lasted for ten days and then stopped suddenly. It probably stopped because western media began to cover the flag hysteria. Western diplomats in Ankara implied that Turkish nationalism was irreconcilable with the EU's democratic principles. The military would not be served well by the world public learning of the role it plays in Turkish politics. More revelations of this role would moreover increase the pressure and demands from the EU for weakening the role of the military if Turkey's ambitions of EU membership were to be met in the future. All the same, the flag crisis demonstrated that the Turkish state, heavily dominated by the military, has a strong central authority or 'state' that compels minorities, first and foremost the Kurds, to renounce their demands for certain democratic rights. It also demonstrated that the Kurds are not regarded as full members of the 'new Turk' nation.

Yet the flag hysteria is only the last example of the political duplicity the military and large portions of the Turkish population display, namely national freedom for Turks, tyranny and cruelty for Kurds. The power demonstrations expressed the Turks' right to decide by virtue of being the 'most fit', but the less powerful Kurds just had to endure the oppression because the Turkish hegemony is unchallenged. The more the Turkish hegemony provokes strong demonstrations of its domination, the more the antagonism towards the minority groups will come to the foreground. The flag crisis also demonstrated that the Kemalist state has created deep national antagonisms and it is not capable of finding solutions to the problems it has created. In the Kurdish areas, the legal protection of the individual has always been more ineffectual than in the Turkish-dominated west of the country. Harassment and atrocities by the military are still the order of the day. The area is characterized as a surveillance society by many, including human rights organizations, and the Turkish Union of Jurists and the western consciousness is aware of this.

Turkish intellectuals, opposition parties, reformist politicians and labour organizations did not react to the treatment the Kurds received at the hands of the authorities while the civil war raged in the period from 1984 to 1999. The Kurds were left to their own devices for 15 years. Now for the first time, Turkish intellectuals have joined in the reaction to the flag hysteria. But, as usual, they are accused of being 'supporters of separatists'. On 11 April 2005 the Turkish daily *Radikal* published a declaration in which 200 Turkish intellectuals criticized the reactions to the flag hysteria and call them racist nationalism. But the Turkish intellectuals committed an elementary error by placing Turkish and Kurdish nationalisms side by side. Perhaps Turkish intellectuals have to criticize Kurdish nationalism so that they will not be persecuted or will not receive death threats from invisible powers.

Turkey is in a more serious crisis than the west realizes. The flag hysteria, together with an abnormal intolerance of humane demands that are regarded as totally basic in democracies, have caused many intellectuals, politicians and commentators both within and without the country to describe Turkey as 'the new sick man if Europe'. In an article in the *Wall Street Journal* of 16 February 2005, editor Robert Pollock went even further and described Turkey as having a paranoid behaviour.[10] Many question the psychological state of the nationalist Turkish state. Imprisonment and torture of the opposition is witness to moral and legal decay. The Turkish authorities refuse to solve the Kurdish question by political means but instead attempt to solve it by use of military measures. It is also doubtful whether the powerful military wants a political solution. The military leaders believe that they have a direct mandate from paragraph 3 of the constitution that obliges them to interfere when they feel that the unity of the country or the state structure is threatened by separatists or others. This is the formal justification. But when the military implements extreme measures against so-called separatism through the National Security Council (MGK), it says more about the state of the Turkish rule. The examples below illustrate this:

- Two months before the flag incident, two football teams, one from the small Kurdish district Yeniceoba in mid-western Anatolia and one from a Turkish-speaking district in the same area, met for a match. Two players from the 'Kurdish team' exchanged some words in Kurdish during the match. This caused the referees to stop the match with the justification that it was not allowed to speak in any language other than Turkish. The referees and the Turkish team complained about the football team from

Yeniceoba to the Turkish Football Association. The association cancelled the membership of the Kurdish team shortly afterwards, throwing it out of the football league.

- Edip Polat was imprisoned for many years. He was convicted for having collected different kinds of flowers from Kurdish areas and given them their original names in Kurdish. According to Turkish law, this was naturally a crime because it is regarded as separatism.

- During the flag hysteria, the well-known Turkish author Orhan Pamuk gave an interview to a Swiss newspaper. He stated that Turkey killed one million Armenians during the First World War and 30,000 Kurds during the civil war in the 1980s and 1990s, something the Turks deny. This was enough for prominent persons in many local communities to ask people to remove his books from bookstores. Pamuk was also disliked because he had, both in the USA and Europe, publicly condemned Turkey's war against the Kurds and repeatedly spoke warmly of the Kurdish struggle. Pamuk, who received the Nobel Prize for literature in 2006, is declared a traitor in Turkey. The attorney general in Turkey has indicted him and 60 other writers and publishers. This led the EU ambassador in Ankara, Hans Jörg Kretschmer, to criticize the Turkish authorities' assault on freedom of expression.[11]

- Human rights activists in the Human Rights Association (IHD) are constantly persecuted. Eren Keskin is Kurdish and the lawyer of four others who run the association's rehabilitation institute for torture victims in Istanbul. The institute founders have been accused for establishing the therapy centre and, in addition, have been convicted for not being willing to disclose the identities of their patients to the police. All the same, many think that they should be glad for being indicted because many others did not even get this chance and were tortured, sometimes to death. According to *Özgür Politika*'s 18 April issue, Yusuf Alataş, the leader for IHD, told that the association had registered 837 people who were tortured in 2004. He added that he believes the real number runs to several thousands but that they could not document the true extent because people dare not come forward and tell of the torture.

- A well-known Kurdish lawyer and human rights activist, Medeni Ayhan, was shot on 6 April 2005 in Ankara. He only just survived. He is one of several hundreds who shared the same fate.

The Turkish state is suspected of being behind the murder attempt. Just before the assassination attempt, Ayhan had given a lecture at the Turkish Lawyers Union in which he said that the principle of self-determination must apply also for the Kurds. In a press conference on 27 May, Ayhan revealed classified documents from the vice chief of the general staff, Ilker Basbug, who had appealed to the attorney general in Ankara and asked that Ayhan be indicted for the speech he had made at the lawyers union.[12] Such a procedure is not allowed by the law but the military all the same use it frequently against the opposition. Ayhan was sentenced to three years in prison for his opinion.

- At least three Kurdish politicians from the party DEHAP were sentenced to 10 months in prison and many more were charged for their referring to the leader of the Kurdish insurgence, Abdullah Öcalan, as *Mister* Öcalan. In Turkey, it is strictly forbidden to use this designation for him and many other Kurdish politicians.

- The independent labour organization of state employees, Kamu Emekçileri Sendikaları Konfederasyonu (KESK), held its congress on 13 May in Ankara. The labour minister was invited to the congress. The minister criticized the labour organization from the speaker's chair for not having raised the flag within the premises and on the congress building. Around the same time, a district court banned a labour organization – *Egitim Sen* – which has 200,000 members because it had included in its program the demand for education in the mother tongue for minorities. The organization has filed a suit at the European Court of Human Rights in Strasbourg.

- Three guerrilla soldiers from the PKK were killed in the province of Siirt in the middle of May 2005. Witnesses told the newspapers that the corpses of the guerrilla soldiers were hung behind military vehicles and dragged through the streets.[13] Human rights organizations accused Turkey of violating the Geneva Convention, which stipulates a humane treatment of prisoners of war. Turkey committed innumerable similar breaches in 1980s and 1990s when the corpses of guerrilla soldiers were hung from helicopters and flown over Kurdish cities and towns to frighten the population.

- On 1 June 2005 Turkish newspapers reported that the Ministry of Defence had filed a suit against the families of five dead PKK soldiers for compensation amounting to 3,000 pounds sterling to be paid to the family of a Turkish soldier who was allegedly killed by the five.[14] The parents of the five reacted to the resolution and threatened by appealing to the European Court of Human Rights in Strasbourg. The lawyer for the five families, Fahrettin Kaya, asserts that the resolution of the ministry conflicts with international law. But it is not only within the borders of the country that the Turkish authorities violate international law.

- A Kurdish family of nine from Syria had been visiting close relatives in Sweden. After the holidays, the Mahos were to travel from Stockholm to Damascus via Istanbul on 3 June 2005. They had bought their tickets from the Turkish airline company THY. All the family was stopped when they passed through the last ticket control, which was manned by an employee of the Turkish airlines company THY. The family was told that they could not travel by Turkish plane because one of the family members was called 'Kurdistan'. It is usual to use 'Kurdistan' as a girl's name among Kurds in Syria. The Maho family appealed to the police at the Arlanda airport. The incident was given much publicity in Swedish media. THY refused to comment on the case. Meanwhile, the International Aviation Organization issued a statement that accused the Turkish airline company of discriminatory treatment of people because of their ethnic belonging. The statement said: 'No one shall be prevented from travelling because of ethnicity, language, culture, religion or race. Those who break this rule by discriminating against people shall be convicted according to the international aviation law'.[15]

- While the flag hysteria and the innumerable violations of human rights continued, one more crisis arose, this time between Turkey and the EU. Austrian Gerhard Pils, who was employed as a biology teacher at St George College in Istanbul, had used the word Kurdistan in his lectures. Although Pils had used the word Kurdistan as the name of a geographic area and not in the sense of a country, it was more than enough reason for firing him. Austria twice took the case up with the EU after Pils lost his job and the vice president of the European parliament, Hannes Swoboda, was urgently sent to Turkey to discuss the case with the Turks. Swoboda thinks that the Pils case is one of the many examples that demonstrate the poor conditions of freedom of expression in Turkey. And, of course, the conditions of freedom of expression cannot be understood independently of the political course the Turkish authorities set, and it is unclear who actually sets the political course. Formally, it is the government that should form the policies but many believe that the military exercises a decisive role through the so-called National Security Council where the powerful generals sit. The EU has tried to reduce the influence of the National Security Council but it is still doubtful whether it has succeeded. The National Security Council is supposed to have only an advisory function but everyone perceives the 'council' as the most important organ of power in Turkey. Many are of the opinion that the government does not have the power to set the political agenda. There are many examples of the military still playing the major role here and these are discussed in greater detail below.

When political incidents, both of internal and external nature, happen in Turkey, it is the chief of the general staff who makes a public statement first, as in the flag incident. He presents the military's view of the incident, based on its principles. Thereafter, he places the incident in a military context with an evaluation of what it will mean for the security and future of the state. In his evaluation, he clearly and unambiguously expresses that the military has the right to decide what valid policies are for the future of the country, to define what is in the country's best interests, and to exclude, humiliate or declare to be illegal those forces that attempt to harm the country. He leaves no room for doubt about who has power and makes the decisions.

The principal views of the chief of the general staff are understood as a political framework within which the politicians must act. He lays down rules for how people should think and how the politicians should treat the case. The politicians come forward after the chief of the general staff's statement and express themselves within the framework the chief of the staff has set, a process that was also repeated during the flag crisis. After the chief of the staff's statement about the flag incident both Prime Minister Erdogan and the leader of the opposition, Baykal, and many other politicians came forward and condemned the conduct of the youths with the flag.

But the chief of the general staff does not only make political statements. The political development must also be evaluated, and this is public. One concrete example of how the chief of the general staff controls the political course came on 19 April 2005 when the chief of the general staff, Hilmi Özkök, made his yearly throne speech at the War Academy in Istanbul. This was termed 'the general staff's yearly throne speech' in the Turkish media. In the west, the term, throne speech, is usually associated with heads of the state and therefore the usage, throne speech and not just speech, is worth noticing. The chief of the general staff's throne speech lasted a full 90 minutes and was published as the main news in all Turkish media and characterized as extremely important for the future of the country. As a rule, the throne speech of the chief of the general staff is broadcast live by TV channels. In his throne speech, the chief of the general staff went through all the topical political issues concerning Turkey. He set out his views on Turkey's EU policies, the process of negotiation with the EU which would start on 3 October 2005: the reform process; Turkey's relations with the USA; the USA's Middle East policies; Turkey's relations with Iraq in general; the Kurdish demands for self-rule in Northern Iraq; the Kirkuk question; and Turkey's relations with the Far East, the Middle East, Armenia, Caucasus, Central Asia, Cyprus, Greece, the Balkans and other neighbours. The general further stated opinions on the internal political situation, the situation of the religion, the PKK and so forth. He criticized the government for being passive in connection with the PKK and the Islamists. And he had a clear message concerning the political development both within Turkey and internationally, and emphasized which issues in the country's politics should be solved, where and how they should be solved. All these issues were considered in the light of Atatürk's ideas.

The chief of the general staff's throne speech did not have the characteristics of one from an appointed official but rather one from a leader elected by the public. The next day, one could read in the Turkish newspaper columns that the general's statement was characterized as an alternative to the country's elected president or prime minister. Some compared the chief of the general staff's throne speech to the official throne speeches that kings or presidents deliver when they open their respective parliaments every year. A veteran columnist, Oktay Eksi, from the largest newspaper in the country, *Hürriyet*, questioned the general's conduct cautiously and asked: 'Are there chiefs of the general staff in EU countries or other democratic countries who publicly evaluate or judge the political situation in his country?' He asked also why the general used only 15 minutes for what he should actually be speaking about, namely military issues, and used the rest of the time for what many think he should not speak about. Another columnist, Hasan Cemal, from *Milliyet*, described the general's speech as a plain political interference and an attempt at undermining political continuity. Two days later spokespersons for both the government and the opposition came forward with full support of the chief of the general staff's speech. Prime Minister Erdogan characterized the chief of general staff's speech as brave.

This typical example demonstrates that the politicians are deprived of their capabilities for manoeuvring or the space for action that must exist before democracy begins to function. The military leaders are the real masters of Turkey. No matter what opinions the elected government may have, it functions only as an advisory organ. Government resolutions must be adjusted to the opinions of the military apparatus before they can be implemented. The opposite is unthinkable. No government decision can be implemented if it conflicts with the views of the military apparatus.

Another example of how the military controls the elected politicians and compels them to silence is from a newspaper interview in the winter of 2004, where an elected member of the parliament expressed his reaction to Atatürk's portrait in a military uniform displaying a field marshal's insignia that hangs in the main hall of the parliament. The member of parliament was from the province of Adiyaman in Eastern Turkey and belonged to the government party AKP. In the interview, the member of parliament expressed his wish that the picture with the military uniform be taken down, to be replaced by another picture of Atatürk dressed in civilian clothes. This was more than enough to create uproar. The chief of the general staff came forward at once and condemned the member of parliament with crass words and demanded that the member of parliament be prosecuted. The chief of the general staff accused the member of parliament by referring to the resolution of the then-parliament that had honoured the founding father with a field marshal's rank. However, that parliament was not elected but appointed by Atatürk himself. After the chief of the general staff's statement, politicians came forward one by one and condemned the member of parliament publicly, although their facial expressions told something else. Prime Minister Erdogan, who was a fellow party member, called the Party Control and Disciplinary Committee together to exclude this 'unfortunate' man from the party.

Another member of parliament from the ruling party was elected the leader of the Defence Committee in the parliament, just before this incident. But the military disliked this choice because he was previously dismissed from the armed forces because of his religious belief. The chief of the general staff posed an ultimatum in which he demanded that the parliament must remove him from the position of leader of the Defence Committee. This was done the same day.

The situation of the Kurds is no better than the treatment these two members of the parliament received. They cannot participate in politics on an ethnic basis; that is to say, they are refused the right to present themselves as Kurds or Kurdish ethno-politicians. Turkish law does not allow it even after the reforms that were adopted to meet the EU's demands. The policies of the Turkish state still aim at making the Kurds deny their ethnic background. The Kurds will be terrorized through coercive methods until they admit Turkish identity. The Kurds must present themselves as Turks in order to participate in politics. That is, they must do so based on Turkish premises. Kurds are met with heavy punishment when they try to participate as Kurds. Political parties that oppose the 'indivisible unity of the state', for example Kurdish parties and parties that work against the secular character of the state, such as certain Islamic parties, are forbidden by law. Also, parties representing class interests, represented by the Communist Party, are forbidden and labour organizations are not allowed to have political activities. The Kurds have tried to establish many legal parties since 1992 without naming them Kurdish. Some of the best known are People's Labor Party (HEP), The Democratic Society Party (DEP), and The People's Democracy Party (HADEP). But all of these were banned by the Turkish authorities. In addition, the Turkish authorities have banned 18 parties after the military coup in 1980, including the largest ruling party, the Welfare Party of the previous prime minister, Necmettin Erbakan, in late 1990s. One of the methods used is to silence by threats.

For the time being, Kurds are active in the Kurdish friendly parties such as DEHAP and Party of the rights and freedoms (HAK-PAR),[16] but both these parties are indicted by the Attorney General with the demand they are banned. The former party is charged with separatist activities and the latter is charged with its leader making his opening speech in Kurdish at the party congress in 2004. One can be sentenced to 20 years in prison according to paragraph 49 of the Turkish penal code if one uses any language other than Turkish at political meetings. The leader of DEHAP and most of the party leadership have already been sentenced to prison. Many leaders of the guerrilla movement, the PKK, have also been charged and some have received death sentences that have been commuted to life imprisonment after pressure from the EU. Others have been sentenced to life imprisonment and many more have been sentenced to many years in prison. There are a total of 6,000 political prisoners in Turkish prisons, the majority being PKK members.

In March 2006, Turkish security forces killed 14 guerrilla soldiers in the province of Bingöl in Eastern Turkey. Kurds marched in large demonstration parades during the burial ceremonies, which took place in Diyarbekir, Batman, Mardin, Van and Yüksekova. They protested against the Turkish security forces, which they claimed had used chemical weapons against the PKK guerrilla soldiers. But the security forces answered using extensive force against the relatively peaceful demonstrations. Thirteen demonstrators, of whom three were children from 6 to 8 years old, were killed by the security forces. Up to 800 people were arrested, among them 80 children under the age of 14. The children were subjected to torture during interrogation, according to the *Economist*, which spoke with their lawyers. The prosecutor asked for prison sentences of up to 24 years for participating in the demonstrations (*Economist* 6 May 2006).

Most of the children were punished by up to 24-year prison sentences although no one could prove that the children had participated in the demonstrations. The court justified the lack of evidence thus: 'Nobody has seen that these children were involved in the riots, but if the police have arrested them, then there is no doubt about their guilt' (*DIHA* News Agency 6 May 2006). The Turkish press defended the sentence by portraying the children as guilty and the security forces as innocent.

After the demonstrations, the Turkish authorities decided that the corpses of the killed PKK guerrilla soldiers would not be handed over to their families from then on. They would be buried where they were killed, without the presence of their families. At the end of April, Turkish newspapers reported that the bodies of 18 Kurdish guerrilla soldiers were buried in a mass grave with their clothes on. This allegedly took place on the Cudi mountain where they were killed.

The examples above are only a few I have used to illuminate certain issues. Hundreds of similar incidents, often more brutal and gross violations of entirely fundamental human rights, happened in the period I was carrying out field work. The cases stretch from forcible movement of families that the authorities suspected of helping PKK members, disappearances, political murder, killing children and youths, torture, raping politically active women, to arresting a series of authors, publishers, journalists, jurists, human rights activists and many others arbitrarily without any legal basis, and open humiliation, harassment and debasement of people in the worst thinkable manner. Many human rights activists and journalists were among the victims. I have also met many people who were crippled as a result of either the civil war or torture in the prisons. It is all about an extremely fascistic core that has placed intolerance and oriental racism at the heart of a state authorized system.

Human rights activists I spoke with were of the opinion that Turkey has never been capable of defining human rights. They ask, 'When the Kemalist ideology has refused to recognize the Kurds as a people and still does so, how can this same ideology be capable of defining this people's identity, cultural, social and political rights?' and add, 'Here in Turkey, even the most fundamental right of man, namely the right of life, is in danger. One never knows what comes to happen with one. One can disappear anywhere and anytime, one can be liquidated or arrested. So people constantly live with such a fear. And this kind of fear is widespread in all social layers'.

The small 'democratic' space is shrinking. A counteroffensive connected with the EU membership has started. This offensive is led in the first place by the military leaders who act as the dogmatic defenders of nationalism and have assumed an extreme role in Turkish politics. It seems that they are inclined to use this role to prevent Turkey from making the transition to a democratic and pluralistic system, something that has been asserted by the aforementioned EU report (Oostlander 2003). In the report, the EU demands a new constitution that will end the military's dominating position in Turkish politics. It seems that this has caused the military leaders to step back into authoritarianism in order to maintain the Kemalist state structure that they think different governments have weakened by unrecognizably distorting Atatürk's state nation-building project. They are leading a struggle in Atatürk's spirit by threatening the fundamental premise for democracy and civil society that lies in 'the rule of law and democracy'.[17] And the offensive by the military is supported by ultra nationalistic forces organized in the Nationalistic Action Party (MHP) and not the least in Atatürk's own party, the Republican Party (CHP).

The political development in Turkey has created concerns within the EU and, increasingly, many within the EU countries are becoming sceptical towards Turkey's EU membership. One EU politician expressed the scepticism thus: 'The EU is beginning to be rather tired of asking Turkey repeatedly to solve her problems by democratic and humane methods. A Turkey which does not respect the language, name and alphabet of her own inhabitants (Kurds) has nothing to do in the EU' (*Özgür Politika* 6 June 2005).

The reasons for authoritarianism

Critics of the regime agree that Turkey has been a totalitarian country, but in the last 5–6 years of EU adjustment the country is described as authoritarian. Turkey is a partially free country, according to the Freedom House (2005). Independent political experts agree that the cause of authoritarianism is the unsolved Kurdish problem in the country. Chris Patten, member of the EU Committee for External Affairs puts it thus: 'Atatürk placed the military as a state within the state. He saw ethnic and religious minorities as a threat to the unity (the state). Therefore, Atatürk gave the military a political key' (*Özgür Politika* 25 May 2004).

Many have difficulties with understanding the temperament of the Turks and therefore ask; what is it that the Kurds want that makes Turkey to react so brutally? The question of an independent Kurdish state is not even a topical issue shown by the Sevres Treaty, which was proclaimed by the victors of the First World War and by which Kurds were promised a state of their own. The Kurds can justify their demands by referring to the right of self-determination, a resolution that the United Nations has proclaimed, but the Kurds think realistically and know that complete independence is unachievable because they are surrounded by Persians, Arabs and Turks, all of whom regard the Kurds as their enemies. Therefore, none of the Kurdish parties or opposition groups in Turkey aims at an independent Kurdish state. They demand the right to speak, to write and to be educated in their own language. They want to cultivate their own culture within the area where they are the majority of the population and they want a certain degree of self-government. They demand local self-government, appointment of local Kurds in the administration and the police force, mother tongue education in Kurdish in schools, and recognition of the original Kurdish names of places, areas and cities. They demand usual legal protection so that they can live in peace and feel secure in their lives and property, which have previously not been protected, and they demand freedom of expression to take care of their cultural identity. They demand the abolition of the village guards system that was established by the military authorities in 1980s and that consists of Kurds to oppose the PKK. The village guards system does not consist of volunteers; it is an imposed arrangement with the aim of using Kurds against each other.

Their demands are reasonable and amount to basic human rights. The Kurds are not the problem. They demand the introduction of democracy. But Turkey cannot stand even discussing a limited self-government for Kurds. Any demand for a certain form of self-government is regarded as a separatist attempt. All forms of self-government, be it federation or internal autonomy, are defined as separatism in Turkish law. Neither are civil rights at a minimum level tolerated. The core of the problem lies in what the EU ascertains in a report on Turkey from 2003 in connection with Turkey's application for EU membership: Kemalism is irreconcilable with democracy and it can be the most important reason preventing Turkey's EU membership (Oostlander 2003). Consequently, if modernity represents a society with manifold cultures, democratic and representative government, individual's right of expression and so forth, then it must be said that what the Kurds are fighting for and representing is modern; what Kemalism represents is anti-modern. For the Kurds, it is all about looking forward patiently and continuing to build institutions in the spirit of freedom, reason and progress.

The policies of the Turkish state, its praxis including the reform process, the flag hysteria and the prevalent attitudes among ethnic Turks defeat the ideal of an ethnically neutral nation where all citizens have equal rights and opportunities notwithstanding ethnic and cultural origin. The road to achieving an ethnically neutral nation, which is also a prerequisite for EU membership, is very long. Politically, the military leaders still operate as the primary actors in today's Turkey and hamper this goal. The Kurds are kept out of the reform process, which started after Turkey was officially recognized as a candidate country in 1999.

When, in addition, the powerful military acts in an authoritarian and undemocratic manner towards the elected representatives, this illustrates how democratic structures and institutions are threatened by authoritarian powers. With the strong position of the military in Turkish politics, the cultural and ethnic antagonism between the Turks and Kurds becomes more intense and the mood between them is full of hatred. The EU believes that when the influence of the military on politics is reduced, the process of democratization will move forward. But this is doubtful. There are historical reasons that the authoritarian powers can still mobilize the masses against the process of democratization. Turkey has never had the opportunity to go through the same processes that Europe has gone through, namely the Renaissance, the Reformation and the Enlightenment.

First, the Ottoman Empire prevented the Turkish society from being influenced by western thinking. After the dissolution of the

Ottoman Empire, Atatürk took over. Atatürk combated religiosity, traditionalism and nobility, on which the Ottoman Empire was based, but he introduced a dogmatic nationalistic ideology. It lacked the political ideals of democracy, egalitarian rights and freedom for the individual, and other fundamental human rights. His thoroughly nationalistic indoctrination of the Turkish society functioned as an iron cage in connection with modern thinking. Atatürk, with an aggressive nationalism, prevented the population from experiencing or becoming familiar with the processes of modernity. In other words, Turkey has not had its Renaissance, Reformation or Enlightenment, and is still a stranger to the values these historical processes have contributed in the transformation of the west to the present society it is.

Atatürk's followers, mainly the military, continued the tradition of intolerance. They have hindered every renewal in a democratic direction and they still prevent such a development. When members of the opposition are imprisoned because of their statements, books are confiscated because they criticize the political system, songs are banned because they allegedly imply Kurdish separatism, people are sentenced to prison for many years because they have given species of flowers their original Kurdish names, political parties are banned because they do not agree with Atatürk's ideology and wish to change the political course of the country, Kurdish politicians and human rights activists disappear mysteriously or are killed or imprisoned, all this shows that Turkey acts as a bandit state, according to the critics of the system. Turkey is similar only to itself as long as the military, and not the elected government, has the real power. The military functions as a state within a state and prevents all attempts to renew the country or to break with its brutal past. The result is that the population of Turkey is not familiar with western concepts, thinking and culture at all, except western dress and the Latin alphabet. This makes the people liable to be easily manipulated by authoritarian forces.

Descriptions of Atatürk in large sections of western literature or media do not reflect the reality. In older school books, it was written that Atatürk was a dictator like Franco, Mussolini, Hitler and Stalin and he oppressed his people and especially mistreated the minorities. At other places, particularly in encyclopaedias (see for example *Cappelens leksikon* 1994), it is written that Atatürk introduced a radical modernization process. Such a description is rather an expression of western naivety, which allows history to be extremely

influenced by Turkish propaganda. According to the Turkish histo-
rian Aykut Kansu (*Radikal* 27 June 2005), Atatürk had conservative
and very authoritarian views on social and economic issues.
He says:

> Atatürk's many statements at the Turkish national assembly,
> especially from the period 1920–1923, contain hard criticism
> against fundamental Western values and principles. He even
> criticises Western attire. The transition to the Latin alphabet,
> secularism, women's rights including the right to vote and be
> elected and the right to become teachers, were reforms which
> were already realized or about to be realized by Atatürk's pred-
> ecessors (Young Turks). But Atatürk collected all the honour
> and this is unjust. Atatürk's international policies were oriented
> towards the West but the rest of his policies are antidemocratic
> and anti-modernist.

Kemalism was an anti-modernist movement in Turkey. It was
against liberal principles, it did not want competing political principles, and it believed trade and investments must be done by the state
and moreover it was strongly opposed to a western-type society
divided into classes.

Another critic of Turkey, the sociologist İsmail Beşikçi, characterizes Atatürk's modernization process as a typical Turkish bluff that
does not reflect the reality. If a survey was to be carried out in Turkey
with questions about how many have heard of the central personalities in European culture, politics and science who have heavily influenced the formation of modern Europe, it would not surprise me if
only one out of 50,000 or maybe rather one out of 100,000 have
heard of Voltaire, Einstein, Freud, Kant or Marx. Even fewer will say
that they have heard of Shakespeare, Ibsen, H. C. Andersen or
Brecht.

The dominating value system, cultural heritage, history, tradition
and national memory in Turkey are essentially different from the
West. It is very difficult to pinpoint something concrete that the
Turkish republic has created that can be described as modern.

A known Turkish critic of the system, Professor Murat Belge,
reacting to the flag hysteria had written this in the newspaper
Radikal on 17 April 2005:

> There are people and institutions in this country who want to
> keep the awareness of the population at the lowest possible level.

The entire political system rests on this level and reproduces itself constantly. Because this political system will not abandon the national genetic heritage it is built upon.

The Turkish military apparatus has a dominating influence in Turkish politics. Comparable influence is difficult to find in any developed democratic country, as it has been asserted in three EU reports on Turkey (the last was published on 9 November 2005). The EU demands that the influence of the army on politics be reduced but meets with resistance from the military. The chief of the general staff, Hilmi Özkök, said: 'The army in Turkey is part of the nation', in a reply to EU's displeasure. He emphasized the army's role in politics. By portraying themselves as part of the nation, they aim at creating a legitimate basis for military intervention, ultimatum and military coup. Through this, an understanding is established that what the military does is the same as what the people do, because they do it on behalf of the people. The military coups in 1960, 1971 and 1980 and removal of Erbakan's government in 1998 were justified precisely by such interpretations. Therefore, the military cannot admit that it is an institution within the state, and its leaders do not like to admit it. They define themselves rather as the owners of both the state and the nation. There is also a widespread belief among the people, with the exception of the Kurds, that the military never makes mistakes. The civilians get the blame if something goes wrong. The almost 'holy' military must be protected; it must not be criticized or struck. The obvious mistakes of the military must not be discussed.

The chief of the general staff said this in connection with the 82nd anniversary celebrations of the republic: 'The Turkish army, which serves the nation, is the most important and most resolute guardian of national unity and existence, the sovereignty and the indivisible unity of the state, national interests and the form of government of the republic' (*Milliyet* 29 October 2005). The general's statement refers to paragraph 35 in the Turkish constitution which says: 'The duty of the military is to protect the country of the Turk's and the Turkish republic as is established in the constitution' (taken from the 1982 constitution).

Today, Turkey's greatest problem, which is discussed intensely thanks to the EU adjustment, is whether the military will allow the country to move in the direction of becoming a state governed by law. The government and most of the population would like to enjoy the advantages of being in the EU. But the military does not desire closeness to the west. The military leaders also feel that they are responsible for the future of the country and they do not wish to leave this political responsibility to the civilian politicians. This is because the military does not want to lose power and economic advantages through social changes and democratization. Politics becomes unreliable under such circumstances. Nobody dares express his true opinion. Nobody dares resist the military. Much of what the politicians say is perceived to be false, because they themselves do not believe in what they say, but they must say what they should. Therefore, political ideas cannot develop under such circumstances.

Totalitarian language

A civilian language does not exist yet in Turkey. A military language and terminology still dominates the country. It is still the military that defines nearly everything. The most important is that the military defines the republic and citizenship. Those who accept this definition are regarded as 'good citizens' and those who do not accept it are regarded as 'bad', 'harmful citizens' or 'enemies of the people and the state'. The usage of language is very totalitarian and is reminiscent of the use of language under the Soviet regime. In democratic countries, those who criticize the regime are perceived as oppositionists, while in the authoritarian and partially totalitarian Turkey, they are still called 'traitors' or 'elements hostile to the state'. A prominent Turkish journalist who wanted to be anonymous said this to me:

> All media in Turkey have received instructions from the chief of the general staff about how they should treat the Kurds. All editors have had such instructions since 1980, that is since the military coup. Military authorities want that each and every Kurdish action or resistance must be depicted as 'terrorist', 'inimical to the state', 'traitor' and similar.

A prominent Turkish journalist, Mehmet Altan, adds:

> Turkey is the world champion in misusing popular concepts. They are clever to change the content of the concepts and to give them false meanings. For example, to portray the Turkish republic as democratic, present militarism as modern and interpret

Kemalism a left oriented ideology. I hope that the EU process makes it easier for us to learn the original content of the concepts.

(www.gazetem.net 21 October 2005)

A society of informers

I will round off this chapter with a short description of the usual methods the military authorities use to maintain their control of the Zaza society. The sight of modern military buildings and mosques dominates all over Eastern Turkey. And each of them symbolizes fear that has made deep impressions in the region. The former are based on physical power, while the latter are based on fear of God expressed through Islam. (The circumstances relating to Islam are treated in Chapter 11 on religion.) Fear of the military refers to persecution, arrests, torture, mistreatment, breach of fundamental human rights and so forth, which the military have been behind for decades. Therefore, the people perceive the military as the very symbol of oppression. The region has been subject to martial law since the military coup in 1980. The military has governed the region by use of extraordinary laws. In this way, the military has run the 'dirtiest' forms of politics, namely spreading fear, political violence and general terror. These have been the usual methods for keeping control. The fear has spread among the population. Everybody suspects everybody, people save themselves by denouncing others, and a lack of political democracy and legal protection characterizes daily life. General fear has spread so much that people apply auto censorship to avoid expressing unwanted opinions. What the Norwegians experienced during the Second World War, the Kurds are experiencing today, and in many ways to a worse extent.

The censorship in the Kurdish region is still strict and the region swarms with police spies. I was told that the military authorities and the feared MIT have planted their people, called *collaborators* by the local population, in every village. Others call them agents. The collaborators inform on suspected 'separatists' in the villages and towns. PKK people keep to the mountains; they do not work among ordinary people. Those who are suspected of being separatists are not PKK people but ordinary people who work for democracy on a legal plane. All democracy activists working in the Kurdish region are accused of separatist activities by the military because the military claims their activities benefit the PKK, although many of them do not have ties to the PKK. And any tendency towards liberal political resistance is crushed if it is discovered.

The collaborators are not professional agents; they do not have any training. They operate on an amateur basis and are often exposed. They are men from poor families and belong to the lowest rank. These men work on assignments for the military or the MIT. Their most important task is to inform the military authorities about who in the village has contact with the PKK guerrillas in the mountains in the area and who sympathizes with this movement.

In addition to this kind of denouncement, the collaborators also report what goes on in the village, who from the outside has been visiting the village, whom they have visited, what people usually talk about and so forth. Those found guilty are sentenced to prison. They also lose their jobs if they are working in the public sector, or they are blacklisted.

The collaborators receive a modest payment from the military for their activities. The Zaza society has developed into a society of informers where political denouncement has become quite widespread as a result of these activities. People do not trust each other any longer. It is even hard to trust members of their own families. The situation has not changed, although the Turkish authorities formally have repealed the extraordinary laws in 2002 as a consequence of the application for EU membership. People's experience is that the cancellation of the extraordinary laws has taken effect only on paper. And this is confirmed by the human rights organization IHD in the provincial capitals Bingöl and Diyarbekir. The military still has extensive powers, which it continues to use to spread fear and terror, and the collaborator arrangement is not yet abolished. This has led to people in this area as well as the neighbouring Kurdish areas becoming nervous and frightening themselves by exaggerating secrets. Such incidents happen in social situations where everyone tries to influence everyone else, which quickly results in spying on and exposing each other. This situation is to be explained by the fact that the military maintains its power by creating insecure situations and impersonal processes which enable it to control the inhabitants.

Zaza Kurds perceive the Kemalist state as tyranny. They have painful experiences with this state. The tyranny has not made the Kurds happy. It has deprived them of joy, freedom, self-confidence and faith in the future. Many Zaza Kurds portray the state as an evil that destroys all they have developed throughout history. Most people in this region know that the state practises very oppressive policies towards them. The oppression is sanctioned by the constitution based exclusively on ethnicity, regulated by legislation that expressly emphasizes that Turkey is the country of the Turks, which is also expressed in daily politics. People also express this, often with irony. They say this openly when dangerous elements (collaborators, official people) are not present. However, although they apparently look at nationalism with awareness and are not enthusiastic about policies of oppression, they actively contribute to the conceptualization of the oppression they are subjected to, by associating the evil of the Turkish rule with the artificial contradiction between secularism and religion. Among the Alevi Kurds, one gets the impression that the Alevi society is oppressed mainly because of its religion, because they claim that the Sunni population is a majority in Turkey and has power, while the Sunni Zaza society claims that they are discriminated against because the state is secularist and people with Alevi backgrounds occupy central positions and oppress them because of their religion. This means that people are far removed from the reality in a cultural perception, which we can, after Bourdieu (1972), term an unreflected knowledge living in their daily actions and habits.

Chapter 9

Culture and identity

I will start this chapter with the concept of culture. Culture is counted as an important aspect of human conduct; it gives form and meaning to existence, regulates manners of action and permeates all human activities. One can say that culture both forms and is formed by the activities of human beings.

The Zaza culture is little known internationally. Until now, no one has described what characterizes the Zaza culture and what it consists of, how the Zaza people assess their cultural forms of expression, and, perhaps most importantly, how cultural expressions have developed or survived under Turkish domination. Does Kurdish culture have the right or the prerequisites to survive in a country such as Turkey? The political situation I described in the previous chapter does not seem to be promising for cultural plurality.

Similar to other population groups, the culture of the Zaza population, first and foremost, consists of common traits such as religious belief (Islam), life experience, knowledge, skills, traditions and values they use collectively. At the same time, these common characteristics form the basis of a common understanding of the reality that people acquire. They communicate this to each other through a common language. But this does not mean that the cultural commonality is unproblematic. Meanwhile, there are two conditions that prevail. First, most conduct of the Zaza population appears to be stagnant. It often appears to be resistant to change and refuses to adjust itself to new circumstances. In most cultures, as we know from literature, one often has a learnt behaviour that changes by acquisition of new knowledge. The way things are done, ideas and values spread speedily and widely by this. I experienced almost the opposite in the Zaza region. They have a proud perception of their culture but they dare not talk about changing it. Perhaps there is a lack of actors with well-developed abilities and self-confidence who could play this role. Maybe they fear new impulses and influences from without if they come closer to other cultures or maybe they feel that individual behaviour is not capable of influencing their common behaviour in the society to which they belong. Their transmission of knowledge is tradition based rather than education based.

Second, certain cultural differences exist in the form of local, regional and social variations, which separate people from each other. Sometimes the variations within a group may be larger than between groups. These differences may split the inhabitants of an area from time to time. However, there are fewer differences than what unites them, since the Zaza society is so small compared to other significantly larger population groups, for example the Turks. Although the Zaza society is also part of a world in which people, ideas, opinions, impulses and so forth cross cultural and social boundaries, there is plenty within the Zaza culture that the members share, despite the fact that many people with Zaza backgrounds travel far and wide to earn an income for themselves and their families. Zaza Kurds have clear boundaries in relation to other cultures, for example to Turkish or Arabic culture. On the other hand, there is no cultural homogeneity within the Zaza culture. In some areas there is considerable internal variation and in other areas it is difficult to see cultural differences.

The internal variation is mainly due to confessional differences within Islam that divide the Zaza population more than anything else and that have appeared to be more divisive than the variation between different groups. The Zaza population is divided down the middle due to confessional differences. About half of Zaza-speaking Kurds belong to the Sunni denomination while the rest belong to the Alevi denomination (see also Chapter 11 on religion). These two religious denominations are quite dissimilar and partly antagonistic. Some concrete cultural expressions connected with the two denominations are given here: the Sunni followers use the mosque for prayers while the Alevi use the *Cem Evi* for prayers; the Alevi denomination has a more liberal view of women; working Alevi women are more numerous than working Sunni women; the Alevi population is strongly secularist, they are loyal to the 'secular' ideal of the Turkish republic and strongly against religious state institutions, which are actively engaged in promoting Sunni Islamic interests; the Sunni population is mainly conservative and opposes separation of religion and politics; and, generally speaking, the Sunni population is more prosperous than the Alevi society.

These variations can also be found in modern, complex societies. However, political use of culture creates problems. The Turkish state is an example of this. This state is built on a brutal and oppressive Turkish nationalistic ideology and promotes special group privileges for the Turkish-speaking population at the cost of other minorities. The state discriminates against minorities to this end. Turkey has manipulated the aforementioned cultural antagonisms between Sunni and Alevi Kurds for years and played these groups against each other. A concrete example of this was shown when the Sunni Zaza population rose against the central state in 1925. The rebellion received wide support with the exception of the Alevi Zaza population. The elderly with Sunni Zaza backgrounds claim that the rebellion was suppressed by the Turkish state with help from the Alevis. When the Alevi Zaza population rose against Turkey in 1937 (the Dersim Rebellion), the Turkish state sought support from the Sunni Zaza population to suppress the rebellion this time. This has marked the Zaza society for a long time. For example, contracting marriages between Sunni and Alevi Zaza has been out of the question, with justification based on religious antagonisms. Interpersonal relations between them have also been minimal.

But the Turkish state not only makes use of the *divide and rule* method, but it also has its collaborators within the Zaza society, as well. The sheikhs and some of the mullahs play on the antagonisms between the Sunni and Alevi Zaza populations. In Chapter 5, I mentioned that the sheikh in the Solhan region makes use of the *divide and rule* method. This can be expounded with an example of how the sheikh plays on religious antagonisms in his propaganda in the Zaza society. In the summer of 2003, I did field work in the village of Xirbizun. In June, a middle-aged woman died. There is a rich tradition of condolences in the Zaza society. When somebody dies, relatives and friends come from far and wide; mainly men but also women visit the family to offer their condolences. In the first three or four days, thousands of people had come. At this point, the sheikh of Solhan was in the village of Yekmal, of which he owns half. The sheikh waited until the rush of visitors was over. After four days, the sheikh visited to offer his condolences. When he appeared, 80–100 people were sitting outside the deceased person's house. The family had placed chairs outdoors where people could sit while they carried out the ritual of offering their condolences. Everybody rose and lined in a queue to welcome the sheikh. Everybody took and kissed his hand. He began kindling the dislike for the Alevi population's belief as soon as he paid his condolences. He himself took up the subject and said the following in a pedantic manner: 'The Alevi are much worse than the Christians because the Christians have a belief although it is wrong, but they believe in their religion. On the other hand the Alevi do not believe in any religion. They are infidels'.

The sheikh was very self-confident in his statement and communicated his message in a condescending manner. And all who listened to him only nodded in confirmation: Yes, your eminence, it is such. You can see everything between the earth and the heavens, on the earth and under the earth, you see everything, you know everything, you are right and so forth. The sheikh does not consider the Alevis as Muslims at all. He believes the Alevis are downright infidels and, therefore, he regards them as legitimate targets of attack. Although he did not directly state that the Alevis were enemies, there was no doubt about what he thought.

After the sheikh had left, I had the opportunity to speak with many of the villagers who had waited on the sheikh. I asked how they perceived the sheikh's statement about the Alevis and whether they thought that the statement had ethnocentric nuances with its justification in religion. In Europe, such statements would meet with negative reactions, be classified as a racist attack against the religious rights of other minorities and be prosecuted because the sheikh's statement was openly discriminating against a religious minority. I heard from the inhabitants that this statement was not new. They told me that the sheikh says this at every opportunity and so far nobody has reacted. It was said that, on the contrary, he becomes more popular with such statements, especially among the elderly. But the opinions were divided among the young. Some of them were of the opinion that one must respect the beliefs of the Alevis. Others thought that what the sheikh said was not grounded in Islam. They said it was propaganda, but people in this region cannot always differentiate between propaganda and what is religiously correct.

But despite the sheikh's statements and influence, the general picture has gradually changed in the last 15–20 years. The antagonisms between the Sunni and Alevi Zaza population have been reduced after the Kurdish liberation movement (the PKK) started its armed struggle against the Turkish state in 1984. The PKK has been organized among both of these groups and most of the Sunni and Alevi population perceive the PKK as their only protection. In this context, an organization based on common political ideology can be seen as a strategy to overcome the cultural antagonisms. This strategy has already produced results. The cultural antagonisms between the Sunni and Alevi population have been considerably reduced. Fewer conflicts appear, especially among the younger people. It is a sign of greater integration between these groups. It seems that people with Alevi and Sunni Zaza backgrounds can marry each other for the first time in history. So, the ideals of liberating the Kurds from the Turkish domination create common opinions. This, in its turn, has led to the boundary between Zaza Kurds and Turks becoming even more marked. But the antagonisms among the older generation are still present.

Another condition that has contributed to the creation of a certain degree of conciliation within the Zaza population is the common way of life and cultural pattern that these two groups have developed. Their way of life has proven to be viable and certainly will last a long time into the future despite continuous attempts of assimilation by the Turkish authorities. Presumably this will also lay the foundation for a common understanding of what is to be a line of guidance for their conduct. When they have common ways of life they also share many types of common understandings. I will expound on this now.

A study of the Zaza population's political life must necessarily cover their discourses on the past. As we will see later in this chapter, there are no written sources on this population group. We are dealing with an oral culture. According to Bronislaw Malinowski (1926) and Edmund Leach (1954), oral cultures constitute a form of mythological documents and contracts that explain, justify and strengthen the current power relations. One experiences that, in many contexts, the Zaza population's tales on the past contribute to legitimizing their political structure. The political struggle they are conducting now is in many ways inextricably connected to a production of tales and arguments about the past. The Kurds conducted an intense armed struggle against Turkey from 1984 to 1999, in which the Zaza population participated actively. This struggle needs to be seen in the same context as the flourishing social construction of the nation or a national fellowship. Liberation struggles and their praxes also, at other places in the world (see, for example, Krohn-Hansen and Vike 2000), to a striking degree, centre on the production of history understood as a set of social relations and narratives of the past, present and future of the same relations. All communication about the past is both a product of and contributes to the structuring of the liberation struggle that the Zaza Kurds are conducting. The example below about the transmission of tradition or previous experiences and knowledge that can clarify this situation may illustrate that the past is understood as symbolic forms giving inspiration to the political struggle the population is conducting.

Since 1920s, the Kurds, including the Zaza population, have at various times conducted many wars of liberation against the Turkish colonial power, sometimes in small groups and sometimes in large collective groups. The rebellions were suppressed brutally each time. They have cultivated their leaders and made them into great martyrs after each rebellion. Their heroic efforts are told and the leaders are remembered at formal occasions. In the Solhan region, people have sanctified the grave of Sheikh Abdullah to a *Quva*. He was the leader of the Solhan region when the Kurds rebelled under the leadership of the Zaza population less than two years after the Turkish republic was established. People come to this holy grave and pray for help during difficult times, such as when an epidemic strikes the people. Every martyr's magical and ritual powers are explained and justified through accounts of earlier rebellions. The true knowledge about previous rebels exists only in oral form and most people relate to this form of transmitting knowledge as a truth. The oral knowledge is administered by the elderly and is transmitted to the younger generations. An important aspect of the administration of this knowledge is that it is kept secret from the Turkish authorities. They think written forms are censored by the authorities and therefore they do not trust Turkish sources. This is understandable considering that the Turkish institutions have systematically tried to deprive the Kurds of their past and have depicted them as something totally different from reality.

Knowledge about earlier rebellions is referred to frequently in political discussions and their relevance brought in with respect to the present struggle against Turkish domination. Often, knowledge about the positions of leadership during earlier rebellions presents a model of organization deciding who can have political positions today and it is first and foremost the alliances between the participants of the rebellion that define the positions of their respective descendants. Experiences from the rebellions contribute to legitimizing the organization of present political relations in the region. The descendants of past rebels are highly respected and get prominent positions more easily, especially if they have not cooperated with the Turkish authorities in the meantime.

The thoughts on the history of rebellion communicate and reproduce the population's resistance or will to seek political freedom in a brutal colonialist landscape. Therefore, knowledge of earlier rebellions is political; to communicate about earlier rebellions is their way of saying 'no' to oppression. For today's Kurdish freedom fighters, previous rebellions are far from rhetoric preserved because of their nostalgic pride. The experiences from previous rebellions are reproduced in many ways as a source for liberation from Turkish domination. Therefore, the knowledge about previous rebellions and resistance communicates a moral system and ideas about justice. The continuity in the constant struggle against oppression, especially in the time after 1920s (an oppression that spans from political murder, forcible deportations of the population from 3,400 villages[1] and extreme torture[2] to the present state tutelage and gross exploitation), has been more than enough to reproduce thoughts on previous rebellions as a living power, a source of inspiration and meaning in daily life.

The example about the transmission of tradition from previous rebellions demonstrates that the Zaza population's political struggle is based on an anchorage of the present to the past. The present is organized through the social organization of the past. They try to legitimize their political struggle against the colonial power Turkey by use of their own ideas about the past. Meanwhile, their ideas about the past must not be regarded as immutable and timeless opinions. Their conceptions and arguments about the past are presented as a result of specific historical processes that spill over time. Meanwhile, their political struggle presupposes inspiration as all other liberation movements. Where do they receive it from? This is the topic of the next section.

Sources of pride among the Zaza population

National pride is something nations or cultural fellowships must construct to create an existential basis and self-assertion. Seen as such, pride constitutes a part of the group's identity. Pride appears as a central value in all cultures of the Middle East. Many in this area portray themselves as proud people by displaying hospitality, helpfulness or courage, and so forth. I illustrate this with a well-known example: in western tourist brochures marketing Turkish beaches to attract more tourists, one can read from time to time that the Turks are *hospitable, helpful, kind* and so forth. I can also agree with such a statement without second thoughts. But this form of hospitality is not just a Turkish tradition; it characterizes all cultures in the Middle East region. Another topical example is that Arabs both in Iraq and Palestine often emphasize their pride in the struggle against the foreign occupation of the USA and Israel, respectively.

National pride is also a very important value for the Zaza-speaking Kurds. It is perhaps one of the most important sources of inspiration in their struggle against oppression. During celebrations of the national day – Newroz, 21 March – and in connection with the flag affair described in the previous chapter, Kurdish national pride has demonstrated a powerful strength for mobilization. They are generally a proud people. But since the founder of the new Turkish republic, Mustafa Kemal Atatürk, prohibited the Kurds from acting as a separate people, the Turkish state has exercised an enormous psychological pressure to force them to assimilate. They had to regard themselves as Turks. This entailed, among other things, to see themselves through Turkish eyes; that is to say, they had to perceive themselves as the state perceived them. Consequently they should perceive themselves as something different than what they were. The pressure aimed to make the Kurds despise their ethnic background. Despite a heavy process of assimilation, they do not hide their background as Kurds. But their historical awareness is characterized by a wounded national pride, as among the Arabs after the defeat by Israel in 1967. After the PKK started its armed struggle in 1984, the wounds gradually healed and the historical pride seems to be asserted again, especially from the late 1990s.

Generally, the Kurds receive their inspiration for national pride from four different quarters. The first one is that the Kurdish region with its natural beauty and stunning mountains is like a river that carries water to the inner sea of Turkey, Syria and Iraq. This concerns first and foremost water that springs forth from the innumerable river sources in the Kurdish highlands, collecting in the Euphrates and the Tigris, on which Turkey has built large dams for production of hydroelectricity. One of the larger rivers, the Murad, which joins another river from the Dersim region to form the Euphrates, runs through the Solhan district without the population in this area benefiting economically from the hydroelectric power.

The second source of national pride is the innumerable popular uprisings and the military effort the Kurds have exerted against Turkey and Iraq from the 1920s to the present. Two of the largest rebellions in Turkey were led by the Zaza population. Despite the defeats by Turkey, it is asserted even to date, particularly by the elderly, that the Kurds were braver and more loyal than the Turks.

The Kurds lost because they lacked weapons and ammunition, and they did not receive support from abroad. This bravery and loyalty is supported by examples from the present situation in which it is related that the so-called 'invincible Turkish army'[3] could not manage to defeat the PKK. Although Turkey continuously has attempted to systematically deny the existence of the Kurds and lately has tried to suppress public expressions of Kurdish nationality, the resistance against the Turks becomes a symbol of Kurdish identity.

The third source of pride is connected with the traditional lifestyle that the Kurds have preserved through centuries of constant oppression. This type of pride is connected with culture, pride of one's kin, ballads, popular music, the family institution, religious beliefs and feelings connected with nature. The Turks appealed to the Kurdish religious pride for fraternity but at the same time they kept the Kurds out of superior positions and prevented the development of Kurdish institutions, which led to the Kurds having to take care of their own institutions.

And finally, and especially in the twenty-first century, it appears that another source of national pride, which also involves the debate on democracy in Turkey, is that the Kurds fought alone against the governments dominated by the military in 1980s and 1990s. The Turkish opposition was split and infiltrated by the state by this time, which cost the Kurds heavily. In the fight against the military power, 37,000 people lost their lives and the majority were Kurds. In addition, around 4,500 Kurdish fighters and human rights activists disappeared without a trace and around 2.5 million people were deported from 3,500 villages to large cities in South and West Turkey.

Oral culture

The Zaza people have a culture without a script. They have an oral culture in which everything is based on experience and memory. Necessarily, much knowledge is lost. Most pages of the Zaza people's history have disappeared without a trace. But the younger generation is trying to search for its roots. They are trying to recreate and transform their identity.

The lack of sources is caused by the fact that their language, culture, history and tradition have been strictly forbidden in Turkey since the republic was established in 1923. The Kurds were not allowed to develop their culture and identity during the Ottoman

Empire, either, that is the period before 1918 when the empire disintegrated. However, since Kurdish culture was not banned by law, this was, despite everything, much better than the later times under the so-called new and modern republic. This is underlined by both the Kurds themselves and experts on the Kurdish issue abroad. To forbid the Kurdish culture and deny the existence of the Kurds, and consequently prevent the Kurdish culture from flourishing by all means, was one of the most important tasks of the young republic and its founder Mustafa Kemal Atatürk. This ban on the Kurdish culture lasted up to August 2000, when the authorities had to repeal the ban because of Turkey's application for EU membership. But the Kurdish language and culture is still practically forbidden because the authorities do not adhere to the new law and because there are still many restrictions in its way that hinder the Kurdish culture from flourishing. After the newly resolved reforms in 2004, it was supposed to be possible to start language courses in Kurdish dialects on a private basis. The Kurds took the initiative by opening Kurdish language courses shortly after the reforms. They got permission from all the relevant authorities. But when the language courses were opened in four Kurdish cities, the police arrived and sealed the premises. The pretext for this was that the doors ought to be 8 cm wider than they were.

The reforms were supposed to open the way for parents giving their children Kurdish names, but they have been refused so far by reference to its being irreconcilable with Turkey's homogeneous unity. This strictly conflicts with the international agreement on children's right to learn their mother tongue that Turkey signed in 1992. Laws to lift the censorship were also passed. But in the book shops, one can observe clearly that the censorship is still valid in relation to the Kurdish question.

The ban has struck the Zaza dialect particularly. However, the other Kurdish dialect, Kurmanji, has done relatively well because it is spoken by far more people. Moreover, Kurmanji is also spoken by people who live in other parts of Kurdistan, that is in Iran, Iraq, Syria and Armenia, while Zaza-speaking Kurds live primarily within Turkey's boundaries. This was the reason that Kurmanji could become a written language, by doing so first outside of Turkey's boundaries. In Iran, Iraq and in Soviet Armenia, radio programs in Kurdish were broadcast as early as the 1940s. The Zaza people did not have the opportunity to establish a written culture because of the ban in Turkey. They are trying to do this now for the first time. The Zaza

Kurds are publishing a popular linguistic periodical, *VATE*, in the Zaza dialect as a contribution to transition to a written culture. *VATE* was published first in the 1990s in Sweden and is now published in Turkey.

People's thinking, culture, tradition and world view develop differently in a society without writing. My impression is that the Zaza-speaking Kurds imagine reality in a different way than do people living in a society with writing. They have another awareness, another experience of time, other concepts they relate to, and they live in a kind of isolation and distance from modern societies in which rational values nearly completely dominate. Some examples that are specific to the oral culture and tradition in the Zaza society are given here. The language in an oral society consists of utterances and thoughts that flow by speedily. Most people do not communicate with each other through writing. The communication is less rational; it is more emotional and less analytic. Written communication takes place between those who have a command of Turkish, who are not many, and then they write only when it is necessary. People rely on oral agreements when they are buying and selling goods or services, which are often based on credit (see Chapter 7 on the economy). They do not draft any written and formal contracts with reference to laws and regulations and signing documents. If the transaction is not based on payment in cash but is carried out through credit, the parties will assure each other with oral promises or agreements, sometimes in the presence of witnesses, at other times without witnesses.

Oral poetry and music

A series of Kurdish poets, first and foremost Cegerxwin, Ahmed Arif, Ahmed Telli and many others, have published collections of poetry that express sadness and melancholy, oppression and hopelessness, loneliness and alienation, longing for freedom, and the Kurdish struggle for survival. The sadness and melancholy does not concern only the heroic individual who has sacrificed his life for his people. It is an entire culture, a complete cultural landscape that one mourns over. A good deal of this poetry is accompanied by music and, especially in the art of singing, many beautiful songs known across the country's borders are created. But as already mentioned, preventing Kurdish music from flourishing is still a task given a high priority by the Turkish authorities. Two recent examples illuminate this situation.

First, a court in Diyarbekir decided to ban the popular song 'Keçě Kurdan', by Aynur Dogan on 27 February 2005. The CD was confiscated all over Turkey after the court decision. The court's justification was that the song was suggesting Kurdish separatism. Kurdish politicians reject the assertions about separatism. Their opinion is that she was banned because she became popular in Turkey and the authorities partly were intolerant of her popularity and partly feared her influence among the masses. Just before the ban, Dogan had appeared on the cover of the *Time* magazine. The same court has banned a total of 12 other Kurdish music albums.[4] The same justification is given, that is the songs are suggesting or encouraging Kurdish separatism (*Ozgur Politika* 28 February 2005).

Second, a court in the Kurdish city of Bitlis sentenced seven leading politicians from the Kurdish-friendly party, DEHAP, to five months in prison on 2 May 2005 because they had allowed Kurdish music to be played during the local party congress that took place on 11 May 2003 (*Hurriyet* 3 May 2005).

Music is an important part of the cultural life and a large portion of the Zaza music, especially the older music, which has become classical, is characterized by traditional transmission. Traditionally popular music has had political undertones and has been an outlet for frustrations of the Kurds and other oppressed peoples. The music is not based on written texts but transmitted orally. This tradition is reminiscent of the aesthetics of the European Classicism, which valued poetry higher than music, probably because reason is expressed most clearly by words and music is wordless. For Zaza-speaking Kurds, the spoken language is the foremost seat and means of expression for reason. Music is ranked as low by them because it is not as capable of communicating a message as poetry. Without musical instruments, the singer can easily awaken feelings in the audience and the audience can concentrate more on the meaning of the text. The singers will not act with background music or they will not only entertain. They will place their songs within a more general cultural or social context. The songs are a mixture of human suffering, courage, fantasy, adventure or love. They also have a strong characteristic of sadness; their message runs in many directions but is covered by a popular social context. In addition, there is a widespread tradition of lamentation songs in the Zaza society. Especially after the 1925 rebellion, many singers who resisted the Turkish culture or did not want to be conciliated with it flourished. These figures have operated independently and may have been in conflict internally, but all the same externally they appear as a united force of resistance, a reaction with great strength in the local society.

Both men and women compose poetry and create verses, often in a fabulous way, sometimes in a courting fashion. From about the 1940s, it has become usual to have female singers and today there are many female stars with Zaza background both in Kurdistan and in Europe. Local poets are not influenced by modern thoughts relating to natural equality of all human beings. But such thoughts dominate the music of those singers who have asserted themselves at a regional level or throughout the country. The texts of the local singers often attack the hypocrisy practised in the name of the morality of righteousness, which is fundamentally different from the dominating melancholy music in Turkey called *arabesk* music. The *arabesk* or the fantasy genre is oriental inspired pop music using electrical versions of both western and traditional Kurdish instruments. The *arabesk* genre is very popular both in Kurdistan and the rest of Turkey and has created Turkey's greatest musicians such as Ibrahim Tatlises and Mahsum Kirmizigül. Both are Kurds, from Diyarbekir and Bingöl, respectively. Much of the Zaza music deals with liberation from the autocratic governments, which were represented by both Atatürk and the Ottoman sultans. Consequently, the music deals with mobilizing the individual's reason and freedom.

Memory is important in an oral tradition. It is powerful among the Zaza population and people remember the words of many songs. Most things are remembered but not all that is said and done can always be remembered. This is perhaps the weakest aspect of the unwritten Zaza culture. One often experiences that most of the things one hears are floating by, some can be remembered but much is not retained apart from knowledge or incidents considered to be important. Such incidents cover previous rebellions, sufferings, insults, norms, rituals, principles, proverbs and phrases. The passage from an oral to a written culture is slowly beginning, although the process may take a long time. Musicians of the 1980s and 1990s, especially from the Bingöl, Dersim and Siverek regions have begun to cultivate and renew the Zaza music. They renew the older classical Zaza music, its language, its heroes and its events. Music gets a more prominent place here. Instrumental music and the text are placed on a par. Instrumental music is also used to accompany dancing at feasts. A type of bass drum (*dawul*) and the oboe-like *zurna* are the most important instruments. But new musicians are also taking the classical music into their style as they attempt clarity in their message, set within a general cultural context, and they attempt to establish rules for artistic activity.

The older classical Kurdish music is a solemn culture that often emphasizes the distance between the authorities and the people. The people are kept in the background. Despite everything, there are differences between authorities and the people. The music represented the spiritual and the physical powers, sheikhdoms, principalities, nobility and tribal chiefs. Their power over the subjects is exercised through music, among other things. The new generation of Zaza musicians, such as Said Altun, is trying to change this tradition by focusing less on the rulers. They choose topics from people's daily lives more often than from history, religion and the bourgeois life. *Govend*, a very popular and widespread Kurdish folk dance, is an example. This attempt, which reflects society's orientation towards liberation, makes young musicians popular, especially among the poor and the most oppressed rural people who dream of political freedom and affluence. *Govend* also has influenced the other non-Kurdish cultures in the Middle East. Both Turks and Arabs have started using this dance lately, although the nationalists in these countries prefer to present *govend* as belonging to the entire Middle East and not only to the Kurds, for ideological reasons, an assertion that they cannot scientifically document. *Govend* is highly esteemed and it is the most representative form of popular music in Kurdistan.

To involve the aforementioned authorities or rulers is to contribute to the divine and the superhuman hegemony on which the rulers base their powers. New musicians consequently attempt to reduce this distance. As mentioned, they emphasize the daily and the mundane where the music is placed preferably within a popular context. This strategy puts an end to a period in which musicians supported and glorified feudal hegemony. They hope that by use of this music, people will learn how to use reason and think for themselves instead of just listening to and believing the authorities. They are trying to reshape their music; maybe more correctly, they are creating a mix or a hybrid, rather than separating old and new music because both forms of music take the suffering and the liberation of the Kurds as their point of departure.

Despite deficiencies, problems with remembering, lost knowledge and weakened development as a result of Turkish oppression and intolerance that have caused human tragedies, it can be asserted that the oral Kurdish culture has many impressive aspects. The Zaza population's ideas and notions about the past (compare the example about previous rebellions) demonstrate how a people can create and maintain an orally transmitted culture, reproduce the conception of the past and use this as a means of legitimization in the present struggle against oppression. This Zaza perspective of their own history enables them to maintain a cultural and political milieu which cannot be denied by the colonial masters any longer. Oral culture can hardly be perceived as independent of the ideas about the past. This is the topic of the next section.

Internal connections between the old and the new

The Zaza people's society and culture refers to life experience, knowledge, customs, habits and traditions. This constitutes norms, values and lifestyles they themselves have created and developed. It does not necessarily follow that the Zaza society always functions without failures or that it is logically and functionally coherent. But when the cultural aspects of the society are connected with phenomena such as the institutions of kinship, sheikhdoms, tribal groupings, the rule of mullahs, bazaars and so forth, this forms a kind of totality without taking it for granted that this totality is lasting and stable. As I described earlier, some of the aforementioned institutions (for example the tribal institution, the bazaar and, in part, the sheikhdom) are quite fragmented and in a slow process of change, but there is an internal connection between the different institutions and people's daily lives.

Today, it appears that some common characteristics of the Zaza culture are in a transformation through which they are being changed with modulated and redefined knowledge, skills and values because the environs compel this. The following example can clarify this development. We can take as our starting point the Kurdish liberation struggle. Since 1920s, the Kurds have staged many rebellions against the Turkish state, which rejects the Kurdish demands for being acknowledged as a separate people. The Turkish state has answered with even more forcible assimilation of the Kurds after each rebellion was brutally suppressed. This presupposes that the Kurds relinquish their own culture and become a part of the dominating Turkish cultural values, norms and traditions so that their original culture disappears. When the Kurds do not bow to the Turkish wishes or resist them, they are accused of terrorism, separatist activities or other forms of activities hostile to the state, while for the Kurds the issue is resistance, self-assertion and identity.

However, globalization, increase in the international trade and internationalization of the economic life have gradually led the Zaza-speaking Kurds into the world economy at the start of the twenty-first century. Planes, communication satellites, mobile phones and the Internet have reduced distances. Independent satellite channels such as CNN, BBC and others are also available to the Zaza population. They must relate to new means of communication, other cultures, modern markets and monetary economy. Globalization refers to processes or social relations that bind different societies together, where decisions made in entirely different places influence societies far away. The world has changed with globalization. Processes taking place in the outer world are forming or influencing the Zaza society. Therefore, the Zaza people must relate to this development. National belonging has become more important due to the assimilation pressure from the Turkish state and the processes of extensive global change in the twentieth century. These developments have strengthened the demands of many Zaza Kurds for an extended policy of culture and identity. They are aware of the need to protect the traditional cultural forms in order to avoid an identity crisis.

This does not mean that the Kurdish freedom struggle is only about conserving traditional norms, lifestyles or a social pattern anchored to religion or tradition or that it will adjust itself passively to changes created at the centre. The ideologies and cultures produced by the Kurdish society are not necessarily defective copies of what is going on at the centre. To a larger degree, the Kurdish struggle of liberation refers to democratization, greater individualism, secularization, scientific orientation, rationalization and cultural plurality. In other words, the Kurdish freedom struggle is about tying the old together with the new, and thereby creating a historical continuity for this people under extreme pressure.

The Zaza population is among the most traditional and peripheral population groups in the world. But this does not prevent their relations with modern societies. Most of the traditional cultures or societies have active and comprehensive relations with modern societies. It can be mentioned that the Zaza society is increasingly influenced by mobility. Many people move to cities in search of work. Simultaneously, more children go to school; some get a higher education, take paid jobs and settle down in the cities. Some of them have paid jobs in the industries in larger cities and their lives are influenced by the fluidity of the world economy. Communication flows across ethnic boundaries and moves between areas of culture.

But this does not lead to a reduction of the distance between traditional and modern societies. Such modernizing changes do not necessarily change culture, since the Zaza population is still engaged in keeping household animals and agriculture and they hold on to their cultural and socioeconomic traditions. There have not been fundamental changes for those who have moved to the cities, either; there may have been some material changes, but in terms of lifestyle, many things are still the same. There have not been changes in the conception of ethnic belonging, either. On the contrary, Kurdish national awareness has become more widespread among in the cities than among their relatives and neighbours in the villages. Urban life as we know it from the literature was supposed to liberate people from their social bonds. This is the only case to a limited extent and then mostly among young men. Women's attire, conduct, relationship patterns and so forth remain uninfluenced by life in cities. Actually, in many cases, people with a rural background in cities become more conservative than their relatives who still live in the villages. They want to avoid the anonymity that characterizes city life. Therefore, they must recreate themselves and their world in the cities. Here they protect their lifestyles even within the complicated global network with which urban life is to a large extent marked.

People with Zaza backgrounds will identify themselves as belonging to their ethnic group in most contexts. There are few who are compelled to present themselves as Turks in certain situations, for example to gain employment with a Turk. Otherwise, one is compelled to redefine his ethnic background to gain a political position. This belonging demonstrates that, although the individual framework changes and they become more dependent on conditions of urban life after they move to the cities, they do not want to break with their local belonging. The ties of loyalty and the feelings towards the group one belongs to are too strong for this to happen. It can be because those who moved away have not yet got a foothold in city life, which, according to many, means more alienation. But these people regard themselves first and foremost as bearers of a culture and tradition who are forever reproducing themselves and in this manner creating a sought-after continuity.

It can be said slightly more generally that people stress differences wherever in the world they may live. We know this not least from

North Europe. For example, we know that immigrants from other countries, particularly those from the developing world, cultivate their homeland's culture and tradition, although most of them are born and raised here in Europe. Integration of immigrants does not only mean that Europeans and immigrants have become more alike, but also they have become different in different ways.

The identity of the Zaza Kurds

Many groups of people have been subjected to oppression similar to the Zaza Kurds, for example Indians in the Latin American continent, the Sami in the Nordic countries, Berbers in North Africa and so forth. These groups of people have often developed two identities, a public one and a private one. The first one can be exemplified by a Sami coming into contact with the environs and presenting himself as a Norwegian because he is vulnerable, insecure and because the outer world expects it. But when the same person is at home in his own environs, he feels himself to be a different person, more secure but at the same time more isolated.

Within sociology identity is understood as an existential and constructed concept connected with the socialization process between the individual and the society. This requires a certain consistence or coherence in the behaviour, opinions or wishes of the individual or the group. There is agreement among researchers that a series of sociocultural factors take part in the formation of identity. As a culture strongly oriented towards the collective, there are a series of social and cultural conditions that limit the choices of the individual in the Zaza society. People in the Zaza society are entirely socially formed and individual persons perceive themselves in the light of and as a product of their social relations, because their need for fellowship and belonging appears to be the most important and deepest urge for them. This brings them together and forms their society. Experiencing closeness and acknowledgement from their environs, for the good or the bad, gives meaning to their lives. Consequently, there is no room for personal identity. Individuality and personal choices are not well developed in the Zaza society, as mentioned earlier. So far, the Zaza society has not allowed room for individual choices. Fellowship, for example kinship-based fellowship, the sheikhdom, the mullah network and so forth, has great power over individual persons. But the people are not totally powerless. Each of them participates in the processes of the fellowship, influences and is influenced by the fellowship to varying degrees and contributes to maintaining it and, if necessary, also to changing it.

There are a series of aspects and properties that influence and form one's identity. There is a general agreement that language, race and ethnic relations, place of origin, family, lineage or kin, religion, tradition, age, gender, lifestyle, education, occupation, politics and class are the most important identity markers (see, for example, Eriksen 2000). These markers both separate and unite people, that is, they create fellowships and simultaneously limit the fellowship with respect to others. But these characteristics are general; they are not valid for all types of societies. In societies based on kinship or in those without writing, characteristics such as education, occupation or class membership either do not exist or they are rather foreign phenomena. There are few who identify with the characteristics of modern society. In social sciences, there is disagreement about which of the general characteristics mentioned above are the most fundamental ones. It seems that for the Zaza Kurds, notions of common origin, place of origin, common language, common cultural perceptions, ethnic belonging, family, kinship, religion, tradition, lifestyle, politics and common experience of oppression are the fundamental characteristics that form their identity.

The relations of the Kurds with the state are regulated through citizenship. In this way, one tries to tie them to the state and give them a 'national identity'. Formally, they are Turks since they are Turkish citizens, carry Turkish ID cards, travel abroad with a Turkish passport and are subject to Turkish law. But they are denied the same formal political rights as the ethnic Turks. When this 'national identity' lacks fundamental political and civil rights, it is natural to expect that fewer will identify with the state and its other citizens because it does not contribute to their national feelings and loyalty. Therefore, when asked how they perceive themselves, most Zaza-speaking Kurds will define themselves first and foremost as Zaza Kurds. Very few of them will identify with the Turkish state. Still fewer will regard themselves as Turks by birth. This brings us closer to looking at the difference between national identity and ethnic identity. In the Turkish political debate, which is strictly controlled by the state authorities, national and ethnic identities are often confused. Any ethnic identity apart from the Turkish one has been taboo. In the western debate, particularly in social sciences, one differentiates between national identity and ethnic identity.[5] National identity as it is used in social sciences is a relatively new phenomenon and describes new identities in the western democratic societies after the industrial revolution, while ethnic identity has existed for longer in both modern and traditional societies.

Seen ethnically, the Zaza population is not Turkish but Kurdish, because ethnic identity is connected with birth, history, culture and myths of origin. Since Zaza Kurds believe that they have a common birth and have survived as a culture-bearing group through generations, they form an ethnic group or a people, but one without a state. They are not considered to be included in the Turkish state, either; they are not perceived as part of the Turkish state formation because the Turkish state is based on a principle of Turkish ethnicity (see the Kemalist state formation). This is clarified by the name of the state defined in the constitution being related to the ethnic Turkish group, where it is stated that everyone who lives within Turkey's boundaries must consider themselves as Turks.

Differences of culture create identity. The dominating understanding (see, for example, Eriksen 2000) is that symbolic expressions of being the same as some but different from others contribute to persons becoming bearers of an identity. Functionalist researchers, especially the Chicago School, which gained reputation in this field (see, for example, Park 1950), asserted that ethnic differences would disappear gradually. The Functionalists meant that ethnic differences were dysfunctional residues from previous historic epochs that would gradually melt into the majority and, in the end, ethnicity would disappear in the modern industrial society. Marxists also interpreted ethnic antagonisms and conflicts as expressions of class antagonisms. The Marxists claimed that ethnic antagonisms are created artificially by the ruling classes with the aim of concealing class antagonisms. Functionalist and Marxist interpretations were dominant until the 1980s both within sociology and social anthropology. Marxism arose in a time when class antagonisms were deep. In order to dampen these antagonisms between the classes it was necessary to play down ethnic differences.

The fall of communism in Eastern Europe and its aftermath proved that a greater importance is attached to ethnicity than to class membership and citizenship in many places in the world, even in modern states. Generally, among research milieus worldwide, ethnicity has acquired a new and dramatic role, although not in all countries. Studies of ethnicity have practically been banned in Turkey since Atatürk's time. In book shops, one can clearly observe that a lack of literature about ethnicity does not only concern Kurds but also all ethnic minorities, and this is no coincidence. However, there is an abundance of literature about different Turkish-speaking ethnic groups all around the world. Translated western literature on ethnicities is also subjected to systematic censorship. Translating literature that supports the struggle of ethnic minorities is deliberately avoided. In Turkish book shops one finds a small selection of this kind of literature, for example Ernest Gellner's analyses, which does not answer questions about nationalism and nation-building but is more of a description of how nations were formed, particularly in Europe, and how nationalism creates homogeneity in cultures. The Turks like to read Gellner's studies of the nation-state's significance for industrialization of the society. Such analyses correspond well to the Turkish official ideology.

Social identity

The socially created identity may be far more important among the Zaza population than in most societies. This is valid both among the people in villages and among those who have moved to other places. Through cooperation with others, one acquires an awareness of who one is, which groups one belongs to, with whom one identifies and how one should relate to others. An increased awareness and the social roles tied to the social groups one belongs to are created in cooperation with others. The example below from the larger cities illustrates ethnic symbols with which the Zaza population identifies.

Up to 5 million Kurds are living in the cities of Adana, Mersin, Antalya in the south and Izmir, Bursa and Istanbul in the west. They moved here mainly in the 1980s and 1990s, partly because of unemployment, poverty and the civil war, partly because of deportations. People with Zaza backgrounds are well represented here. The cities are physically ethnically segregated, which means that the Kurds live in certain sections of the cities. They either live in the poorest slum areas or have very little informal contact with Turks who live nearby. Ethnic boundaries are maintained because relations between the groups are either non-existent or meagre. Here, the Kurds maintain large portions of their culture and their network of social contacts is largely based on ethnicity. Sameness of their identity is mainly based on common origin, coming from the same place, genealogy, common language, cultural perceptions, lifestyle, ethnic membership and common experience of the oppression they have gone through when originally living in Eastern Turkey. Birth and place of origin were clearly the most important criteria for identification. They create security and support through these common properties, which makes friendship and confidence more likely; feelings of fraternity, equality, solidarity and, not least, appreciation are developed.

Feelings of identity through birth and place of origin are prevalent not only among the grown-ups; many children and youths born away from their homelands nevertheless consider Kurdistan as their real home. A small number of the youths feel they belong to the cities they live in and they often speak Turkish. For them, feelings of belonging to a place seems to override ethnicity. But the majority feel the opposite. That identity is connected to birth and place of origin is not confined to Zaza Kurds. In all societies, certain rights, feelings and duties are connected to birth and place of origin. Dialects, attire, etc. signify who we are. We know from Europe (see, for example, Eriksen 2000) that second- and third-generation immigrants consider their grandparents' country of origin as their 'real' home, although they have never visited it.

Some also refer to experiences of being rejected by the Turks when they try to get to know them or being excluded if they try to become like them. That they are rejected and excluded leads to a stronger internal unity and makes the feelings of common identity more stable. When the Turkish authorities incessantly apply pressure on the Kurds, this works against its aims; the Kurds feel that their identity becomes the more important the more it is subjected to attacks from without. The unity is especially maintained in crisis situations, for example the flag crisis, because then the external pressure is most tangible. But it must be said that the Kurds have not been able to maintain their unity at all times. This fellowship broke down under extremely violent pressure, especially in the 1990s while the civil war raged (see the section on the informer society in the previous chapter). Turkey has created a picture of the enemy in relation to the Kurds. The enemy image is simultaneously used to dampen the internal conflicts and strengthen the Turkish feelings of identity.

The example of Kurdish life in large Turkish cities first shows that ethnic belonging structures the distribution of housing. They establish a fellowship of identity based on notions of common origin and other similarities that they identify with. Second, they maintain their differences from the Turks through these ethnically determined housing concentrations, because the differences are important for identification. The example also demonstrates that it is in relation to the Turks that the Kurds can define themselves; perhaps they cannot be themselves without their *relation* to the Turks; their fellowship perhaps would not have risen without rejection by the Turks and their inner unity perhaps would not have been as strong as it is now, without the pressure, the coercion and the oppression from the Turks. This demonstrates that relations between groups do not always soften the ethnic boundaries; maybe more often the opposite is the case. At times, the relations can create harder boundaries. The boundary has become sharper in the case of the Kurds and the Turks. The self-representation of the Kurds in their meeting with the Turks, and the Turks' reaction or perception of the Kurds, have led to a new view of identification among the Kurds.

Alternatives to national identity

The Turkish national state is not perceived as an independent power in relation to the Turks and the Kurds. It is not a neutral actor, but serves the Turkish majority population. Turkish nationalism easily spills over to aggressive national self-assertion, at the cost of general rights and freedoms of the minority groups, as the flag crisis also demonstrated. The Turkish state stands in contrast to demands for cultural and ethnic plurality with its constitution and praxis. It also stands in contrast to the liberal thought practised in democratic countries and which claims that political unities are voluntary communities of independent citizens. The Turkish state does not treat ethnic minorities similarly; for example, freedom of expression and equality before the law is not valid to the same extent for Turks and Kurds. The Turkish state has consciously attempted to create a homogeneous nation based on Turkish culture and identity, as we saw in the previous chapter, and insists that all who speak languages other than Turkish should subordinate themselves to the Turkish reality and ways. In other words, the minorities are presented with a pattern of life from without. They have received orders about how they should think, act and behave, without consideration for their own ways. Consequently, the state is accused of discrimination based on ethnicity. When the Turkish state does not function in agreement with principles of formal equality but unilaterally relies on ethnic Turks, refuses to recognize the Kurds as a separate people and undermines the political ideals of democracy, then it is not surprising that Kurdish ethnic awareness acquires an increasingly important role, because Kurds are largely foreign to the Turkish ways. They feel that their own ways are trampled on. Against this background, the Kurds demand the right to be different but at the same time to be equals. When their demands are not met, it forms the basis for a new political organization with demands of greater independence as an alternative to Turkish nationalism.

Turkey practises a deep identity policy that is strongly based on Turkish ethnicity. The Turkish state has used enormous resources for many decades to demonstrate to Kurds, other ethnic minorities and many Muslims that Turkish ethnic identification is much more important than their own ethnic and religious identities. When the Turkish state's view of humanity is based on a declared aim to destroy transmission of other cultures and forms of life, we can imagine the tragic consequences this leads to for the entire life basis of the Zaza Kurds and their culture. Throughout history, the Zaza Kurds have had to defend their identity against intolerant systems that have tried to impose on them 'the only true identity', with brutal methods. To be born into an ethnic minority that has been subdued by a master people for centuries provides good reasons for subscribing to a distinctly and clearly defined ethnic identity. Experience of this oppressive system tells something about why group feelings among Zaza Kurds and other minorities are strong. Because it is these groups who experience the external pressure the strongest. Forcible assimilation does not automatically lead to the removal of boundaries of identity. Most studies of ethnic processes show that actually the more similar people become the more they become preoccupied with looking different from each other (Eriksen 2003). I illustrate this with a topical example from the neighbouring country Iraq: the Kurds in Northern Iraq have run a persistent campaign for their rights after Saddam Hussein's regime fell in April 2003. The struggle for surviving as a culture-bearing people has never been a problem for the Arabs of Iraq in recent history and, therefore, Kurds and Christian Assyrians had a clearer ethnic or religious identity than their dominant neighbours in contemporary Iraq.

The relation between external pressure (Turkey's demands for assimilation) and internal unity (ethnic group feeling among Zaza Kurds) is clear. But strong group identification and internal unity among Zaza Kurds do not only arise as a result of external pressure. They are also related to the perceived source of the pressure. Since the Ottoman Imperial period, supporters of an Islamic nation have struggled for the creation of an Islamic state consisting of different ethnic groups, without some of them dominating the others. This has not influenced the internal Kurdish relations particularly. Neither Alevi Zaza Kurds nor secular Sunni Zaza Kurds have been concerned with this discussion. But as mentioned earlier, the arch-enemies Alevi and Sunni Zaza Kurds united against the military when the Turkish military subdued the Kurds with the 1980 military coup. This reaction has been the reason that they both re-established and, in many cases, reinforced their boundaries of identity in relation to the Turks. Those who break with this unity can pay a high price, first and foremost in form of social exclusion, but other forms of sanctions are also used.

In addition, it is important to say that common origin and blood ties create obligations, a spirit of self-sacrifice and group loyalty among members of the Zaza society. Different cultural traditions based on common origin and blood ties with their own experiments, experiences and different qualities of life represent an alternative form of life to the purely ethnic Turkish national identity. Their experiences provide them with a subsuming meaning of life, legitimize their struggle ideologically, and make their fellowship function in some sense. Their ideals about their own dignity demand that the right to live according to one's own culture is respected.

Chapter 10

Gender relations, family and division of labour

The Zaza society is one of the most gender-divided societies, after the Arabic countries. In the latter countries, the society is more gender divided than among the Zaza-speaking Kurds. Nevertheless, the Zaza division between men and women is very clear and the gendered behaviour is anchored to traditional institutions. This society has not yet had modern institutions such as schools, mass media and public debates that can contribute to the creation of greater variation and more possible social adjustments for women. It is true that Turkish schools and media have affected women's position in society, but these are foreign elements to Kurdish culture and the local population does not speak the language of these institutions. Lack of modern institutions results in the segregation of the genders in all social contexts.

Biological and social conditions form a basis for a perception of gender differences. To reinforce the differences between the genders, manliness as the essential is greatly focused on and cultivated. It is legitimized, among other things, by the fact that men are generally physically stronger than women and therefore tasks that demand more muscle power are left to men. These tasks include forest work, clearing and cultivating the fields, cutting grass for the animals, tending household animals, construction work, etc.

Biological differences such as masculine strength, physical skills and characteristics are given as the reason that division of labour between men and women is pronounced both in the sphere of production and in the private sphere, and as the reason that work life is dominated by men in the Zaza society. Division of labour is determined culturally in many contexts because attitudes towards gender and gender-specific manners of action are culturally constructed and are not necessarily biologically conditioned. This is otherwise well documented in anthropology and gender studies (see, for example, Mead 1974, 1978; Butler 1990; Broch 2000). It is also well documented that gender is culturally determined, that is, to be a man or a woman varies from society to society. Gender roles are learnt through socialization processes in the Zaza society, similarly to other societies. The socialization process has clear aims. Boys and girls and men and women are attached dissimilar practical and symbolic or intentional significance through the socialization process. They learn clearly what it means to be a boy or a girl, a man or a woman. In the socialization process, many effective mechanisms are used in the upbringing and these shape the gender roles: a culture-specific pattern of proscription and prescription, physical punishment and reward, social control and social exclusion, upbraiding, gossip, praise and recognition, and a collective understanding are emphasized at the household level where all members participate in different gender-determined tasks. Obedience to the elders is a usual means people use to achieve socially acceptable gender roles. Different collectivistic kinship ideologies, for instance, patrilineal, matrilineal and patriarchal viewpoints (see Chapter 2 on kinship) operate together in the socialization process and are reflected in the conduct of men and women. The socialization process does not appear to be thoroughly planned but it is routine and ritualized to a great extent.

Zaza-speaking Kurds regard gender-determined ways and actions as 'natural' and the only socially acceptable ones. It is usual to see the pattern of gender roles as rooted in the quasi-biological conditions. Boys are associated with natural power and strength – they are strong and tough, leaning towards theoretical capabilities, responsibility and practical tasks – while the girls are usually associated with weakness – they are careless and dutiful with a tendency towards tasks of caring. In this lies an implicit point of view that gender differences lay down the premises for certain types of tasks. The differences make development of specific forms of behaviour possible, which means that the adjustment strategies of the individuals are directly transmitted to their issue through socialization.

From a sociological point of view, one cannot, of course, deny that biological dispositions are relevant for social behaviour. But my impression of the Zaza society and many other Islamic societies is that biological dispositions are both manipulated and exaggerated. They overlook the cultural and social character of gender roles. Typical women's tasks or occupations need not have 'congenital' reasons but are due to social and cultural conditions because cultures are constructed socially and they are transmitted in different forms of common values through processes of learning. Some of the afore-mentioned tasks that require muscle power can be executed by women, too. A single woman milking a large flock of sheep twice daily in the traditional way in reality has a heavier physical burden than cutting grass or shepherding animals, which are considered to be manly tasks. Tasks that are typically associated with men are also partly carried out by girls of 15 years of age or older who actively participate in such work, with the justification that girls help their fathers. (These tasks include forest work, clearing and cultivating the fields, cutting grass for the animals, tending household animals and construction work, as mentioned above.) Moreover, women carry water from the springs, which often lie at least a kilometre away from the house, and this is a physically demanding task. Furthermore, women collect firewood and carry it over several kilometres. Otherwise, they carry out other heavy agricultural work. Such tasks demand muscle power and often are reckoned to be as heavy as men's tasks. So, masculine power as a justification for the division of labour is not entirely valid.

But I believe one physically determined condition that the Zaza society generally emphasizes can be an important explanation for men's dominating position. This is men's fighting skills when it is necessary. Fights and quarrels have been part of their survival strat-egy. Use of physical power has traditionally been widespread and still happens, both in villages and towns, although it is not any longer so frequent as before. Stones and sticks are important weapons in fights between the parties. In more serious conflicts pistols, rifles and automatic firearms are used. This demonstrates how actual use of or threats to use physical power still affect the society.

I was told that in the last 25 years Solhan has been an important arena for power duels between the tribes. When conflicts arise between two or more parties in the village, Solhan often becomes the place for the physical clash. This is particularly valid for those vil-lages in which groups belonging to different tribes of equal strength live, as this situation means that none of the groups can reckon with defeating the other. Therefore, they move the conflict to Solhan with the hope that more of their members will arrive to help when the clash takes place, because many members from both tribes live here and also members of the tribes from other villages often meet here. The point is that these clashes create local heroes. Active or successful participants of fights, that is, persons who have caused the opponents' defeat or pain, are rewarded with hero status. This leads to a strong personality cult. Willingness to fight is portrayed as valour or a heroic deed and it gives high recognition and prestige, to which nobody can say no. Valour and heroic deeds have an important place in Kurdish awareness. This is expressed particularly in Kurdish music and literature. A considerable part of Kurdish music deals in particular with valiant personalities, how they fought against Turkish domination and oppression, how they defeated brutal attacks, how they revenged themselves, but also how brutally they were treated, were pained and were victimized. The process of a personality cult proceeds as follows: first, people begin by preparing oral stories about their valiant or victimized personalities. These stories are told orally for a considerable time; they spread from mouth to mouth. Thereafter, they write down in poetry form about the heroes and the incidents that took place. In the end, they put them to music and such songs are an important symbol of Kurdish identity. This tradition is transmitted to the younger generations. The point with a personality cult is both to remember the heroes and to respect them. The interpretation is that the heroes deserve a respectable place in the history of the Zaza population.

Family

Marriage is perceived as a fundamental social institution among an agricultural people with a strong patrilineal and patriarchal kinship system such as the Zaza society. The concept of the lasting monogamous marriage is dominant and forms the basis of establishing families in the Zaza society. The most important reason for the institution of family is a desire to perpetuate the kin. People marry early in life because marriage and the accompanying family life provide status. Being married leads to being recognized as an adult. Most people marry between the ages of 15 and 25. The boys should preferably marry before they go into military service, that is before they are 20; if not, they marry right after completing their military service. The girls must preferably marry before they are 21. If not, it is perceived that no one wants them.

The marriage institution is mainly interwoven into the Islamic moral system based on Islamic marriage laws but also partially adjusted to the local principles of descent and rules of settlement (see Table 2.1). Most marriages are not contracted at the 'legal' institutions such as the municipal administration but in the presence of a mullah. When they choose the mullah, they are expressing an opinion that the institution of marriage should not be regulated through legislation of the society. A formalized marriage contract is not perceived as genuine or proper. Therefore, it is formalized much later, preferably many years after the marriage takes place. Often when the children are registered at the Census Register, it becomes necessary to obtain such documents and then the marriage is formalized. Moreover, there are many who are not registered because the secular authorities recognize a marriage contracted in the presence of a mullah.

Marriage contracts that are not formalized lead to negative consequences for women. In the case where the woman divorces her husband and does not have formal documents of her marriage, she cannot demand any form of property rights according to Turkish law. And in practise, the right to a divorce belongs only to the husband and not to the wife. The woman does not have any parental rights after a divorce, which is a rare phenomenon in the Zaza society. When the divorce becomes a reality, this entails that she moves away from her children and ceases to be a mother to her children. If the ex-husband remarries – and most of them do in such a situation – the new wife takes care of the children. If he does not remarry, his mother takes care of the children. If the mother is not alive, either an unmarried sister or the wife of a brother takes care of the children. A modernization of the Islamic marriage's gender roles seems to progress slowly with some steps forward (see *preferential marriage* p. 51), but also with backlashes.

Polygamy is also practised in the Zaza society.[1] This form of marriage is exceedingly oppressive and hits some women very hard. Polygamy creates large problems within the family, among relatives and neighbours but, fortunately, there are relatively few who practise polygamy. On average, around 2 per cent of the population practises this form of marriage. Many reasons are given for polygamy. The first one is that a man marries anew if he does not beget a son with his first wife. It is immaterial whether the couple has many daughters. According to the established mentality, others own the girls; when the girl is married off she belongs to the husband. It is expected that the first wife will show understanding when the husband takes the initiative to marry anew.

Second marriages also occur among men who are dissatisfied with their first wives. There are many justifications. Some men try to justify their second marriages by arguing that the first marriage was involuntary. It was the wish of the parents and the couple could not resist it. Others justify their second marriage by referring to the fact they were much too young when they got married, which means that it was an immature decision, and now when they are mature it is their right to try again.

A third explanation of polygamy is the obligations connected with the agnatic line of descent.[2] Therefore, levirate occurs frequently, in which widows marry a brother of their deceased husband. If the deceased does not have a brother, it may happen that his wife marries an uncle or a cousin. An essential reason for this is said to be to avoid the woman leaving the children.

A fourth category of men who marry anew are those who cannot resist temptation and think it is their right to enjoy women. They can be poor or affluent. But often this is a type of man who is perceived as tough and felt to be handsome and attractive by women.

This description of the marriage institution in the Zaza society cannot be explained by anything else other than that women are totally subordinated. Islamic legislature and a patriarchal system that dominate this area stress the woman's actual subordination to the man and render the woman completely powerless in relation to the man. Women are also depicted as ignorant, unpredictable and dangerous, and are therefore treated with a deep suspicion. A typical example is that the man does not tolerate the woman discussing her situation with him; he gives the impression that he knows best and dictates to the woman about how she should be. His ambition is boundless. The woman's freedom is experienced by him the same as being without honour, a feudal characteristic according to which to be honourless means to die every day.

Gender-determined contact network

Gender is an important principle of classification in the Zaza society. Culture-specific methods are used to maintain certain divisions between the genders, and there are large differences between the social networks of men and women. Such gender-determined differences structure the social contact between men and women. In many contexts, women have their own contact network without the men being directly involved. But men are informed about such contacts by their wives, sisters or aunts. They want to keep a certain overview of what is going on among women. These forms of contact take place in the neighbourhood and are entirely informal. Men have contact with their relatives and friends more often than women do and they have many good friends who are present. These differences have to do with the man's dominating role in this society.

Men and women sit separately in their free time. Men often gather at the home of one of their circle of friends. When they come together they often sit in the assembly room (*diwon*). It is usual that each family has an assembly room reserved for *diwon* meetings. These rooms are also called guest rooms. Men spend most of their free time in such guest rooms. If a man spends his free time at home, he is mocked. He is characterized as a 'henpecked husband' or a 'man ruled by the hag'. Women are also supposed to nag the men that they should participate in such assemblies. This is so that the man avoids being mocked.

The men's meetings are regulated very hierarchically. Those who are advanced in age and have high status have most power and influence in the assemblies. Those with high rank sit on mattresses with fine cushions at the upper side of the room away from the door, are listened to most and get the most attention, while men with low status sit at the lower end of the room closest to the door, only on mats without cushions. Age is also a factor of regulation for how and where people are to sit in the assembly. The youngest men sit among those with low status at the lowermost end of the room. The latter groups should show respect for the elderly and the ones with high rank; they should sit humbly and talk as little as possible. Consequently, the contact network is choreographed in such a way that it reflects the hierarchies and lines of division that exist in the daily life. This principle also structures the eating patterns of the genders. Men and women eat separately, especially if an outsider is present. Men eat first, often in the family's living room. Sometimes, certain children of the family, the most spoiled ones, are allowed to eat with the men, but at other times, when the family has guests, the children are not allowed to do this. The women must wait until the men have finished eating. Only then can they eat the rest of the food and they must eat in the kitchen with the children.

The women often sit in the kitchen or the alley in their free time. No guest room is reserved for the women. They can use the family's assembly room only if it is not in use by men. Women would only go into the neighbour's house after they have finished the day's errands. Women's assemblies are also hierarchically regulated. Ageing women are shown respect. Advanced age is associated with life experience, wisdom and sound judgement. The society appreciates such characteristics. Therefore, the elderly women sit uppermost, they are listened to and they function as guides for younger women. These older women exercise a considerable influence on the female society. Younger women are associated with lack of experience and judgement.

Contrary to men, the women work at the same time as they sit and talk. They are engaged in handicraft and are often weaving woollen socks, gloves, sweaters and the like. The women's assemblies are often more disruptive than men's. They are not peaceful at all times and the assemblies often end with intense quarrels. The quarrels often arise between younger women and are dampened by older women.

The pattern of social networks among Zaza-speaking Kurds is very different from what is usual in urban areas of Europe. This is valid whether social contact, competency or economic rationality is considered. The pattern of contact among the Zaza people emphasizes good, close and stable relations between human beings and these relations are totally informal. The informal network of help and support is close knit. The contact among neighbours is characterized by transparency of relations, which also extends to the external relations one may have. For example, if you have contact with an outsider, you cannot hide it from the neighbourhood because they find out anyway.

Attire

Attire among the Zaza Kurds is gender differentiated and it continuously evolves in different directions. But attire may be the area that is least affected by religion. One seldom sees women with a black shawl, which is the foremost Islamic symbol. Women's attire is more marked by the traditional Kurdish way of dressing, with many colours. Women's clothes are usually more expensive than are men's. They keep expensive clothes and use them at special occasions such as feasts, weddings and other social gatherings. Western attire is increasingly becoming the model for men, but to a lesser extent for women. Zaza men's dress is also characterized by ornamentation to a large degree, but all the same they hide their bodies rather than display them; this perhaps emphasizes the fact that they want to be modern but their work and status does not always justify it.

Women's attire is characterized by variety; it is colourful with an abundance of textiles with plenty of pleats and folds. Each woman should preferably dress in a distinctive style and the clothes must be colourful and artistic. Women use fine clothes more often than men, who dress up especially for feasts such as weddings. Weddings are popular and they often act as the arena for making acquaintances and perhaps for courting. Girls especially are eager to participate in weddings. The boys and the girls do everything to impress each other. Beauty is important in the Zaza culture. When one is looking at a boy or a girl, the first thing one should notice is the beauty of the person, how he/she looks. One looks for inner values thereafter. But in recent years, materialistic values have acquired precedence among the girls. When girls choose a boy – to the extent they have that option – they attach more importance to the boy's wealth, job, education, material conditions and so forth. Consequently, marriages are seldom based on mutual love.

Most of the adult and elderly women generally wear traditional Kurdish clothes often including the headscarf and a long skirt, which covers large parts of the body. They dress in this way both to demonstrate their belief and out of respect for tradition. Consequently, there is a polarization of attire that strengthens the polarization of gender roles. Although the attire has been simplified among some young women, for example the skirt is drawn up a little above the ankles, this has not changed women's attire radically. When some women try to shorten their skirts up to knee level, they are met with negative reactions, first and foremost from moral guardians such as the mullahs, sheikhs and the elderly. But comment also comes from the neighbourhood and the locality. This is because people think that exposing the female body is indecent, according to their perceptions. Therefore, it must be warned against, almost hysterically, with the justification that the social fabric of society is disintegrating.

So women's attire has not yet gone through large-scale changes. They must wait for a while before they experience a year like 1965 when western women wore the miniskirt for the first time, which was the beginning of the changes in women's attire in western societies and which has continued with new fashions ever since. The change in attire in western societies was described as a break with the past and a more traditional society, and the introduction to women's liberation.

Sexual morality

In the Zaza society, sexual morality is defined according to Islamic morals and it is strict. The connection between Islamic morality and oppression of women can be illuminated in many ways. This morality does not contain any political or economic freedom for women. Islam does not make the same demands from both genders with respect to sexual morality. It entirely favours men, clearly and expressly. Polygamy is the best example of this. All the same, most Zaza Kurds live in a lifelong monogamous marriage, a marriage sometimes grounded in spontaneous feelings, at other times based on more rational decisions, and seldom based on mutual love. In many cases, the consideration of survival is more important than thoughts about love. As the consideration for love is devalued, at the same time arranged marriages and in certain cases forced marriages also take place. Forced marriages occur more frequently among families loyal to their kin among which patriarchal relations are still strong. Some forced marriages are also connected with polygamy.

Consequently, there are many similarities to the sexual morality of Christianity as it was practised in the Middle Ages. Young and unmarried women are expected to be virgins. A girl who is not virgin has difficulties with being accepted by her spouse or his family. In that case, she is returned to her parents. Therefore, child upbringing is traditional and very strict in the Zaza society. Girls especially must be continuously controlled and followed. On the contrary, there is a certain acceptance of the young unmarried boy acquiring sexual experience before he marries. But the experience shall not be had in the local milieu. He can acquire such experience in larger cities or go to bordellos far away from the local society.

There is an unwritten rule that the husband can indulge in certain affairs and extramarital relations, while the wife cannot. This is justified by the thinking that the man's sexual drive is uncontrollable and it is the woman's duty to tame it. Some extramarital relations occur here, as they do in all other societies. Some are swept under the carpet, others are uncovered, and a few have caused murders, especially of women. The common perception is that the husband's honour is dependent on the wife's fidelity. Therefore, the woman's self-respect and recognition increases with her fidelity and loyalty towards her husband. Where else can the woman receive respect and recognition than from the husband and his family? Since she has no role or job outside the home, it is precisely the family that has authority over her and can show respect for her behaviour.

Traditions of honour are entirely central and still functional in nearly all contexts. Highly valued and highly respected actions are praised with honour, while lowly and unacceptable behaviour is punished with negative reactions, shame and various forms of exclusion. Yet in this society, allocation of prizes of honour is dependent on which gender one belongs to, because there are different rules for men and women about what is right and wrong. A simple example to illuminate this: when a girl and boy elope with the aim of contracting a marriage – based on their free will – this is judged according to which of the parties has taken the initiative for the elopement. If the initiative has been taken by the boy, it is seen as a courageous act and often accepted by society, because it is his duty; but if it appears that the girl has taken the initiative, that the girl has led the process, she is not allotted the same recognition as the boy. It will rather be depicted as virtually unacceptable behaviour and many will say that the initiative was not *manly* and, therefore, not courageous enough. The topic can also be illuminated with another example: in certain situations, a woman can play a decisive role of arbitration between two conflicting families by virtue of her kinship relations. But even if she succeeds in bringing the opposing families together, in the end men receive the honour for it. This happens by arranging a public meeting, often in the presence of prominent men from the local society, where the conflicting parties are brought to speaking terms and peace between them is declared.

There are different rules of honour for the genders, as the examples above indicate. Another example for this is that sexual unfaithfulness of women is regarded as highly insulting and the sanctions against it are extremely strict. In some cases, it leads to people being killed and the action is described as an *honour murder*. This has to do with the allocation of honour prizes to the man. For the husband to be deceived by his spouse is the greatest shame and for the woman to be marked out as unfaithful is the greatest disgrace. To save his honour, the deceived man must either kill both his wife and her lover or turn her out as a sinner. Such actions are considered to be fair because they aim to save the family honour. It is still acceptable to kill women when they have committed the so-called crime of affronting the family honour, that is to say when they have been unfaithful to their husbands.

However, the opposite is not possible; for example, if the wife is deceived by the husband it is unthinkable for her to save her honour in the same way as the man. More often than not, the man avoids punishment when he commits the same error. This must be understood against the background of distribution of power and position between the genders. It is easier to put the blame or the shame on the woman since she is defined as the weaker gender (compare *manliness as the essential*, p. 172).

All the same, most men in the Zaza society do not practise such double standards of morality. The average man can be described as reliable; he goes to the mosque regularly, displays responsibility for his family, is sexually monogamous and keeps to the principle of being faithful to his wife. Men who juggle lovers are strongly disliked and they are met with social sanctions. They are often described as coming from the lower social strata; they do not provide for their families, represent lower morals, have no manners and shame, and so forth. Having an affair is more widespread among those men who have moved to Europe. Research I carried out in 1998 showed that eight out of ten men from Muslim countries were unfaithful. The ratio of unfaithfulness among women from the same countries was much lower, perhaps 'only' two out of ten.

Yet, the sexual morality of the Zaza society is totally different from the sexual morality of western societies. A free sexual morality that does not connect sexuality with marriage is an entirely foreign thought. The thought of being free, uncommitted, independent and individualist is also a foreign phenomenon. The concept of sexuality itself is nearly non-existent. Sexuality is a taboo, and religious norms and rules, or more correctly, prescriptions and proscriptions that dictate how people should live, are referred to; no one must talk about it, at least in the common space. Each individual must not only act based on the moral law but also should follow custom and habit. The guardians of the morals are, first and foremost, patriarchs, mullahs and sheikhs who constantly encourage people towards a morally conducted life, with threats of punishment or rewards of the hereafter. From time to time, sexuality becomes the subject of conversation in the private sphere but then it is kept strictly secret. This society is not yet capable of perceiving sexuality as something oppressed and therefore to be freed. The modern, rational and scientific thinking necessary for this is not known yet. Extending the stage for reason, taking the individual as a starting point, is a prerequisite for talking about taboo subjects openly.

Consequently, religious and traditional perceptions determine how marriage and relations between the genders should be conducted. Old-fashioned rules for etiquette hamper progress and prevent life from unfolding. It does not seem that the traditional pattern of the gender roles will change in a foreseeable future. A change in this area demands certain prerequisites. Economic growth is entirely fundamental for new occupational groups to come into being. In connection with EU membership, the European Commission demanded that Turkey forms a separate economic plan for the Kurdish region in Eastern Turkey. Economic development will lead to a decline in agricultural occupations. A class of wage-earning workers, a stratum of public employees, a middle class and bourgeoisie will arise, which will lead to a considerable change in the occupational composition of the population. Such a development will lead to changes in the family institution, as well; the extended family will be replaced with nuclear families with fewer children than is the case now. Family life becomes less central when children become fewer. Then, women will have time for tasks in the society other than giving birth to children and raising them. The society will be more differentiated and bourgeois lifestyle and middle-class culture will be preferred to the traditional lifestyle and culture. After that, the society will be able to change the traditional pattern of gender roles to a more modern or bourgeois sexual morality. The aforementioned structural changes will necessarily lead to changes in women's attire, too; women will likely then follow the new fashions, with shorter skirts, jeans and new variants of dress that will reflect women's new roles.

Men's and women's positions

The connection between women's oppression and Islamic morality can be illuminated in other ways. Gender segregation is pronounced in the Zaza society and Islam operates as an ideologically legitimizing factor in this area. For example, there are clear social norms that regulate the relations between the spouses. Women only participate in defining the moral norms to a small extent. It is mostly men who express their opinions and make decisions. The feudal perceptions and views that the strong one, the man, should protect the weak one, the woman, and that the man should act chivalrously are still dominating. From a modern point of view, a woman is not to be provided for, but she should take part in the development of the society in education, economy, politics and so forth. Equality between the genders is rejected in most of the traditional societies in the Middle East. As mentioned earlier, in all Muslim societies there is a widespread view that men are superior to women or that the masculine is the stronger gender. Therefore, each gender has its specific tasks. Equality between the genders need not mean sameness; it can also mean complementarity, as the secular laws emphasize. One gender is not superior to the other; they have different capabilities.

It is striking that women in the Zaza society do not have the same rights and opportunities as men. In the economic plane, it is obviously unreasonable that women do not have access to all occupations. They do not participate in the working life on the same level as men. The justification is partly based on biological perceptions and congenital differences between the genders and partly on the monotonous toil of the life of the traditional wife that holds the women down, and prevents them from using their talents. Therefore, only very few women work outside their homes. Most have been left to the private sphere. Nearly all women are homemakers and mothers. They are active in housework, which is not a chore ranked highly. The attitude is that the house should be clean and tidy. Women have a certain influence in the household sphere, where most of the time is spent on taking care of the children and the elderly in the family. One hears this often from men, too. They complain that the wife is the boss at home and she decides everything and gets her way. The woman's strong position at home is often the subject of conversation in the neighbourhood, too. By way of example, let us suppose you are coming from outside and wish to appeal to a certain family to borrow a thing or ask for services or the like, which is a quite common situation in this society. Traditionally, one thinks of appealing to the man in the family but this is not always so. You may be advised by neighbours that you should first appeal to the woman in the family because she is the one who decides, they will tell you. Of course, this does not apply to all women. There are relatively few women who govern the household. Moreover, the woman's exercise of power at home cannot be compared to the man's exercise of power outside the home. Compared to men's power, women's is too modest, insignificant and often exaggerated.

Choices that one makes in one's youth often beget consequences for the rest of one's life. But on the whole, women have few possibilities for choosing. Men make choices and priorities on behalf of women. Specifically, her father decides for her when she is young and her husband decides for her when she is married. Consequently, the future of the woman is formed by the man and this constitutes a pattern of fundamental conflict. The situation can be described as follows.

After a man and woman are married, she will move in with his family. Since there are no modern institutions such as kindergarten, clubs, sports facilities and so forth, the family has the responsibility for the socialization of the children. This constitutes part of the household tasks for which the woman is responsible. Here she gives birth and has the responsibility for the childcare, she cooks, washes clothes, keeps house for the whole family, takes care of her husband's ageing parents and so forth. For example, cooking and laundry are entirely foreign phenomena for the man. In addition, she spends a great deal of her time tending the animals, which are the family's main economic basis. The work with the animals involves milking the cows, sheep and goats and washing the barn in the winter (see Figures 10.1 and 10.2). It is also important to mention that there are no childcare institutions in this region, which means that much of the woman's time is spent taking care of the children. The women must take care of the children until they reach school age, in addition to the 'trivial' daily chores.

The worst effects of the women's position are felt by the newly married women or daughters-in-law (*vew*). These have the lowest status in the family. They often marry between the ages of 14 and 18.

Figure 10.1 A woman ready to milk the sheep
Photo: Zozan Kaya Asphaug.

Figure 10.2 A woman preparing milk products. She is shaking a sack made of sheepskin hung from a tripod. First, she has fermented milk to make yoghurt, then she shakes the yoghurt in the skin sack to churn butter. The result is butter and sour milk.

Photo: Mehmed S. Kaya.

They are often subjected to extensive oppression and are treated like housemaids. Also, newly married women are often a source of problems in the family. The relationship between the mother-in-law and her son's spouse can be particularly problematic because the mother-in-law demands continuity in her relations to her children and grandchildren. The mother-in-law is also afraid that the social bonds between her and her son may become weaker because of his spouse. In this way, the mother-in-law involves her daughter-in-law in a competition for the son's bonds of loyalty. Conflicts of this type last for a long time in many families, and they sometimes lead to the married couple moving out of his parents' house.

   Men in the Zaza society have great power over women, as in all the other Muslim societies. They have authority and are associated with the power to dominate women. Boys become socialized into an ideology of masculinity from an early age (ideas of men's manliness). Men hold all the political and religious offices. Only men can become mullahs and interpreters of Islam. Perhaps the most important

fact is that they control the economy. Put simply, men carry out economic transactions, form ideologies, sit at both formal and informal
positions of power, make political decisions and conduct religious
ceremonies. Men are valued as protectors in a society practically
without legal institutions. This is probably the most important reason that men's activities are always attached more importance than
women's.

For the women, the opposite is the case in the Zaza society. Women
are clearly subordinate. They do not get the opportunity to become
economically self-sufficient. They do not have a voice in decision-
making, they do not hold any religious office, they do not take part in
the formation of ideologies and they do not participate in forming
political resolutions. Men consider them as their property. They are
controlled with all conceivable means, if necessary with physical
power and with their lives being at stake. It seems as if men's values
and authority are legitimized at the expense of women's. Women
often try to show their loyalty to the tradition rather than demand
their rights. This can be interpreted as accepting their lower place-
ment in the gender hierarchy. They do not appear to be capable of
offering resistance, at least not publicly, but at home they have a certain possibility for limited power. It is also obvious that men do not
take women seriously. Forms of expression used by women are
regarded as nagging or gossiping; they are childish and so forth.

The problem is that what women do is first and foremost over-
looked, and thereafter it is perceived as less interesting and, finally, as
less profitable than what men do. Women in the Zaza society, as in
most other societies, execute a comprehensive amount of gratis work
in form of housework and socialization of children. Then one can
ask why this society is so much dominated by men, since men do not
contribute more to the economy than do the women. Perhaps it is
because men's economic contribution is spectacular and visible, and
a big issue is made of it. Women's economic contribution is evaluated as modest. But this alone does not explain why men in this society exaggerate their own contribution at the expense of women's
contribution. Women's capabilities are heavily underestimated,
although they often participate in physically demanding work such
as tending for animals and other heavy agricultural work. Women in
the Zaza society and in Muslim societies are appreciated very little.
They are grossly exploited, often without most men actually realiz-
ing that they are oppressing their wives. A large portion of the
oppression is due to the lack of capability and will to see one's

actions. But, to an even more serious degree, this is due to the fact that the collectivistic kinship ideologies (patrilineal and patriarchal) prevent people from reflecting about the consequences to which these taboos have led.

According to the patrilineal and patriarchal ideology, only the man has the capability to take care of his family – perhaps the most important task connected with the masculine ideal. Let me describe an example that can illustrate the relation between gender relations and the economy. The district of Hun consists of Zaza-speaking Kurds and lies to the south-west of the provincial capital Bingöl but administratively belongs to Palu, a district subordinated to the neighbouring province of Xarput to the west of Bingöl. The large river Murad, which is a tributary of Euphrates, flows through the district of Hun and is the reason that agriculture in this area is relatively productive. Hun society has a way of life that can be compared to Solhan. The people in the district of Hun are engaged mainly in agriculture, sheep farming, gardening and some trading. All have gardens, at times quite large, a result of the fertility of the land. They cultivate many kinds of fruits and vegetables and sell the agricultural products to the markets in the neighbouring towns. The division of labour is based on gender as in other places in the Kurdish region. Men have the responsibility to clear the land while planting, weeding, harvesting and further treatment is the women's responsibility, apart from marketing and selling a possible surplus, which will be done by the men. Women gather wild fruits and vegetables, as well, and men are engaged in extra buying and selling. Women are not allowed to trade. Nor do they seem interested in it. Although the men use up considerably more time for clearing the land and tending the sheep, it is the trade activities that take a central position in their self-image, and this is so even though they earn far less through trade than agriculture or sheep farming. This is because trade imparts higher status and prestige. This is an example of how men control the tasks to which higher prestige is attached in the society and also how the culture attaches authority and value to men's roles, something corresponding to their idea of manliness as the essential.

Horticulture, which consists mainly of women's work, often brings larger incomes into the household than both sheep farming and trade. In this society, it is the 'skilful' tradesman who is honoured, not the industrious woman. In this case, social status does not have an immediate connection with more work and more income. It also concerns power and prestige, and if selling flour sacks is regarded as more dignified (see the example Emin and Baki in Chapter 7, p. 104) than to cultivate fruits and vegetables, it is of little importance that fruit and vegetables bring in more income than selling flour sacks.

In this chapter we have seen that the strongly segregated gender relations that prevail in the family structure, in the division of labour between men and women and in many other situations in the Zaza society are legitimized through religion (Islamic legislation, Islamic sexual morality, polygamy, patriarchal structure and so forth). Therefore, it is important to expound on the topic of religion. This will be the subject of the next chapter.

Chapter 11

Religion, collectivism and individualism

In addition to kinship as a collective fellowship, there is also another collective behaviour, namely religion, and in particular Islam, which has been highly valued and has held the Zaza society together. Religion has been one of the central topics in sociological and anthropological research since the 1800s. Sociologists and anthropologists have documented that belief or religion affects nearly all parts of the society. It marks people's thinking, affects decisions, kindles or dampens diverse conflicts, regulates peoples' behaviour, social adjustment and economic life, influences individual and social moral and ethical standards, concerns sexuality, disease and healing (see the example of Fatma in Chapter 2, p. 18–20), life and death, and so forth.

The Frenchman Emile Durkheim is the most influential sociologist in the interpretation of religion. The social function of religion was important for Durkheim, especially his idea that, seen at a deeper level, religion is worshipping the collectivity. Religion is a prerequisite for the social collectivity of human beings and it brings people together in a moral fellowship. He thought that such a moral foundation was necessary for the integration of the society. Taking this as my starting point, I will describe Islam's place in the Zaza society. Here, Islam is looked at as an influential social institution in the Zaza society.

The Islamic view of life has left deep marks on the spiritual life of the Zaza society as well as the daily life of the population and can be described as a line of guidance for a moral way of living and also as a model for both individual and collective life. The Sunnah[1] establishes that Islam attaches decisive importance to building a society based on more permanent relations and moral obligations, in which the choices and wishes of the individual must give way to what is best for the collectivity. In other words, Islam has been a conserving factor for the society and, therefore, often opposed individualism.

Islam requires individual sacrifice and total devotion to the laws (Sharia) of the society. The individual is not encouraged towards individual development or independence, but to develop a harmonious equilibrium in all life situations. Having a set of very restrictive common normative values in the form of prohibitions, prescriptions and ritual duties, Islam does not allow the individual Muslim, particularly a practising one, to choose another form of life than the Islamic one,[2] wherever in the world he or she may live. These normative values symbolize fear and are used effectively to limit the free development of the individual. Islam has clear references for how a Muslim should think, live, behave and so forth. The majority of the Zaza society tries to keep strictly to this lifestyle. I first give an account of the Zaza population's relationship to Islam before I analyse Islam's dominating role in this society.

Confessional boundaries

Zaza-speaking Kurds in Eastern Turkey, like the vast majority of the rest of the population of the country, are Muslims. They believe in Islam in the general sense, but in varying forms. About half of the Zaza population in Eastern Turkey belong to the Sunni/Shafii sect, while the rest belongs to the Alevi sect. The Sunni/Shafii sect represents the most conservative and orthodox variant of Islam. The Alevi sect originated in the 1800s and was disliked by many from the start. This is, among other things, because the Alevi regard Ali, son-in-law of the prophet Muhammad, as divine or the natural follower of the prophet. He became number four among the divine caliphs. The Alevi sect is a less orthodox Islamic sect than the Shia or Sunni Islam and they have been subjected to oppression and propaganda from Sunni Islam for a long time. The Alevis are quite secular and have characteristics both from Islam, Christianity, Judaism, Zoroastrianism and shamanism. This is the reason that many think the Alevis are a breakaway sect of Islam. Although the theological foundation is the same in Shia Islam and the Alevi sect, there are clear differences. The popular religiosity in the Alevi sect has given Alevism distinctive traditional and cultural features; it is less theologically characterized than the Shia Islam of Iran. Zaza-speaking Alevis are tolerant to other religions. According to them, religion is a private matter – a matter between Allah and the individual. They believe all individuals are responsible for themselves.[3] But they are accused of celebrating many Christian holidays, using bread and wine in their rituals, and for having relinquished the use of veil by women.

Contrary to Sunni Islam, the Alevis do not have the yearly fasting month Ramadan, but a shorter fast of 12 days (Imam Days). They do not go on pilgrimage to Mecca and they do not pray in the mosque. They have their own house of worship which is called *Ki Cem* (*Cem Evi* in Turkish) where women and men together carry out the rituals, which may be dance, mourning and *zikr* (remembrance, a form of meditation). Alcohol is not prohibited in the Alevi tradition; it is among the Sunni that alcohol is strictly prohibited. Women in the Alevi society have relatively high status. The Alevis consider themselves to be liberal, democratic and secular. They also support separating religion and politics. For this reason, there has not been a religious political mobilization among the Alevis. The previously mentioned Dersim rebellion led by the Alevis was a national rebellion demanding national rights for the Kurds.

All people in Solhan and around belong to the Sunni/Shafii sect. But they are not fundamentalists. There are also few who have a moderate relation with Islam. Most of them regard themselves as traditional Muslims. They keep close contact with the mosque (see Figure 11.1) to carry out their religious duties, first and foremost in the form of prayers (*nimaj*), fasting or Ramadan (*rueji* or *roji*), the feast of sacrifice (*roshon qorbonon*), alms (*zika*) and other solemn Islamic occasions. They maintain their own view of life through the ritual praxis.

Part of their primary identity is anchored in Islam through the primary socialization process. Islamic concord is a key concept for understanding their upbringing, their way of thinking and acting. Concord is understood as a spiritual and social process in which the past and the present are included as a whole in the daily life. Zaza people acquire an Islamic view of life through the religious socialization process. One's life view marks one's way of acting and it spans more or less through all one's existence.

Islam has a strong position among the Sunni portion of the Zaza population, both in the districts of Solhan and the neighbouring areas. It has a considerable influence on the society, culture and the individuals. For Muslims, the definition of Islam is generally not separate from that of social morality, as has been possible in the case of Christianity in Northern Europe. Islam regulates people's patterns of thinking, conduct and life, and is closely integrated into their daily lives.

Figure 11.1 Ulu Cami in Bingöl. Mosques are prominent all over the Kurdish-dominated Eastern Turkey. The mosque symbolizes fear of God expressed through Islam.

Consequently, Islam has an enormous ability as a regulator and claims to be entitled to interfere in all social conditions because it is interpreted to be a perfect system. During my field work, I witnessed several episodes that unfolded in one of the villages relating to this. One was in the fasting month, Ramadan, when it became known that a couple of boys in their 20s broke the rule about fasting. Although they did it in strict secrecy, they were nevertheless discovered. The reaction from the population, especially from the adult men and the elderly, was very strong. They interpreted the young men's conduct as a sign that they had acquired a different lifestyle and, therefore, they must be declared infidels and heretics. The 'heretics' were also met with social sanctions in the form of being excluded from each and every social occasion.

The example tells that the Zaza society attaches much weight to a religious conduct of one's life. There is also wide agreement among people that Islam permeates nearly all aspects of existence and it functions as the spiritual dimension of the daily life and the collectivity. Not only this, it also acts as a guide for the things people do for the rest of their lives.

The Zaza population's general understanding of reality is mainly based on three sources: religion, experience and conventional thinking. Religious orientation shows itself in nearly all contexts among the Zaza population. For example, not many seconds pass before religion is drawn into a conversation and one says, 'Praised be God'. The conversation is referred to religious sources as often as it is possible. One is often reminded of God the almighty who is omnipresent and nobody should go without his blessing. They try to place every conversation in a religious context, consciously or unconsciously. One nearly gets the impression that conversations without a religious content are both uninteresting and meaningless.

The conversations are often routine and unreflective, but the participants preach and moralize nearly endlessly. The attitudes are marked by repetitions. They repeat themselves without moving on. This marks people's thinking and actions, too. In conversations, people try to connect the new with the old, notwithstanding topic and occasion, not primarily to understand the new through old experience, but to assert how wrong the new is because it is not identical or does not correspond to what the Prophet said. Islam, as the Zaza population interprets and practises it, appears as a form of orientation that was typical for pre-modern societies in which the attitudes were quite hostile to progress.

Strong religious orientation and conventional thinking obviously prevent people from reflecting independently. This also hinders personal freedom and creativity. Innumerable conversations that I witnessed and studied meticulously did not seem to have been characterized by rational and analytical thinking. They lack references to a reflected understanding of a rational way of life. The main responsibility lies with the interpreters of Islam, that is, sheikhs, mullahs and other religious figures who do not have a formal education. They only have a religious education. They do not rely on scientific thinking, analysis and methods. Interpreters of Islam contribute heavily to maintaining the prevalent society. As a result, they do not want people to think independently, to be critical of religious taboos, to question the oppressive social structures and, above all, they do not want people to think different from themselves. Islam functions as an instrument of certain groups for exercising power in society. Their interpretation of Islam aims at making people put up with the oppressive social order, with the hope of being rewarded in the hereafter. They say this by expressly quoting the prophet Muhammad.

Kurdish intellectuals have discussed why Islam has such a strong position in the Kurdish society. There is general agreement that it is due to a series of conditions. Education is one condition that is mentioned often and it seems to have an important explicative power. Generally, the level of education in the entire Kurdish region is low, including the Zaza area, very low when compared to the rest of Turkey. Both Kurdish intellectuals and politicians assert that the Turkish authorities have never been interested in building an equal educational system in the Kurdish areas, as they have done in the Turkish part of the country. Many think that the Turkish authorities are too vulnerable with respect to the Kurds and are not at all interested in raising the level of knowledge. The Turkish side is afraid of educating its critics. Some of the Turkish intellectuals are of the opinion that Turkey does not have a high standard of academics. Academics in the country's universities are half-schooled because the authorities do not wish to educate proper academics for fear of their criticizing the political system.

Poverty is mentioned as another explanation for the strong position of Islam in this region. There is a causal connection between economic underdevelopment or poverty and religious orientation. This connection decreases strongly in larger cities where life is characterized by economic progress, as it is to the west of this region.

The religious market

When the level of education is as low as possible in these global times and accompanied by widespread poverty, great opportunities are created for religious manipulation, speculation and exploitation, first and foremost by religious sects and sheikhs, but also by some mullahs. All these three groups operate on religious grounds. Further, people allow themselves to be manipulated and exploited economically and politically. The three former actors together constitute a kind of religious market or bazaar: a bazaar for recruiting to religious groups or sects and a bazaar for economic exploitation where the sheikhs play the main role while the mullahs are somewhat subordinate. Common to all three actors is that they refer to religious belief and religious feeling, and that they claim a monopoly for the profit. The methods these actors use in their relations with people are kept partly secret. There is no state authority that exercises control over the activity, either. So they have a free rein in these kinds of activities. A detailed description of the activities of the three groups is given below.

Religious sects address themselves to all social strata, but most often they recruit youths from the poor social strata. They make promises about mystical insight, holistic healing, myths and the like. The sects use Islam as an ideological instrument. They interpret Islam literally. Through this interpretation, they try to convince others that they are the most correct ones, because they stand for the right interpretation of holy scripts. The interpretation also aims at acquiring a monopoly over Islam. Their appeal is that their aim is to save Islam. They agitate for religious awakening and demand introduction of the Sharia law. One of their foremost aims is to fight secularism and western influence. Scientific cosmology and progress is made suspect by reference to God almighty. The Nurcu movement, the Nakshibendi movement and the Hizbullah party are active in the Zaza region. These movements had relatively more supporters in the 1980s and 1990s. But people are less responsive now because the movements are suspected and have partly been revealed as infiltrated by the Turkish intelligence services.

As mentioned above, the second group that participates in the religious bazaar is the sheikhs. They collect alms, mainly in the form of money, sheep, goats, corn and, sometimes, clothes. Their area of activity for exploitation stretches over the entire Kurdish region in Eastern Turkey and the Kurdish ghetto concentrations in the large Turkish cities. Some of them also travel among the Kurdish milieus in Western Europe. From the Kurds in Western Turkey and Europe, they collect only money and clothes. The sheikhs divide the territories among themselves. Consequently, each sheikh has his own territory where he is engaged in his activities.

The methods that the minor sheikhs use in this context are a form of preaching. He starts by presenting himself as a member of a highly esteemed sheikh's family. The presentation usually includes his family's apocalyptic powers, presentiment of the invisible, an indispensable place with God, their being able to refer to true predictions about the future and his forefathers having been spiritual guides of the people. He gives the impression that his family will always serve Islam and has used its apocalyptic powers and prayers to protect people from all evil. The sheikh aims to convince people that he is in close contact with Islam, he represents the true interpretation of the holy scripts, he is a true representative of Islam and by virtue of this he is the only true guide for people. At the same time, he prays for people. The prayer is very intense and appears genuine, in which he gives the impression that it was commanded or will be accepted by

God. He is admired and gets recognition through this. In this way, the sheikh acquires a form of power based on alleged apocalyptic powers. This religious authority, which aims at making people indebted to itself in God's name, is perceived to be both righteous and legitimate by the people.

When he achieves this, that is, when he becomes a trustworthy sheikh, he is rewarded. But he does not take the initiative for the rewards. It would be mean of him if he himself takes the initiative for alms after so much boasting. He has made a couple of acquaintances in the village in advance whom he visits and with whom he stays. They speak among themselves and agree that the host takes the initiative on behalf of the sheikh and collects alms. The host takes the initiative either directly in the assembly where the sheikh has presented himself to those who are present and has offered his prayers or he appeals to some chosen prominent personalities in the village. These personalities further communicate the message to the inhabitants. The host, together with some volunteers from among the inhabitants, collects a huge amount of alms, about 30 sheep from a village of 60–70 households, in the course of a short time, usually one or two days. In addition, the sheikh receives some money from those who are not engaged in animal husbandry. The sheikh will collect two to three tons of corn if it is harvest time. The alms from one or two villages, depending on how successful he is, will be more than enough to provide for his family for a year. The sheikhs who collect alms do not represent the highest stratum among the sheikhs. Members of the uppermost stratum of the sheikhs are usually powerful enough from the past, they have plenty enough resources to manage; they are considered to be rich and they do not condescend to collect alms because they think to ask for alms is beneath them. Those who do this are often from the lower stratum of the sheikhal hierarchy, but some also come from the middle stratum.

The mullahs are the third group that participates in the religious bazaar. Unlike the sheiks, the mullahs' territory of exploitation is confined to the villages or towns where they are active and carry out religious services. The mullahs are employed either by the inhabitants or the state. They are called imams if they are employed by the state. They are called mullahs if they are employed by the people. Alms collection yields the same proceeds for the mullahs as the sheikhs, that is, money, sheep, goats, corn, clothes and other gifts, but they do this by virtue of the religious services they carry out. The mullahs do not claim that they have apocalyptic powers, presentiment of the invisible or an indispensable place with God, as the sheikhs do. Their primary task is to lead the prayers in the mosque. When the mullah carries out a service in a village or a town, the inhabitants are obliged to reward him. The reward is given in form of alms. The alms are considered to be his wages when the mullah is not paid by the state. But the inhabitants do not give all the alms to the mullah. Some of the surplus alms are given as charity to the poor from the same village or given through the sheiks to the poor in other villages.

First, the description of the religious bazaars shows that it is difficult to separate the religious from the daily in the Zaza society. The boundary between the social and religious life is nearly erased. Religion and daily life complement each other and are significant for the production and reproduction of social processes. Mystical cosmologies and magical rituals live on and flourish periodically, especially in times of economic depression. The relationship between cosmology and daily life is seen in living traditions of knowledge in constant change (see among others, Barth 1987), which are in a complex give-and-take relationship with the world of daily life. Therefore, the bearers of such traditions – the actors in the bazaar – cannot always relate to the traditions in the same way. These traditions are continuously changing, are constantly adjusted to new situations and are applied by different people in different ways.

Second, the description of the three groups – the bazaar actors – tells that what is brought forward in the religious bazaars is a misunderstood interpretation and communication of Islam. These groups do not attempt to describe the genuine religious message but we can say, like Levi-Strauss, that they are justifying the deficiencies of the reality since they are interpreting the mystical aspects of the religion but are simultaneously demonstrating that they are not *tenable*. This move is typical for mystical thinking characterized by false consciousness because it is not subject to being discussed. All the same, it implies an admission that social relations involve an irresolvable contradiction, a contradiction that the bazaar actors cannot understand. Therefore, they translate it into ritualistic acts, for example, into a message to which the users can be receptive so that it makes exploitation possible. The actors play strategic games with power, honour and exploitation. This is a form of a bartering system in which the actors interpret Islam in such a way that religion provides them economic gains, for example in the form of alms but also gifts.

Moreover religious knowledge, as other kinds of knowledge, is unequally distributed among the members of the Zaza society. The example of the religious bazaars indicates that the bazaar actors have relatively deep insight into their own religious traditions. They have 'specialized' in this area. They can construct long mystical stories or false justifications for vague religious statements. They are inventive and can tell dubious stories about their forefathers. Most people in the Zaza society have limited knowledge about religion, especially women, who are often excluded from religious gatherings where religious knowledge is communicated. Generally, people are only acquainted with those rules of Islam that they come into contact with daily because, as mentioned earlier, most people are illiterate. No religious literature in Kurdish or in Zaza dialect exists. People do not have a knowledge of Arabic, which is necessary for familiarity with the religion they believe in. The Koran and the Hadith literature is only translated into Turkish but not every one can benefit from this, either. Consequently, there are few who have access to religious knowledge.

All this makes it possible for various interest groups to use Islam as a commodity. It has not only become the livelihood of many, but also many operators profit from Islam. It is used as an instrument for many aims. Some of these aims are very suspect. Some uncommitted groups use Islam for political aims (i.e. the sheikhdom), others use it purely for economic exploitation of poor people (i.e. alms). At the same time, these same groups use Islam to legitimize their suspicious activities, which are not always compatible with Islam. Can such a development be a sign of Islam becoming weaker?

Is Islam becoming weaker?

Until now, Islam has been one of the pillars of the social organization of the Zaza society, much the same as kinship or economy. Religion has had a power that it exercised over human beings through traditions and religious prescriptions and proscriptions. It is through a strictly ritualized life that Islam has contributed to social fellowship and social order and has been instrumental in that people have felt themselves to be members of this society. But ritual praxis has created social forms such as gender-based division of labour, asymmetrical gender relations, authoritarian systems and social antagonisms connected with a pre-modern society. The reason for the society and daily life to be organized and governed by religious principles does not seem to be valid any longer. Societies based on religious principles do not have an eternal life.

200 The Zaza Kurds of Turkey

This has caused Islam's influence to become reduced. There is much that indicates that Islam, from being a dominating framework of social life, is gradually becoming a lateral social institution in the Zaza society. Not everybody submits to religious prescriptions and proscriptions. Religion is not capable of controlling people's lives as before. Kurdish culture and political awareness connected with demands for recognition of a national identity appears as the foremost challenge to Islam. In many ways, this mobilization acts as an alternative or a replacement for Islam, one which aims at producing a better social order and gives meaning to life. The development of knowledge about political awareness will especially contribute to modernization and promote new expectations, norms and values for social integration, social fellowship and social order. This entails that religion, myths, rituals and traditions, such as alms giving, constantly become less important. Hopefully, the tradition of almsgiving will change both in form and content. Earlier, the Kurdish national awareness was under religious control. Islam had a mobilizing function when the Kurds rebelled in 1925 against the newly proclaimed republic. This is not the case today. Kurdish leaders with whom I had conversations believe that Islam has lost its mobilizing function. They think that Islam no longer plays a role in their struggle against national oppression. Other Muslim societies use Islam gladly as an important propaganda instrument against what they perceive as western occupation or oppression, but in relation to the Kurds the same religion is used both by Turks, Arabs and Persians to legitimize their oppression of the Kurds. Until 1960, Islam was used to highlight the cause of the oppressed, but this is not the case any longer. Today, Islam is used mainly to serve or to assure the interests of the dominant groups or nations.

Kurdish awareness is to a large extent secularized, which can be a driving force for social change. Islam is under pressure from many sides, in addition to a new Kurdish cultural awareness. On the one hand, the religion is subjected to a western cultural pressure that promotes, among other things, individualization, democratization and privatization of religion, while on the other hand, it is under pressure from the growing Muslim fundamentalism, which regards modern life as a morally unbearable situation.

Science as the highest known form of knowledge is perhaps one of the most reliable primary institutions of the modern society. It has a constantly renewed task. Islam is continuously weakened by the progress of science because a continuous and unchallengeable development that institutionalizes change and progress is taking place here. Science constitutes a challenge to Islam because scientific progress contributes to changes in a way that threatens the existing social order, but it can also be used to conserve the old or the surviving. Humanity has generally acquired an increased understanding of social life and a better insight into life with scientific progress. It can provide an account of life. Humanity can increase its reflective power, interpret itself and its situation better, and many people aim at liberating themselves from structures, collectivities, superior forces and traditions, which limit their choices. The greatest problem for the Zaza people is that science is new and seems peripheral for them. Because the society lacks its own modern institutions, it will take time before science gains increased authority. This is the explanation as to why many people still believe in destiny. In addition, there are still existential questions, such as life after death, which science cannot answer. Therefore, a space for many sheikhs, religious sects, magicians, fortune tellers, astrologers and similar 'specialists', which still constitutes a large and lucrative market in the entire region, is created.

All the same, one observes that the strengthened position of science is beginning to lead to consequences for the religious life. The belief in the Koran as the word of Allah and the belief in miracles are being shaken for those who take the progress of science seriously – and this concerns primarily the well-educated younger portion of the population. But if the belief is shaken, it can be won again, too. The challenge and assault of science is met in many ways. The most extreme fundamentalists especially condemn all science and often demonstrate their suspicion of progress. They call to fight against the hegemony of science and technology, and want to break all which is modern and want to relate only to the Islamic lifestyle, which means to have the people tied to the past. Other more moderate interpreters emphasize getting science to work together with Islam. These quarters are constantly stating that Islam should accept the leading position of science in modern culture and should accommodate itself to it. And still others, more traditional interpreters have an indifferent attitude to science. They are of the opinion that religion and science are different things and assert that Islam and science need not contradict each other. Perceived as such, Islam loses much of its political significance. When the social order is unstable as it is now and creed can be interpreted in ways, which have widely different political consequences, it is difficult to supply a trustworthy explanation.

The critics think that Islam is not capable of justifying its moral direction of the society. At this point, it is still too early to assert that the public opinion has changed. But some institutions, which were under religious control, are gradually becoming secular, for example, parts of the marriage contract where religious rules are rejected. Religious engagement and religious congregations are somewhat weakened, although empirical investigations cannot demonstrate a connection between weak religious engagement and secularization. But large gatherings are less frequent than before. And another point that is becoming increasingly relevant, particularly outside the political rhetoric, is that religious knowledge becomes less important when it cannot be used to an end. The general tendency is that this use of Islam is being reduced and perhaps it will be gradually deinstitutionalized. If Islam's institutional function is weakened, its existential foundation will become dependent on the cultural resources it has, and its capabilities for flexibility will decide whether it can live into an unforeseeable future.

The Zaza are collectivist

In most western societies, a fundamental ideal is that the individual is to be raised to become independent, responsible for their own life. On the contrary among Zaza-speaking Kurds, the individual is a constituent of a family unit where the individual is primarily regarded as a member of a group and where the family's demands are set above the individual's. They attach less weight to individualism. All that the individual obtains in form of property, material affluence, success, prestige, honour or loss of it, is allocated to the members of the group to which the individual belongs (see Table 2.1). This strong collectivistic conception prevents the individual from thinking freely and developing himself as an independent individual who can express his own opinions. On the contrary, one does everything to avoid being perceived as deviant. Collectivistic notions are so strong that independent opinions do not have a chance to be asserted.

An example of this was one day, when we were sitting and having a nice conversation in the village of Azad. There were around 20 people present. All, of course, were men. The woman kept to another room or, as usual, to the kitchen. As it often happens, the elderly began talking preachingly. Usually one dares not say anything if one disagrees with them. But this time, a university student from the same village cautiously tried to point out two contradictory principles in the holy book, the Koran. One says that the individual is free and decides his own destiny; the other says that everything is preordained. This remark was perceived by the participants as though the boy was questioning the Koran. But, in fact, he wanted to discuss and perhaps theorize about religious principles. The boy was accused of being a pagan (*kafir*) and he was stigmatized with this. Thereafter, he was humiliated and upbraided. This resulted in him being excluded from the gathering. No one wanted to discuss or have contact with the boy any longer.

The example illustrates a strong tradition preventing the individual's attempts to liberate himself from established thinking. The adults and the elderly have a collective consciousness that builds on common perceptions of creed, convictions and feelings. And they cooperate to protect their common interests. If necessary, they use force towards individuals.

The dominant social perceptions reject individual thinking and can be formulated approximately as such: a society does not consist of individuals who establish a voluntary contract about conforming to certain rules and arrangements. Instead, the society consists of established authorities and groups, connected together in the past and the present, in a collectivity that no individual can grasp. Therefore, the traditions are the foundation of the society. At the deepest level, the traditions are holy because they emanate from religion. The social order consists of institutions, sheikhdom, mullahocracy, kinship groups and family, which all have a religious origin or are organized in conformity with religious principles and divine providence. These are holy institutions that do not exist for the benefit of the individual. The individual is thought to be a nullity with respect to the institutions. It is still an epoch of fellowship between human beings, an epoch in which life is permeated with religious feelings and where the mosque is still the focal point.

Therefore, the individual's conduct in the Zaza society is strongly limited by a dominant collectivistic notion of conduct. For example, parents and grandparents have a strict upbringing strategy for children. They set down strict limits for the life course of the future generations because they are afraid of children becoming independent. They tie the children not to the contemporary modern world but to their own. Parents and grandparents do this by presenting the past to the children. They cultivate the past to create or to maintain a traditional existence in the future. To manage this, they often play on fear. Fear is the most important means to achieve conformity.

Individualism

Individualism is a classical philosophical school of thought that stresses the individual human being's freedom and independence, emphasizing the individual's value and his or her right to assert himself in relation to collective perceptions. This *Weltanschauung* accentuates the individual's struggle for freedom from duties and conventions. Another interpretation of individualism is that the modern society with its differentiated institutions and roles entails a larger space for the individual to be something else and something greater than his or her role.

There has been general agreement among researchers that individualism replaces kinship-based fellowships and family relations in many societies. The industrial revolution, which happened in Europe in the mid-1800s, weakened family and kinship ties. But at the same time, the European revolution emphasized the individual human being's freedom and independence. This strengthened individual creativity by which individuals could assume responsibility for, and liberate themselves from tradition, church and local fellowship. The increasing individuation of the human being has to do with the urbanization and modernization of the society. Urbanization individuates, 'urban life liberates' from the old society's monitoring, gossip, intrigues and traditional forms of social intercourse. And modernization refers to processes through which the social relations are transformed from 'traditional' to 'modern' ones. Economically, this involves the growth of industrialized production of goods. Politically, it means that traditional institutions are subjected to democratic government. Culturally, it entails increasing individuation of the human being. But such processes have not yet begun in the Zaza society. It is a society with no particular room for individualism and in which collective values are entirely dominant. The close-knit kinship based on solidarity and various collective regulations (patriarchy, sheikhdom, principality and the mullah priesthood) in the Zaza society results in individuals not getting opportunities to form their individualities. These forces control individuality and prevent it from developing. The individual is not raised to make independent choices in adult life and take responsibility for those choices and their consequences. Individuals here are brought up to regard themselves as members of the collectivity and to respect the choices the collectivity has made. There is much more acceptance of the duties towards the kin taking precedence over personal considerations. The loyalty is 'inbuilt' in a kinship collectivity. In some contexts, kin and family are one and the same. The extended family lives under the same roof. The parents spend much time integrating their children with the rest of the kin. Grandparents exert extra effort so that children will display respect for the society around them. 'Children should know their roots and where they belong' is an established norm that should not be broken. This becomes an expression for a deep moral obligation to take care of the fellowship values.

In some cases, certain individual strategies play some role, for example, in relation to choosing a spouse where the concerned person may forward his or her wishes and proposals, but then within the premise that the family can accept the proposal and it does not conflict with the family's wishes and evaluations. Such situations arise quite often and create intense discussions both within the family and the local society. Many people involved themselves in such cases. The central question is how the person will manage this dilemma and which strategy he/she will follow, because the person is in the middle of a difficult situation. On the one hand, the person must primarily take their own wish into account although their wish does not always correspond to the family's, and on the other hand, their wish must be conciliated to the wishes of the family and the kin if the person is to have any chance at all to achieve their goal. In a case where the concerned person makes a proposition that does not conflict with the expectations of the family, that is, the response is positive, the process will be accelerated. But if the proposition does not satisfy the family's expectations, that is, the response is negative, the process will be hindered. This is an example of how kinship collectivities regulate themselves and maintain control rather than satisfying individual needs. I will next describe an example that illuminates the dilemma.

In one of the villages there was sudden news about a young boy and a young girl who allegedly thought about marrying each other. This news became a conversation subject for a long time. According to rumours, they had been sweethearts for some time. They were from the same village but they were not relatives. The boy was barely over 20 and the girl was 18. Neither of them had education above the primary school level. The boy is from a relatively affluent family, which allows the boy and his family a larger arena of action, while the girl is from a somewhat poorer family. A larger scope for action is locally expressed as follows: 'If you have a good economy, you can get any girl you want in this area.' Economic status imparts different esteem and rank to the families. The boy's family regards itself as an esteemed and prominent family in the village. They believe they belong to the upper echelons of the village hierarchy. The boy's family places the girl's family among the low status groups in the village. This was more than enough for a confrontation between the families.

The father took up the case with his son after the news became known. The boy allegedly admitted that he could think of marrying the girl if his family allowed him. But the boy received a stubborn 'no' from his father. The father justified his resistance by indicating that the families were not equivalent, there was no equality between the families and the families belonged to different classes. Therefore, there would be no question of a marriage between the boy and the girl. This was the father's clear message. After this, the boy's family began speaking in a condescending manner about the girl's family while the girl and her family kept a low profile.

I left the village two months later. There had not been any conciliation between the families until then. The relations between the families were very cold. They were not on speaking terms. The girl's family claimed to have received threats from the boy's family. And there were rumours that the girl would elope with the boy if his family did not give in. This is a well-established solution when the families do not show understanding and it is the last way out, which many use. It is said: 'This is the only language the parents understand'.

The impression is that if the families had somewhat equal social status, the boy would probably have had the opportunity to come forward with a compromise proposal and his family would have accepted a contract of marriage with the girl, although we do not know for sure that this would happen. The example demonstrates above all that the boy could not manage the situation that arose. The situation is a power game. My impression of this episode is that the boy appears to be powerless. This results in his inability to follow his own strategy, because among other things he is also oriented towards the collectivity. He cannot act differently. He cannot think independently, either. He obviously has limited choices, which results in his inability to make an independent decision vis-à-vis the parents and the kin, because he cannot withdraw from the collectivity since he would lose his rights (see Table 2.1).

Many experts believe that industrialization and globalization will cause great social changes in these societies. Kinship and other collective fellowships will become less important and occupation, education and other individual capital will become more important. According to these experts, the development will lead to individualism replacing kinship and other collective fellowships. It remains to be seen if this does happen. What is certain is that the development will create a debate in the Zaza society, too. Some will assert that the collectivity will always be more important than the individual person while others will assert the opposite, that is, they will be of the opinion that the individual is inviolable and more important than the collectivity. The collectivity-oriented people will claim that human beings must have common rules and principles for human conduct and humans can realize their humanity only in a close-knit sociocultural fellowship. They will also point out the need for a local-based fellowship that imparts feelings of belonging and security. While individual-oriented people will answer that close-knit fellowships conflict with individual interests and rights because the collectivity limits the individual's right to develop oneself freely and the collectivity acquires great power at the expense of the individual. They will also underline that even in the most individual-oriented society the individuals already share a series of common conceptions and values.

As I understand it, there may arise a very interesting and exciting debate on collectivism and individualism among Zaza Kurds in the future because the discussion about the relationship between the individual and the society or the equilibrium between the collective identity and individual rights is already going on. It seems that the tension between the family, kinship collectivity and individual freedom in the Zaza society will continue for a considerable time. Only the development in larger society with a debate on democracy, Turkey's EU membership, and greater possibilities of freedom for the Kurds and other minorities can secure Zaza Kurds the opportunity of a choice between modern and traditional lifestyles.

Notes

I Introduction

1 For a further description of the Beritan tribes, see Harald Skogseid (1997).

4 A patriarchal society

1 Classificatory kinship is the designation for using the same kinship terms for different people of the same category (based on age, gender, etc.), often without reference to biological kinship.

2 Endogamy is the rule that marriage is to be contracted within the kinship group.

5 A society with its own authorities

1 For more information on the Nakshibendi movement in Kurdistan and other Islamic societies, see Martin van Bruinessen (1992).

2 For more information on political executions, see the Susurluk Report, published by the Prime Minister's Office (Savas 1998).

3 *Fatwas* are issued when people regret an act they have committed, for example, when a man decides to divorce his wife but after a while changes his mind and turns to the mullah and asks him to annul the decision. Then the mullah must consider issuing a *fatwa*, but it must be based on the religious rules. Otherwise, a *fatwa* can be issued in many situations. In times of war, both the mullahs and the sheikhs have issued *fatwas* for mobilizing the people.

6 Reciprocity among the Zaza population

1 I want to stress that 'exchange of girls' is not the same as exchange of married women or wives. Among Zaza Kurds, this distinction is clear. Exchange of married women has never occurred among Zaza Kurds and is a foreign phenomenon. On the other hand, exchange of girls, that is

unmarried girls, is a totally accepted phenomenon. It must also be stressed that although men play the main role, it is not only they who exchange girls, but the families altogether. It is a new relationship, an event that engages the families from both sides with their kin and to a certain degree the neighbours who all contribute in different ways.

7 The economic system of the Zaza society

1 Beritan is a large nomadic tribe, one of the large Kurdish tribes in Eastern Turkey. The tribe wanders between Urfa province on the Syrian border in the south and Bingöl province in the north. In winter they use the grazing lands in the provinces Urfa, Diyarbekir and Mardin, and in summer they use the highlands on the Bingöl and Erzurum plateaus in inner East Turkey. For more information on the Beritan society, the brilliant work of Harald Skogseid is recommended (1993).

8 Turkey, a nationalist state in conflict

1 For more insight about the state direction of Turkish universities, the Turkish sociologist İsmail Beşikçi (1978a) can be recommended.
2 Atatürk means the father of the Turks. He got this surname after the foundation of the Turkish republic in 1923. But not all Turks regard him as the founding father. Ordinary practising Muslims, Islamists and Kurds disagree strongly. They emphasize that the designation of founding father was conferred by the then parliament that was not elected democratically but appointed by Atatürk himself.
3 For a closer insight on this theory, see the world-famous Turkish sociologist İsmail Beşikçi (1978a, 1978b).
4 For a closer description of the countless Kurdish rebellions, see Martin van Bruinessen (1992).
5 The statement was published in a feature article in Dagbladet on 3 March 1999 written by Thorvald Steen. By that time, Beşikçi was in prison as a prisoner of conscience. Amnesty International and the Norwegian Authors Union were engaged in Beşikçi's case.
6 In his 1978b book, the Turkish sociologist İsmail Beşikçi has documented thoroughly how Atatürk ruled the country. Beşikçi was sentenced to more than 200 years in prison. He served a total of 17 years and was released after massive pressure from Europe. All his books were confiscated and prohibited. He was also expelled from the Atatürk University in Erzurum, where he was a lecturer.
7 Paragraph 5816 of the Turkish Constitution prohibits offending the founder of the republic, Mustafa Kemal Atatürk. Breach of this law is to be punished immediately.
8 See also the newspaper Radikal on 18 April 2005 or other Turkish newspapers from the same date for Demirel's further exposition of the role of the military in Turkish politics.
9 For a more detailed report of the 'martyr' affair, see Hürriyet on 27 May 2005.

10 Robert Pollock is an expert on Turkey and has close contact with the White House. In the article, Pollock makes an unusual attack on Turkey's paranoid behaviour and places Turks side by side with the Nazis.

11 For more detail about the polemic between the EU representative Hans Joörg Kretschmer and the Turkish authorities on Orhan Pamuk and the other writers and publishers, see the Turkish newspaper *Radikal* on 3 March 2005 and other newspapers on the same day.

12 For the press conference and more details about the assassination attempt against Ayhan see the Kurdish Internet newspaper at Gelawej.org, Kurdistan-Post.com or other daily papers.

13 For more detail about this incident see *Özgür Politika* from 11 May to 22 May 2005 and other papers from the same period.

14 This case was reported by the Internet editions of *Hürriyet* and *Milliyet*, Wednesday, 1 June 2005, among others.

15 For more information about this incident, see the Swedish newspapers from 5 June or Kurdistan-Post.com and *Özgür Politika* on 6 June 2005.

16 Hak-Par is short for Hak ve Özgürlükler Partisi (Rights and Freedom Party).

17 Through military coups in 1960, 1971, 1980 and several interventions, the latest in 1997, and through convictions by the courts called DGM (the State Security Courts), the military has effectively set 'the rule of law' aside.

9 Culture and identity

1 Kurdish society in Eastern Turkey went through a deeply tragic development in 1980s and 1990s. The population experienced a civil war against the central authorities in Ankara. The war cost many people their lives and around three million people were forced to leave their homes by the Turkish authorities.

2 Torture has been widespread in Turkey for decades. The authorities still use torture extensively in Turkish prisons according to human rights organizations and the opposition. It is particularly directed at the Kurdish resistance movement. For more detail on torture, see the reports published by Amnesty International and the largest human rights organization in Turkey, IHD. The country has been repeatedly convicted by the European Court of Human Rights but this has not helped. The government of Recep Tayyip Erdogan says that torture does not take place any longer while IHD and the Kurdish opposition say the government is lying, which is thoroughly documented by the IHD reports for December 2004 and January 2005. IHD has for many years documented that political prisoners have been systematically and deliberately tortured. The Amnesty report (see also the daily newspapers *Radikal* on 30 March 2005 and *Hurriyet* on 3 May 2005) criticizes the Erdogan government for defective practice and lack of follow up with respect to the reforms: The authorities have not implemented effective measures for stopping the violation of basic human rights. People are

arrested without being registered; they are tortured and set free after traces of torture have disappeared from their bodies. People also disappear and are killed without being brought before a court. The authorities do not investigate cases of disappearances either. Security forces and police officers who commit such crimes are not punished. Instead, human rights activists are arrested. The critics of the system say that an independent commission must be appointed to follow up any reforms that are implemented.

3 The enormous Turkish propaganda apparatus has created an impression that 'the heroic Turkish army is invincible' since the days of Kemal Atatürk. This is heard nearly daily in state propaganda.

4 On 4 and 13 February, the court in Diyarbekir banned the following Kurdish music albums 'Devrane', sung by Sehmuz Kaya; 'Ji bir nabin', sung by the group Koma Gula Xerzan; 'Doktor Zeke', sung by Pismam-1; 'Welat Xwina Sehidan', sung by the group Koma Cekdar; 'Rojda', sung by the group Koma Azadi; 'Roje Sube Ez Hesirim', sung by Gula Serhedi; 'Tina Roje', sung by Diyar; 'Dilana Besinor', sung by the group Koma Ciya; 'Cenga Jina' sung by Diyar; 'Mezopotanim Ez', sung by the group Koma Rojhilat; 'Ava Evine', sung by Kawa; 'Beje', sung by Aydin og; and 'Ay Dil', sung by Heme Haci (*Ozgur Politika* 28. February 2005).

5 For the difference between national identity and ethnic identity, see among others: Michel Foucault (1979), James C. Scott (1998) and Bruce Kapferer (1988).

10 Gender relations, family and division of labour

1 Polygamy is a marriage system in which a man can have several wives at the same time according to Islamic law – the Sharia law.

2 An agnate is a member of one's paternal lineage, that is, the notion that one follows first and foremost his paternal descent group.

11 Religion, collectivism and individualism

1 Sunnah means Islamic tradition contained in the Hadith literature that explains how the prophet Muhammad acted in daily life.

2 For more insight into Islam's restrictive normative values, limitations and value sets, see the Koran and the Hadith literature.

3 For more insight into the Alevi population, Elwert (1998) can be recommended.

References

Barth, Fredrik (1987). *Cosmologies in the Making. A Generative Approach to Cultural Variation in Inner New Guinea*, Cambridge: Cambridge University Press.

Barth, Fredrik (1991). *Andres liv – og vårt eget*, Oslo: Universitetsforlaget.

Beşikçi, İsmail (1978a). *Science-Official Ideology, State-Democracy and Kurdish Question*, Istanbul: Alan yayıncılık. (In Turkish.)

Beşikçi, İsmail (1978b). *Bilim Yontemi, Turkiye'deki Uygulama 2 Turk Tarih Tezi, Gunes Dil Teorisi ve Kurt Sorunu*, Istanbul: Alan yayinlari. (In Turkish.)

Bourdieu, Pierre (1972). *Outline of a Theory of Practice*, Cambridge: Cambridge University Press.

Broch, Harald Beyer (2000). 'Kjønn, alder, kropp', in F. S. Nielsen and O. H. Smedal (eds) *Mellom himmel og jord: Tradisjoner, teorier og tendenser i sosialantropologien*, Bergen: Fagbokforlaget.

Butler, Judith (1990). *Gender Trouble: Feminism and the Subversion of Identity*, New York: Routledge.

Elwert, Georg (1998). 'Switching in we-group identities: the Alevis as a case among many others', in K. Kehl-Bodrogi (ed.) *Die Kizilbas/Aleviten. Untersuchhungen uber eine esoterische Glaubensgeminschaft in Anatolien*, Berlin: Schwarz.

Eriksen, Thomas Hylland (2000). 'Sosial identitet, etnisk tilhörighet, nasjonalisme, tid og sted', in F. S. Nielsen and O. H. Smedal (eds) *Mellom himmel og jord: Tradisjoner, teorier og tendenser i sosialantropologien*, Bergen: Fagbokforlaget.

Eriksen, Thomas Hylland (2003). *Hva er sosialantropologi?* Oslo: Universitetsforlaget.

Evans-Pritchard, Edward Evan (1951). *Kinship and Marriage among the Nuer*, Oxford: Clarendon Press.

Fortes, Meyer (1945). *The Dynamics Clanship among the Tallensi*, Oxford: Oxford University Press.

Foucault, Michel (1979). *Discipline and Punish. The Birth of the Prison*, Harmondsworth: Peregrine Books.

Geertz, Clifford (1963). *Peddlers and Princes. Social Change and Economic Modernization in Two Indonesian Towns*, Chicago: University of Chicago Press.

Gellner, Ernest (1987). *The Concept of Kingship and Other Essays on Anthropological Method and Explanation*, Oxford: Basil Blackwell.

Helle-Valle, Jo (2000). 'Fra modernisering til globalisering', in F. S. Nielsen and O. H. Smedal (eds) *Mellom himmel og jord: Tradisjoner, teorier og tendenser i sosialantropologien*, Bergen: Fagbokforlaget.

Heradsveit, Daniel (1999). 'Sekulære mottrekk til islamismens framvekst i Tyrkia', *Internasjonal politikk*, Oslo: Norsk utenriks politisk institutt (NUPI).

Kapferer, Bruce (1988). *Legends of People. Myths of State, Violence, Intolerance, and Political Culture in Sri Lanka and Australia*, Washington: Smithsonian Institution Press.

Kaya, Mehmed S. (2000). 'Mechanisms which regulate emigration', *Norwegian Journal of Migration Research* 1/2000, Fagbokforlaget.

Keesing, Roger (1975). *Kin Groups and Social Structure*, New York: Holt, Rinehart and Winston.

Krohn-Hansen, Christian and Vike, Halvard (2000). 'Makt og symbolske former – perspektiver på politick', in F. S. Nielsen and O. H. Smedal (eds) *Mellom himmel og jord: Tradisjoner, teorier og tendenser i sosialantropologien*, Bergen: Fagbokforlaget.

Edip Polat (2004). Kürt coğrafyasının flora ve faunasına giriş bilim dilinde Kürtler Edib Polat, Istanbul: Evrensel Basım Yayın.

Leach, Edmund R. [1954] (1981). *Political Systems of Highland Burma*, London: Athlone Press.

Leach, Edmund R. (1961). *Pul Eliya. A Village in Ceylon – a Study of Land Tenure and Kinship*, Cambridge: Cambridge University Press.

Lerch, Peter (1857). *Forschungen über die Kurden und die iranischen Nordchaldœer*, St Petersburg: n.p.

Lerch, Peter (1858). *Kurdische Glossare, mit einer literar-historischen Einleitung*, St Petersburg: n.p.

Levi-Strauss, Claude (1969). *The Elementary Structures of Kinship*, London: Tavistock.

MacKenzie, D. N. (1962). *Kurdish Dialect Studies, 1-2*, London and New York: Oxford University Press.

Malinowski, Bronislaw [1926] (1992). *Malinowski and the Work of Myth*, Princeton, NJ: Princeton University Press.

Mauss, Marcel (1995). *Gaven*, Oslo: Cappelen Akademisk Forlag.

Mead, Margaret (1974). *Male and Female*, Harmondsworth: Penguin Books.

Mead, Margaret (1978). *Coming of Age in Samoa*, Harmondsworth: Penguin Books.

Nasidze, Ivan, Quinque, Dominique, Ozturk, Murat, Bendukidze, Nina, and Stoneking, Mark (2005). 'MtDNA and Ychromosome variation in Kurdish groups', *Annals of Human Genetics* 69, 1–12.

Oostlander, Arie M. (2003). *Report on Turkey's Application for Membership of the European Union*, Strasbourg: The European Parliament.

Österberg, Dag (1999). *Det moderne. Et essay om Vestens kultur 1740–2000*, Oslo: Gyldendal Norsk Forlag.

Paul, L. (1998). *Zazaki: Gramatik und Versuch einer Dialektologie. Beiträge zur Iranistik*, Wiesbaden: Reichert verlage.

Park, Robert (1950). *Race and Culture*, Glencoe, IL: Free Press.

Radcliffe-Brown, Alfred Reginald (1952). 'The study of kinship systems', in *Structure and Function in Primitive Society*, London: Cohen and West.

Sahlins, Marshall (1972). *Stone Age Economics*, Chicago: University of Chicago Press.

Savas, Kutlu (1998). *Susurluk raporu*, Ankara: Prime Minister's Office.

Schneider, David M. (1984). *A Critique of the Study of Kinship*, Ann Arbor: The University of Michigan Press.

Scott, James C. (1998). *Seeing Like a State. How Certain Schemes to Improve the Human Condition Have Failed*, New Haven/London: Yale University Press.

Shanin, Teodor (1971). *Peasants and Peasant Societies*, Harmondsworth: Penguin.

Skogseid, Harald (1993). 'Nomadic pastoralism and land use patterns in Eastern Turkey. The case of the Kurdish Beritan tribe', in H. Palva and K. S. Vikør (eds) *The Middle East – Unity and Diversity*, Nordic Proceedings in Asian Studies No. 5, Copenhagen: Nordic Institute Asian Studies.

Skogseid, Harald (1997). '*Beritan – den siste kurdiske nomadestamme i Øst-Tyrkia?*' in D. G. Bates and H. Skogseid (eds) *Menneskelig tilpasning. En humanøkologisk innføring i globalt miljø*, Oslo: Universitetsforlaget.

Smedal, Olaf H. (2000). '*Blod, sæd, moral og teknologi: Hva slektskap brukes til*', in F. S. Nielsen and O. H. Smedal (eds) *Mellom himmel og jord: Tradisjoner, teorier og tendenser i sosialantropologien*, Bergen: Fagbokforlaget.

van Bruinessen, Martin (1992). *Agha, Saikh and State. The Social and Political Structures of Kurdistan*, London: Zed Books Ltd.

Articles from newspapers and periodicals

Dagbladet, 3 March 1999, 19 October 1999.
Dagens Nyheter, 6 June 2005.
DIHA (News Agency) 6 May 2006.
Economist, 6 May 2006.
Freedom House, Freedom in the World – Turkey (2005).
Gazetem net, 21 October 2005.
Gelawej.org, 6 April 2005, 6 June 2005.

Hürriyet, 15 April 2005, 21 March 2005, 3 May 2005, 27 May 2005, 6 November 2005.

Kurdistan-Post.com, 11–22 May 2005, 6 April 2005, 21 October 2005.

Milliyet, 30 April 2003, 8 May 2003, 13 May 2003, 18 April 2005, 22 March 2005, 29 October 2005.

Özgür Politika, 25 May 2004, 28 February 2005, 9 April 2005, 11 April 2005, 14 April 2005, 18 April 2005, 11–22 May 2005, 6 June 2005.

Radikal, 24 February 2005, 3 March 2005, 30 March 2005, 14 April 2005, 11 April 2005, 17 April 2005, 18 April 2005, 19 April 2005, 14 May 2005, 30 May 2005, 27 June 2005, 19 September 2005, 6 November 2005.

Wall Street Journal, 16 February 2005.

Index

rebellions 64, 114, 116, 124, 135,
148, 151–2, 153, 160, 192, 200
reciprocity 81–95
REFAH (Islamic Welfare Party) 124
religion see Islam
religious sects 196
Republican Party see CHP
reserve workforce 108
Rinnan Gang 66
'Rojda' 211
'Roje Sube Ez Hesirim' 211
roshon qorbonon 192
Ruha (Urfa) 5

Said, Sheikh, of Palu 61, 64
Sami 163
'saving actions' 84
science 200–1
seasonal workers 109
secularism 118, 140, 145, 196, 200
self-employed businessmen 104
self-government, demand for 137–8
semen, value of 20
'senior-junior' axis 51
separatism 108, 112, 127, 128, 129,
138, 139, 157
Septioglu, Ali Riza 65
Serhedi, Gula 211
settlement, rules of 174
Sevres Treaty 122, 137
sexual morality 179–83
sexual services 92
sexuality 182
Shafii sect 191
shamanism 191
Sharia (Sheriat) law 16, 71, 191, 196,
211
sheep farming 7, 97–8, 99–100
sheikhdom 13, 16–17, 88, 163, 182,
196–8, 203
Arabic 58
economic authority 62–3
hereditary tradition 74–5
in Melon 61
network 72–4
political authority 63–7
religious and moral authority 67–70

reputation 70–1
in Solhan region 58–62
Shemsxon 32
Sherevdin Plateau 6, 97
Shexi Melon 58
Siverek 5
slogans 116
slyness 94
social identity 166–8
social status, marriage and 51,
206–7
social structure 74–6
socialization process 172
Solax 32
Solaxan tribe 10, 32, 66, 91
Solaxan 6
Solhan (town) 4
Solhan region 4, 5–6, 7, 8, 69, 101,
173
emigration from 109, 110
Sorani (dialect) 4
Stalin 120, 139
status 177
stories 174, 199
suicide 101
Sun and Language Theory 115–16
Sunnah 190, 211
Sunni/Shafii sect 191, 192
conflict 145, 147–50, 170
women, employment 147
survival of the fittest 95
swearing 49
sweethearts, behaviour of 92
Swoboda, Hannes 130
symmetrical alliances 48

talismans 72
Tatlises, Ibrahim 158
Tavzi 30
tax collection 108
Telli, Ahmed 156
'temporal sovereignty' 79
terrorism 112, 142, 166
THY (Turkish Airline Co.) 130
'Tina Roje' 212
torture 127, 128, 135, 136, 143,
210, 211

.